The Pleasures and Pains of Collecting

A publication by

The Friends of the Oriental Museum

The Pleasures and Pains of Collecting

By Malcolm J. MacDonald

Edited by Alexander Nicholas Shaw

For Malcolm

First published in 2018 by
Friends of the Oriental Museum
c/o The Oriental Museum
Elvet Hill, Durham, DH1 3TH
www.durham.ac.uk/oriental.museum

ISBN 978-1-5272-3198-6

Edited by Alexander Nicholas Shaw
Photography by Kate Weightman
Design by Rachel Barclay and Alexander Nicholas Shaw
Printed by Short Run Press Ltd., Exeter, Devon

Contents

List of contributors

The Rt. Hon. Malcolm John MacDonald, P.C., O.M., was a prominent Cold War diplomat and a prime mover in British decolonisation. During the Second World War he left behind an illustrious parliamentary career as an MP and Cabinet minister to embark upon new adventures as a diplomat and colonial administrator. Malcolm served successively as High Commissioner to Canada, Governor General of Malaya, Commissioner General for South East Asia, High Commissioner to India, Co-chairman of the Geneva Conference on Laos, Governor of Kenya, Governor General of Kenya, High Commissioner to Kenya and Special Representative in East Africa. He was also a key player in bringing about Anglo-Chinese reconciliation during the Cold War, and a prolific collector across a range of art forms. Malcolm was awarded the Order of Merit in recognition of his lifetime's achievements in the public service.

Dr. Victoria Bagshaw is a niece of Malcolm MacDonald who enjoyed his company in many different locations. She studied Botany at the University of Edinburgh where she gained a BSc (Hons) and a PhD. She was then employed as an assistant lecturer in Electron Microscopy at the University of Glasgow before starting a family and spending nearly four interesting years living in South East Asia. Uncle Malcolm always supported Victoria's interests in wildlife and her appreciation of diverse African and Eastern cultures. Introductions to some of his numerous friends were a welcome and engaging bonus. His own writings were invaluable and helped Victoria in her understanding of life in different parts of the world. Meeting with him was always great fun whether at small family gatherings or larger more formal events. She is delighted to support the publication of her Uncle Malcolm's manuscript *The Pleasures and Pains of Collecting*.

Dr. Craig Barclay is Durham University's Head of Museums with overall responsibility for management of the Oriental Museum, Museum of

Archaeology, Durham Castle Museum, Durham University Art Collections and parts of the university's Biological Science collections. Craig has a keen interest in ceramics and is also responsible for the delivery of all numismatics teaching at Durham University as well as teaching aspects of Museum Studies at postgraduate level. He has previously taught at the University of Hull and held a visiting professorship at the South-West University of Finance and Economics in Chengdu.

Rachel Barclay is Curator of the Oriental Museum. Since 2008 Rachel has been responsible for the complete redisplay of all of the museum's permanent galleries. She also manages the museum's very active programme of temporary exhibitions and installations. Rachel is heavily involved in university teaching across a range of departments on topics ranging from Ancient Egyptian art to Japanese Manga. She previously worked at the Pitt Rivers Museum, Oxford and originally trained as an Egyptologist, participating in excavations in the Valley of the Nobles at Luxor. Outside museums Rachel has several years of experience in international marketing across Southern Europe, North Africa and China.

Alexander Nicholas Shaw is a Cold War historian currently completing his PhD at the University of Leeds. His doctoral research project, funded by the White Rose College of the Arts and Humanities in association with the Arts and Humanities Research Council, looks at the British intelligence community in Singapore during the period when Malcolm MacDonald was Commissioner General. Alexander's other interests include the diplomatic role of western collectors of Asian art, particularly Malcolm MacDonald and John Mansfield Addis. In 2017 he curated the exhibition *Beauty and Diplomacy: The Malcolm MacDonald Collections* in partnership with the Oriental Museum. As a collector of books he is pleased to add this volume to his collection of Malcolm MacDonald's writings.

Acknowledgements

On behalf of my fellow contributors and I, we would like to thank all who have helped us to bring this project to fruition. Most of all, the kind generosity of Victoria and Ian Bagshaw and the Friends of the Oriental Museum has enabled us to finally bring Malcolm's memoir to the public audience it deserves.

The Malcolm MacDonald papers at Durham University's Palace Green Library are a fantastic resource. Navigating this treasure trove has been made all the easier thanks to the help and advice of Francis Gotto, who also facilitated the copyright permissions necessary to publish this book. For granting us that permission, we are indebted to Ishbel Lochhead as holder of the copyright on Malcolm's papers.

The splendid photography in this book was produced by Kate Weightman, who has captured the beauty of some of Malcolm's favourite objects. We took direction from a list of illustrations which Malcolm had wanted to be included if the book were ever to be published, as well as including some of our own favourites.

Without the kindness of the numerous individual private, public and charitable benefactors who helped fund the purchase of Malcolm's ceramic collection for the Oriental Museum, we would not have the privilege of being able to showcase such a beautiful and diverse collection through this book. Many years may have passed, but we remain grateful for their generosity.

As Editor, I would also like to extend my personal thanks to those who have supported me in this journey. I first decided to publish Malcolm's book whilst curating the exhibition *Beauty and Diplomacy: The Malcolm MacDonald Collections* in partnership with the Oriental Museum. Our exhibition of 2017 was a celebration of Malcolm's life, achievements and love of beauty. For that opportunity, and all the others which followed, I would like to thank the entire team, especially Helen Armstrong, Julia Oliver, Gill Ramsay, Mel Smith and Phil Smith. Most of all I am grateful to Rachel and Craig Barclay for their encouragement and for sharing my enthusiasm for Malcolm's story. It was through curating this exhibition that I met Victoria and Ian Bagshaw, with whom it has been a constant pleasure to work on this book. Whilst working on this project, I also met Dr. Claire Sutherland, who enabled me to fulfil a dream to visit some of Malcolm's other collections at the Museum of Asian Art and University of Malaya Art Gallery in Kuala Lumpur. For sharing their stories and making our trip to KL so memorable, I would like to thank A. K. Kamari, Abd Aziz Rashid and the many other people who showed us their wonderful museums. My next port of call in tracing Malcolm's surviving collections will be Singapore, for which I wish to offer advance thanks to Patricia Welch and the Southeast Asian Ceramic Society.

For supporting me in my studies, I am indebted to my PhD supervisors Simon Ball and Adam Cathcart, as well as my generous funders WRoCAH. Caryn Douglas, Clare Meadley and Julian Richards have created a remarkable environment in which to nurture the ambitions of PhD researchers like myself, and have never stinted on the provision of morale support, project funding or pies. Furthermore, without the inspiring teaching of Martin Thornton, I may never have discovered an interest in diplomats like Malcolm MacDonald.

Finally, I wish to give my heartfelt thanks to my family and friends for enduring my growing obsession with Malcolm's life-story. My parents remain a bedrock of support for which I am more grateful than these words can express. I know they will both be glad to finally read something I have written which isn't full of the acronyms of British intelligence agencies. My gratitude also goes out to those friends who visited *Beauty and Diplomacy* and let me share my ideas: Sarah Askam, Aiden Heeley-Hill, Bryony O'Neill and Jo Rodgers. Last, but by no means least, I thank Scott Ramsay and Harvey Rhodes for being there on opening night, for visiting twice, and for learning more about Malcolm MacDonald than they ever wanted to know.

Simplified list of Chinese dynasties

Neolithic period	6200-1600 BCE
Shang dynasty	1600-1046 BCE
Western Zhou dynasty	1050-771 BCE
Eastern Zhou dynasty	771-221 BCE
Qin dynasty	221-207 BCE
Western Han dynasty	206 BCE-8 CE
Eastern Han dynasty	25-220 CE
Period of Disunity	220-581 CE
Sui dynasty	581-618 CE
Tang dynasty	618-907 CE
Five dynasties and ten kingdoms	907-960 CE
Northern Song dynasty	960-1127 CE
Southern Song dynasty	1127-1279 CE
Yuan dynasty	1271-1368 CE
Ming dynasty	1368-1644 CE
Qing dynasty	1644-1911 CE
Republic of China	1912-1949 CE
People's Republic of China	1949 CE – present

The many cultures represented in the Oriental Museum collections have used a variety of different dating systems over the millennia. To provide consistency the Museum uses the dating system BCE/CE. BCE stands for 'Before Common Era' and CE stands for 'Common Era'. The numbering of the years is identical to that used in the BC/AD system.

Notes on terminology

Malcolm MacDonald wrote the main manuscript in 1972. Sometimes the language he used reflects archaic place-names or terminology which has fallen out of favour. Words such as 'Eskimo' and 'tribe' fall into this bracket. In the interests of preserving Malcolm's manuscript as a valuable historical source, we have made minimal editorial changes. Thus you will find Thailand referred to as both Siam and Thailand, maintaining Malcolm's original inconsistency, Myanmar consistently as Burma and Iran as Persia. Although 'South East Asia' is becoming increasingly replaced with 'Southeast Asia', we have maintained Malcolm's usage of the older form and, for the sake of consistency, adopted it in our introductions. For the modern reader's ease, here is a list of the principal archaic city-names Malcolm uses and their modern equivalents. However, as this is primarily a book about collecting, and one in which Chinese ceramics feature heavily, the names of Chinese dynasties and of different types of ceramics have been altered to their more recognisable modern forms.

Archaic	**Modern**
Calcutta	Kolkata
Djakarta	Jakarta
Djogjakarta	Yogyakarta
Luang Prabang	Louangphabang
Madras	Chennai
Peking	Beijing
Tanjore	Thanjavur

Descriptive Guide to Plates

The 32 colour plates found between pages 68 and 69 contain images of individual objects from the Malcolm MacDonald collections at Durham University's Oriental Museum. Malcolm was one of the most important donors to the Oriental Museum. His collections encompass 405 Chinese ceramics, 106 antiquities from South, South East and Central Asia, 3 Korean ceramics, and 79 photographs of Borneo taken by Malcolm's friend, the Sarawak Chinese art photographer K. F. Wong. Out of a total of nearly 600 objects, here are some of the highlights. Many of these beautiful objects are on permanent display to delight the visitor at the Oriental Museum.

Front cover. Detail from Malcolm's favourite bowl

This Song dynasty Dingware bowl was Malcolm's favourite Chinese ceramic. You can see the bowl in its entirety, and read more about it, at plate 15.

Bowl: porcelain. China. 1100-1200 CE (Song dynasty).
DUROM.1969.40

Rear cover. Malcolm preparing for a journey from Canada

In this photograph, Malcolm is preparing to board an aircraft on one of his many excursions. The photograph appears to have been taken when Malcolm was High Commissioner to Canada, and therefore dates from 1941-46.

Photograph courtesy of Dr. Victoria Bagshaw

Plate 1. Tomb figure purchased from T. Y. King

One of Malcolm's preferred ceramics dealers was the doyen of the Hong Kong antiques fraternity, T. Y. King. Along with other art sellers, King relocated his business from Shanghai to Hong Kong in 1949 and reduced his prices to finance his new venture. Malcolm was able to afford some highly desirable pieces including this Tang dynasty tomb figure, probably depicting a Turfan man from west China. He is decorated with a *sancai* (three-colour) glaze of cream, yellow-brown and cobalt blue.

Tomb figure: glazed earthenware. China. 775-825 CE (Tang dynasty). DUROM.1969.31

Plate 2. Xylophone from Sihanouk's gamelan orchestra

Norodom Sihanouk, King (later Prince and Prime minister) of Cambodia, became a close personal friend of Malcolm. This xylophone was part of Sihanouk's gamelan orchestra and was played in accompaniment to the *Royal Corps de Ballet.* One of Sihanouk's daughters was prima ballerina. On their first meeting, Malcolm and Sihanouk attended a ballet performance together. This xylophone, a gift from Sihanouk, is a rare relic of royal Cambodia to survive the cultural destruction of the Khmer Rouge.

Xylophone: wood, textile. Cambodia. 1900-1950 CE. DUROM.1976.116

Plate 3. Royal teapot

This teapot was also a gift from Sihanouk to Malcolm. It symbolises their personal friendship as well as the high status of Malcolm's position as Commissioner General for South East Asia. Five colour Bencharong ware was originally made exclusively for the Thai royal family, and this piece was presented to the Cambodian royal family. It became a diplomatic gift for a second time when given to Malcolm.

Teapot: porcelain. Thailand. 1850-1900 CE.
DUROM.1979.32

Plate 4. Reservation art or traditional clothing?

This pair of moccasins was made by the Arctic peoples of Canada. Whilst serving as High Commissioner to Canada, Malcolm had little time to appreciate indigenous art, although he admired the maintenance of traditional clothing amongst the Arctic peoples. Only later did he discover the beauty of their craftsmanship. These shoes are probably more representative of commercial, 'reservation art' produced for the tourist market.

Moccasins: leather and textile. Canada. 1900-1950 CE.
DUROM.1980.64

Plate 5. Malcolm's first Chinese ceramic purchase

As described in this book, Malcolm's first introduction to his greatest collecting passion – Chinese ceramics – came about during a tour of Japan, Korea and China in 1929. At the Yamanaka Brothers' store in Kyoto he bought a few examples, including a pair of lion figures from the Ming dynasty which cost him only £5. They would have originally held incense candles for Buddhist ceremonies. With their bright colours and very decorative design, this sort of figure was very popular with some European collectors.

Lion figure: glazed stoneware. China. 1550-1650 CE (Ming dynasty).
DUROM.1969.246.A&B

Plate 6. Chinese ceramics for export to South East Asia

Living in Singapore, Malcolm found it easy to purchase export ceramics such as the Swatow ware piece in this photograph. With its many colours and flowery design, it reflects his earlier collecting tastes. As a result of tuition from his friend S.Q. Wong, he came to prefer pieces made for the domestic Chinese market. He donated the majority of his collection of around 120 export wares to the art museum of the University of Malaya. Only a few examples are to be found in Durham; more are held by the National University of Singapore Museum and University of Malaya Asian Art Museum.

Plate: porcelain. China. 1750-1799 CE (Qing dynasty, Qianlong reign).
DUROM.1969.238.C

Plate 7. A gift from S. Q. Wong

One of the most prominent members of Singapore's Chinese community, the businessman S.Q. Wong became friends with Malcolm due to their shared interests as collectors. Despairing of Malcolm's focus on export wares, 'S.Q.' made him a gift of this slightly chipped Junware bowl in order to lure Malcolm into collecting domestic Chinese ceramics. His plan worked. Later, when Malcolm donated his export wares to found the University of Malaya art museum, he also persuaded S.Q. Wong to join him in making art donations. At the time, 'S.Q.' and Malcolm believed this to be a Song dynasty piece, but experts have now suggested a later date in the Yuan dynasty.

Bowl: glazed stoneware. China. 1260-1368 CE (Yuan dynasty).
DUROM.1969.96

Plate 8. Northern celadon

Malcolm's favourite Chinese ceramics were those of the Song and Yuan dynasties. His utmost preference was for Dingware, closely followed by celadons, Junware and Qingbai ware. This group of Song dynasty celadons showcase the variety of his fine collection. The olive-green coloured dish here is a Yaozhou ware (Northern) celadon with a design of entangled peonies. The carved pattern gives the glaze a contrast of light and dark shades.

Dish: glazed stoneware. China. 1000-1200 CE (Song dynasty).
DUROM.1969.118

Plate 9. Longquan celadon

Longquan ware celadons flourished during the Southern Song dynasty as the great northern kilns producing Yaozhou celadons declined. The glaze is a more bluish-green and the inside of the bowl has a relief pattern showing a pair of fish. In Chinese art, two fish swimming together are a symbol of happiness in marriage. These hidden patterns were a feature that Malcolm found very appealing.

Bowl: glazed stoneware. China. 1200-1300 CE (Southern Song dynasty).
DUROM.1969.104.C

Plate 10. Junware bulb bowl

Junware was another of Malcolm's favourite types of Chinese ceramic, following his conversion to domestic pieces at the teaching of friends such as S. Q. Wong. Junware was produced in kilns in Henan province and the height of its production was the Song dynasty. This drum-shaped piece is a bulb bowl intended for planting bulbs. It showcases a fine variation of the opalescent lavender glaze typical of this particular ware, passing into mauve on the outside.

Bulb bowl: glazed stoneware. China. 960- 1644 CE (Northern Song or Ming dynasty).
DUROM.1969.87

Plate 11. Qingbai ware vase

As well as Dingware, celadons and Junware, Malcolm expressed preference for Qingbai ceramics. Their glaze is white with a faint blueish tint, and they were produced in Jiangxi province of south-eastern China during the Song and Yuan dynasties. Here is a piece from Malcolm's collections: a pear-shaped vase decorated with sprayed copper-brown dots.

Vase: glazed stoneware. China. 1260-1368 (Yuan dynasty).
DUROM.1969.58

Plate 12. Tang dynasty tomb figure

Although Malcolm's favourite Chinese ceramics were from the Song and Yuan dynasties, he was also drawn to tomb figures from the Tang dynasty. Malcolm first encountered these in the Yamanaka Brothers' store in Kyoto during his trip of 1929, and he loved their vivid sense of life and movement. Amongst the tomb figures he collected are models of elegant ladies, male courtiers and many animals: camels and horses, a wild boar, an ox and a ram.

Camel figure: glazed earthenware. China. 775-825 CE (Tang dynasty).
DUROM.1969.19

Plate 13. Ming dynasty blue-and-white stem bowl

Blue-and-white Ming dynasty ceramics are one of the most recognisable forms of Chinese art. They inspired European imitations including the famous Delft ware and continue to be exceedingly popular with both Asian and other collectors. Malcolm's collection at the Oriental Museum includes 37 blue-and-white ceramics from the Ming and Qing dynasties. The shape of this stem bowl recalls bronze *dou* vessels from ancient China. Amongst the floral pattern you can see the reign mark of the Xuande Emperor (the fifth emperor of the Ming dynasty).

Stem bowl: porcelain. China. 1425-1435 CE (Ming dynasty, Xuande reign).
DUROM.1969.341

Plate 14. Underglaze red bowl with bat design

This bowl is one of a pair bought by Malcolm. The decoration depicts flying bats in an underglaze copper red style popular during the Ming and Qing dynasties. Bats represent happiness in Chinese art, and each bowl includes four bats on the outside and one on the inside. In Malcolm's personal preference, this particular type of glazed porcelain was the equal of the more iconic blue-and-white wares.

Bowl: porcelain. China. 1723-1735 CE (Qing dynasty, Yongzheng reign).
DUROM.1969.186.A

Plate 15. Malcolm's favourite Dingware bowl

Of over 400 domestic Chinese ceramics in his possession, in addition to around 120 examples of different export wares, this piece was Malcolm's undisputed favourite. He loved the thinness of its walls, the delicate beauty of the incised pattern, and the perfection of the creamy-white glaze. It was fired upside down in the kiln, leaving the rim unglazed; instead it is bound in beautiful copper. The design shows a pair of Mandarin ducks: believed to mate for life and therefore a symbol of conjugal bliss. At £750 it was one of Malcolm's most expensive purchases. Malcolm's example stands favourable comparison with similar pieces in major international collections.

Bowl: porcelain. China. 1100-1200 CE (Song dynasty).
DUROM.1969.40

Plate 16. Malcolm's oldest Chinese ceramic

This prehistoric pot is the oldest piece in Malcolm's collection of Chinese ceramics, dating back to the Neolithic period. Although some collectors choose to stick to favourite styles or periods, Malcolm's motivations changed once he began collecting for the Oriental Museum. He wished to assemble a ceramic time-line of Chinese history for the benefit of the students of Durham University. The jar is probably a mortuary urn, with ornate geometrical patterns painted on its sides.

Jar: painted earthenware. China. 2800-2500 BCE (Majiayao culture).
DUROM.1969.251

Plate 17. A lesson in forgeries

As he admits in this book, Malcolm sometimes fell prey to forgeries. These could, however, teach him something useful about identifying fakes in the future. Here is just one of his few errors. It pretends to be a Henan ware vase from Song dynasty China, but is in fact a reproduction from twentieth century Japan.

Vase: glazed stoneware. Japan. 1900-1950 CE.
DUROM.1969.80

Plate 18. A Korean variation on a Chinese theme

Chinese ceramics were Malcolm's greatest collecting passion whilst he served as Commissioner General for South East Asia. As a variation on this theme, he diversified into the ceramics of other Far Eastern cultures. Here is one of three Korean ceramics which he added to his collection. All three are celadons from the Goryeo period, made at a similar time to the Song dynasty Chinese celadons with which Malcolm was more familiar. The technique was introduced to Korea from China, but developed its own unique features, particularly the white and black *sanggam* inlay.

Bowl: porcelain. Korea. 918-1392 CE (Goryeo dynasty).
DUROM.1969.236.C

Plate 19. Silverwork from Kelantan

As Britain's Commissioner General for South East Asia, one of Malcolm's most pleasurable duties was to travel round different nations. He made friends everywhere he visited and took advantage of this unique opportunity to collect beautiful items from many lands. He particularly admired the craftsmanship of silverwork which he encountered. In this illustration is an example from Kelantan in Malaysia: a matchbox cover depicting a figure from the *Wayang* puppet theatre popular in Indonesia and Malaysia.

Matchbox cover: silver. Malaysia. 1945-1975 CE.
DUROM.1980.62

Plate 20. Niello-inlaid silver box from Thailand

Thailand was another destination on Malcolm's frequent diplomatic travels. He developed respect for Field Marshal Phibunsongkhram (known in the West as Pibul), whom Malcolm regarded as 'the greatest master of the *coup d'état* then alive' and an 'awful rascal'. Malcolm once found himself having to dissuade the Thai Chief of Police from launching his own coup attempt against Phibunsongkhram. This small box is decorated with niello: a mixture of copper, silver and lead sulphides used to create black inlay.

Box: silver and niello inlay. Thailand. 20th century CE.
DUROM.1980.61

Plate 21. Silver cigar holder from Brunei

Of all the silversmiths across South East Asia, Malcolm believed the best were those from Brunei. As he recounts in this book, he enjoyed sitting and watching them at work just as much as he enjoyed possession of their finished objects. This cigar holder is a true masterpiece of their art. The delicate butterflies float atop springs which would allow them to gently flutter in the smoke made by a lit cigar. Malcolm added the legs himself so that he could use the cigar holder as a table-top decoration at parties.

Cigar holder: silver. Brunei. 1945-1975 CE.
DUROM.1976.139

Plate 22. A cannon from Malcolm's veranda

This bronze cannon was originally made by the master craftsmen and gunsmiths of Brunei for a deadly purpose. The Brunei Bay area was a haven for piracy during the nineteenth century, and merchant ships needed to be well-armed to navigate these waters. Brunei became famous not just for its pirates, but also for the quality and beauty of the cannons it produced for fighting those pirates. This example is lavishly decorated with a crocodile and bird, as well as Islamic imagery in the form of the double-bladed *zulfiqar* sword. Malcolm bought a set of antique cannons to decorate his veranda at Bukit Serene, and even fired them on formal occasions.

Cannon: bronze, wood. Brunei. 1800-1900 CE.
DUROM.1976.117

Plate 23. Lacquer work from Burma

Malcolm once described his duties as Commissioner General for South East Asia as being like a bird on permanent migration. Visiting politicians also brought him into contact with artists and craftsmen working in a huge variety of styles and media. While on his travels, he picked up a number of small lacquer work trinket boxes. This box, in the shape of a duck, is from Burma (modern-day Myanmar).

Duck-shaped box: lacquer. Burma. 1900-1950 CE.
DUROM.1979.34

Plate 24. Borneo people

This wooden figure is a self-representation of one of the indigenous Dayak peoples of Borneo with whom Malcolm was friends. He is a Kayan man, looking very contemplative as he squats on his haunches. Weighed down by heavy rings, his stretched ears are clearly visible. This practice was even more noticeable amongst Kayan women. Amongst local people this was deemed extremely beautiful, but Malcolm remained unconvinced of its merits.

Carving of a Kayan man: wood. Sarawak. 1950-1960 CE.
DUROM.1976.125

Plate 25. Temenggong Koh's head-hunting sword

During his time in Singapore, Malcolm accumulated a number of swords. By far the most precious was this one which belonged to his adopted Iban father, Temenggong Koh. Koh was said to have taken over one hundred of his enemies' heads with this sword. Although outlawed under British colonial rule, head-hunting was revived during the Second World War when Borneo was occupied by Imperial Japan. Koh earned a reputation for bravery and wisdom during this conflict. His sword is beautifully ornate as well as deadly, and is bedecked with human hair.

Head-hunting sword and scabbard: steel, brass, horn, rattan and
human hair. Sarawak. 1890-1940 CE.
DUROM.1976.119

Plate 26. Wooden bowl from Sarawak

Malcolm's favourite destination to escape from his work was Sarawak on the island of Borneo. He fell in love with the different indigenous cultures he encountered, particularly the Iban people of his adopted father Koh. Malcolm enjoyed watching them produce fabulous and functional items, showing off the beauty of their traditional artisanship. This carved hardwood dish was probably made by the Kayan or Kenyah peoples, and although functional, is made decorative through the elaborate dragon's head carvings on each side.

Dish: wood. Sarawak. 1945-1975 CE.
DUROM.1976.126

Plate 27. Everyday craftsmanship from Sarawak

Malcolm enjoyed collecting everyday objects just as much as high status artworks. Spending time with his adopted Iban family, as well as friends from other Dayak peoples, introduced him to many new forms of everyday art. He drew pleasure from watching Dayak women weaving baskets, such as this Kanowit example from rattan and other plant fibres. Amongst Malcolm's collections are many other pieces of everyday craftsmanship, including hats and headdresses, articles of clothing, and woven blankets.

Basket: plant fibre. Sarawak. 1945-1975 CE.
DUROM.1980.53

Plate 28. Stone sculpture from India

Malcolm purchased several examples of ancient Indian stone sculpture whilst living in Delhi as British High Commissioner. Here is the head of a lady sculpted in Chandella style during the rule of the Pala Empire. Although this period is often associated with Buddhism, she is a Hindu artwork, with traces of red paint showing a bindi mark on her forehead. Probably taken from a larger relief, she appears to have been used for votive purposes.

Female head: sandstone. India. 1000-1100 CE.
DUROM.1969.347

Plate 29. The Durham Bodhisattva

This piece of sculpture is now known as the Durham Bodhisattva and is one of the highlights of the collections at the Oriental Museum. Malcolm bought two Bodhisattva heads made in the ancient Kingdom of Gandhara. He eventually gave this one to the Oriental Museum, but kept the other for himself. Gandhara was situated in modern day Pakistan and Afghanistan, and Buddhism flourished there from the first century CE. The size and quality of this sculpture of a bodhisattva (a being who is able to reach nirvana but delays doing so through compassion for others) indicate that it probably belonged to a key icon in a major shrine.

Bodhisattva head: schist. Kingdom of Gandhara. 100-400 CE.
DUROM.1969.346

Plate 30. Indian walking stick

Malcolm accumulated many walking sticks during his adventurous career across many different lands. This one is a particularly elegant ceremonial stick made in northern India. It has a repeating flowery motif carved into the wood, and an impressive lion's head carved in ivory for its finial. Perhaps this is a deliberate reference to the British imperial lion – symbolic of the empire which Malcolm was dedicated to ending and replacing with a Commonwealth of equal nations.

Ceremonial walking stick: wood, ivory. India. 1900-1960 CE.
DUROM.1980.54

Plate 31. Laotian army baton

This baton would have belonged to an army officer in the Royal Lao Army. Laos was a French colony which became independent in 1953. On the silver finial is a three-headed elephant, the official symbol of the Kingdom of Laos and its Royal Army until a communist coup in 1975. Its appearance here makes the baton a fascinating relic of a brief but important period in Laotian history. The baton was given to Malcolm by one of the Laotian princes, probably his friend Prince Souvanna Phouma, to commemorate Malcolm's role in temporarily ending the civil war in Laos in 1962 (either at the time or on one of Malcolm's later trips to South East Asia).

Military baton: bamboo, silver. Laos. 1953-1975 CE.
DUROM.1976.144

Plate 32. Chinese ceramics purchased from Roger Bluett

Even after placing his collection of Chinese ceramics on loan to Durham University's Oriental Museum, Malcolm continued to add to it. He wished to fill gaps in his ceramic time-line of Chinese history. Whilst serving as a diplomat in Geneva, Kenya and throughout Africa during the 1960s, on visits back to his political masters in London he would call on his old friend, the dealer Roger Bluett, and buy more ceramics to send to the Oriental Museum. This Ming dynasty dish with a red, gold and green phoenix design was Malcolm's most expensive ceramic purchase, costing him £1,000 in April 1966.

Dish: porcelain. China. 1600-1650 (Ming dynasty).
DUROM.1969.330

Introductions

Uncle Malcolm

I am so pleased to have met Alexander Shaw, the editor, who together with Craig and Rachel Barclay introduced me to this previously unpublished manuscript written by my uncle, Malcolm MacDonald. I feel honoured to have been asked to write this foreword. It is such an interesting record of the appreciation of one man's passion for collecting beautiful things during a busy political and diplomatic life around the world.

Uncle Malcolm's admiration for beauty was not confined to works of art made by man, but extended to many of God's creations including wild flowers. One of his favourite recreations was bird watching. He kindly encouraged collections of both of these when my brother, John, and I stayed with him in Kenya in 1963. I surprised many Kenyan villagers by jumping out of a Land Rover with a long knife and a plant press to gather specimens for the herbarium in Nairobi. John took many beautiful photographs of the native birds and animals. He went on to have a career in ornithology and nature conservation. During this holiday we also had a glimpse of our Uncle's social entertaining. His guests included members of the Nepalese Royal family and also Sir Julian and Lady Huxley who were attending an international nature conservation conference. Political figures arrived daily for meetings and refreshments. Uncle Malcolm did not usually make these formal occasions as he wanted everyone to feel at ease. At the dinner for the King of Nepal, when other guests were dressed in their 'best', Uncle Malcolm walked in wearing a flowery shirt and invited the men to remove their jackets.

He was always great fun when he was with the family. In 1975 he led a group of British art gallery and museum experts on a tour of China to view archaeological and artistic discoveries made during the last 25 years. After the tour he returned to Hong Kong by train. I met Uncle Malcolm at Fanling Station in the New Territories and took him to our small British Army quarters in Sek Kong Village. Communications must have broken down as later that afternoon there was an urgent telephone call asking if we had Malcolm MacDonald because the Governor of Hong Kong was expecting him to stay at Government

House! Of course he stayed with us but accepted the Governor's offer of the loan of his official Chinese junk. Next day we had a lovely picnic on a sandy beach on one of the islands. Not long afterwards my husband and I were privileged to receive an invitation to a dinner party at Government House.

Back in England our children had a wonderful time visiting his home in Sevenoaks. He encouraged them to dress up in some of his treasured gifts – colobus monkey cloak, warthog headdress and academic cap – and to hold knives and spears. He even encouraged them to jump on his treasured four poster bed and referred to himself as 'Monkey Malcolm'. The visit would not have been complete without him standing on his head and walking on his hands. These same actions were said to have been requested by the Queen Mother to liven up a difficult party. On leaving his house each child was invited to choose one of the many walking sticks from a great collection inside the front door.

Now my children bring their own children to see Uncle Malcolm's *objets d'art* displayed at the Oriental Museum in Durham and we all feel proud that so many students and visitors can enjoy seeing items from his collections which none of us could afford to purchase for ourselves. I support the publication of this book as it is an interesting autobiography and a fitting tribute to his love of beauty and his success as a collector.

Victoria Bagshaw, 2018

'Not the Footballer': Malcolm MacDonald at the Oriental Museum

In 1955 the Rt. Hon. Malcolm MacDonald was appointed to the post of British High Commissioner to India. For the previous nine years he had been living and working in Singapore and Malaysia, where he had successively held the posts of Governor General of Malaya and Commissioner General for South East Asia. While in Singapore, MacDonald had amassed a considerable collection of Chinese ceramics. He did not wish to take this collection with him to India and so sought a temporary home in 'some art gallery where it would be enjoyed by countless visitors'.

Durham University was recommended to MacDonald by John Sparks, the London-based dealers in Chinese antiquities. The company was aware that a new School of Oriental Studies had been established and it was actively seeking collections with a view to creating a new museum to support teaching. MacDonald was not entirely convinced: Durham was a long way from London and he was keen that he should be able to access his pots whenever he visited the UK. Fast forward 16 years, and his initial reticence had evaporated. Indeed, the very same Malcolm MacDonald now held the post of Chancellor of Durham University, working tirelessly to promote the institution and regularly making the long journey north from London.

Today, it is not only Chinese ceramics but also objects from South and South East Asia donated by MacDonald that are displayed in the galleries of the University's Oriental Museum. What brought about this *volte face*? Two individuals must take much of the credit for swaying MacDonald: Thomas W. Thacker and Raymond Dawson.

Durham University was founded in 1832 and from the outset the teaching of non-European languages featured strongly on the curriculum. To begin with, the focus was on those languages connected with the study of Theology – Biblical Hebrew and Aramaic – although in the early twentieth century innovative courses in Arabic were added. At the outbreak of the Second World War however, the range of language teaching offered and institutional interest in Asian cultures was still, in common with most British universities at the time, very limited.

The realities and demands of war brought about a profound change in attitudes. When the UK had needed the skills of specialists proficient in the languages of the many countries impacted by the conflict, it had found itself to be sadly lacking. Professor Thacker, a brilliant linguist, understood this deficit very well. In 1941 he had been appointed as Professor of Hebrew and Oriental Languages at Durham University, but his academic career was interrupted by wartime service as part of Britain's intelligence community. When the teaching of languages in British universities was reviewed in the aftermath of the Second World War, Thacker had very clear ideas about what he wanted for Durham.

Durham University was one of five selected to receive government support to develop teaching in the 'Oriental' languages. A heavy emphasis was placed on producing talented graduates to fill the ranks of the military, diplomatic and intelligence services and when the new School of Oriental Studies was founded, Thomas Thacker's wartime experience provided him with the skills needed to take on its leadership. Early development centred on the existing areas of strength in West Asia, but before long, Thacker began to look further east and in 1952 Raymond Dawson was appointed to the newly-created post of Lecturer in Chinese Philosophy

From the outset, Thacker was clear that the teaching of any language had to be accompanied by efforts to understand the culture of the speakers of that language. For this purpose, he was convinced that his students needed access to a museum with relevant collections. No such institution existed within the North East of England and so Thacker set about building up collections that could be used to form the basis of the School's own museum.

In 1949 Thacker was able to acquire the magnificent collections of ancient Egyptian and Mesopotamian antiquities that had belonged to the Dukes of Northumberland. Comprising more than 2,500 objects, this collection would form the core collection of the planned new museum. Other small donations of art and archaeology began to trickle in thanks to Thacker's skills of persuasion.

In 1953, to mark Queen Elizabeth II's coronation, Dawson arranged an exhibition of Chinese bronzes loaned by A.E.K. Cull. This exhibition, staged in Southend House, proved to be far more successful than Thacker or Dawson had imagined and was followed by an exhibition of Chinese textiles within Cosin's Library on Palace Green. These exhibitions attracted not just specialists but also members of the public. In the wake of this success, Thacker and Dawson began to imagine a museum which might do more than simply support teaching and research for the University.

By 1955, when MacDonald was looking for a temporary home for his Chinese ceramics, plans were moving on at a swift pace in Durham. The School, for example, had acquired a new home in Elvet Hill House, a large Victorian villa sitting on open land to the south of the city. Moreover, Sir Charles Hardinge (Fifth Baronet of Belle Isle) had made a commitment to bequeath his important collection of Chinese jades and hardstones to the University and several other large collections of material from across Asia had been secured.

With the acquisition or promise of such material, Durham University was beginning to develop a critical mass of high-quality Asian art. MacDonald was persuaded that the northern university did indeed represent an appropriate temporary home for his beloved collection and in 1955 agreed to an initial loan period of five years. Arrangements were put in place to ship more than 230 pieces from Singapore, and this was achieved largely without incident.

Malcolm MacDonald had, up until this point, collected for his own enjoyment and enlightenment. As will become clear to the reader of this book, MacDonald had wide collecting interests, ranging from British furniture to South East Asian metalwork. His collecting was driven by his love of beauty: Malcom MacDonald purchased and surrounded himself with the things that he found beautiful, irrespective of their place of origin.

Once his Chinese ceramics were in Durham however, this world-view changed. Records show that, from 1955 onwards, the University would receive regular shipments of additions to the collection. MacDonald had decided that if this was to be a useful teaching collection, it needed to be as representative as possible of the myriad different styles of Chinese ceramic created from the Neolithic period up to the twentieth century. As a result some pieces were added to the collection that MacDonald himself found to be less than lovely, but as he recorded in 1971, his focus had shifted and his aim was now that his collection should be 'available for viewing and handling by young students in Britain who were learning about Chinese culture and arts'.

In 1960 the museum opened. Initially styled the *Gulbenkian Museum of Oriental Art and Archaeology*, it was located next door to the School of Oriental Studies to the south of the city centre. The new building was intended to be the first phase of an ambitious construction project to create three identical blocks linked by glass walkways and Japanese gardens. Sadly the funding necessary to realise the full plan was not forthcoming. The layout of the museum as constructed comprised teaching and research spaces on the ground floor (actually the highest level of the building), surrounding three open plan galleries cut into the hillside below. There was no provision for stores, as the aim was for all of the collections to be on display to maximise their usefulness for teaching.

From the day that it opened, the museum was overcrowded, in part because of the unexpected arrival shortly before its planned opening of a collection of more than 2,500 Chinese jades and hardstones from Sir Charles Hardinge. Hardinge had been a long-time supporter of the Oriental Museum and, as early as the spring of 1956, had lent a selection of pieces from his collection to one of the pioneering exhibitions organised by the School of Oriental Studies. He had long planned to bequeath his outstanding collection to the University, but following a severe fall early in 1960 took the decision instead to gift his collection during his lifetime.

This was a welcome addition to the nascent museum's collection, but its acceptance dictated that the planned gallery layouts had to be quickly rethought. Images of the MacDonald collection on display shortly after opening show cases packed with objects. Surviving labels from the time exhibit equally dense text. The public were allowed to visit the museum, though only for three afternoons a week. Those who came were faced with an academic teaching museum, built around displays and interpretation that made no allowance for non-specialists.

By the mid-1960s, MacDonald was keen to retire from his nomadic existence as a diplomat. However, there was a small problem. For decades MacDonald had lived in grace-and-favour dwellings. He had no home to retire to and no money to buy one. All of his income had been spent on beautiful things.

MacDonald had intended to gift his collection to the museum, but in 1967 was forced to ask the University to purchase the pieces instead. MacDonald had found a house that he wished to purchase in Sevenoaks, Kent. In order to fund its purchase, he offered to sell the collection to the University for one-third of its market value. He would help in the fundraising for the purchase by personally contacting potential donors. What he needed from the University was a commitment to make a payment immediately, so he could secure the property.

A deal was done. The University Treasurer made the required payment (effectively a loan) and the house was secured. MacDonald then set about retrospectively helping to raise the equivalent amount of money so that the ceramics could be given a permanent home in Durham.

Letters on file from the fundraising campaign make fascinating reading as they include personal letters to philanthropists such as John D. Rockefeller III making the blunt plea, 'I have no money of my own!'. By late 1968 all of the funds had been raised through a combination of grants from charities such as the Victoria and Albert Museum Grant Fund, the NACF (now the Art Fund), the Spalding Trust, Pilgrim Trust and other societies and organisations as well as donations from more than 185 individuals. The collection was formally added to the Museum's Accession Register in 1969 so that today all of these pieces retain a museum number which includes the number 1969. The acquisition was formally marked in 1972 by the publication of a comprehensive catalogue. Authored by Irenus László Legeza, it featured an extensive foreword by MacDonald that outlined the history and philosophy of his collecting.

By this point the relationship between MacDonald and Durham University had developed far beyond anything that either side might have envisaged in 1955. In 1971, MacDonald was invited to become Chancellor – or titular head – of the University, a post he was to hold until 1980.

During this period, MacDonald continued to make donations to the museum. Most notably, in 1976, he donated 144 South East Asian pieces ranging from the famous sword of Iban leader Temenengong Koh (plate 25) to a bronze Brunei cannon decorated with a stylised crocodile (plate 22). Ever keen to avoid unnecessary expenditure on shipping, MacDonald offered to pack a few items in with his luggage every time he visited Durham to fulfil his official duties as Chancellor. He even suggests in one letter that rather than catching the train, he could load two or three suitcases onto the bus from London to Durham 'to save the University some money on account of the Chancellor's travel expenses'. Museum staff replied that they would rather arrange to drive down and collect the pieces at the University's expense as, 'you would very likely get arrested at the bus station for carrying concealed weapons, which would produce a very unfortunate headline'. Once safely in Durham, MacDonald dictated extensive notes on these pieces, adding personal information on the people and places they connected him to.

By the time of his death in January 1981, MacDonald had transferred almost 600 objects to the Oriental Museum; making him one of the most important benefactors in the institution's history. Perhaps even more importantly, he had made many friends and won numerous admirers among Durham's students, staff and local residents for his easy manner, sense of humour and great passion for all facets of culture and learning.

Throughout the 1980s and '90s, efforts to raise the money needed to extend the museum continued. However, the focus on such grand future plans meant that the existing galleries were not updated. They accordingly began to look dated and out of step with both the museum's growing function as a public museum and with changes in teaching and research methods.

The funding needed for the major development continued to prove elusive, but in 2000 the Heritage Lottery Fund supported the opening of a new gallery to showcase Chinese art and culture. *Marvels of China*, however, focused on other more recent additions to the museum and the MacDonald collections continued to languish on the lowest level of the museum in a cold and uninviting gallery that was avoided by all but the most dedicated of visitors.

In 2008, museum staff began a programme to completely renovate all of the museum's permanent galleries. High on the list of priorities was the Chinese gallery containing much of the MacDonald collection. Between 2009 and 2011 major grants were secured from the Designation Development Fund and the DCMS/Wolfson Museums & Galleries Improvement Fund to enhance the display and interpretation of our Chinese collections Chinese ceramic specialist Xiaoxin Li was brought in to review the entire Chinese pottery collection in the light of modern scholarship. Equally importantly, the gallery space housing the MacDonald displays was completely refurbished to provide a warmer, more welcoming atmosphere.

Central to the redisplay plan was a decision to reduce the number of objects on show. This might seem like an odd thing for a museum to do. Cases which have previously housed densely-packed shelves of ceramics were re-evaluated and hundreds of pots were removed from display and put into storage. Museum visitors are often amazed to hear how many objects museums have in storage. There is sometimes a perception that somehow curators are keeping all of the treasures for themselves. Quite the opposite is true.

The dense teaching displays, some of which appeared unchanged since 1960, put most visitors off. There was just too much to take in. The aim of the redisplay was to select only the very best examples of each type of ceramic available. These were then housed in a display that was arranged chronologically from the Neolithic period to the modern day: stretching in sequence from one end of the long gallery to the other. In this way the visitor can quite literally walk through time, watching the development of one of China's most important art forms over the millennia.

The redisplay was no easy task, and each case now contains between four and nine pieces. Selecting which example to use was far from easy, but the response of visitors suggests that the effort has paid off. From being the least popular and least visited gallery in the museum, the gallery is now one of the most popular.

The opening of the new MacDonald Gallery in 2011 was followed by the creation of the Roberts Gallery of the Himalayas, South Asia and South East Asia. This gallery now showcases many of MacDonald's other gifts to the museum, ranging from Iban beadwork to Gandharan sculpture (plate 29). In the course of this development many pieces were returned to store but, at the same time, pieces which had never before been on public view were placed before the public gaze.

But what of the pieces now in storage? These do not languish unloved and unused. Just as it was in Thacker's day, the Oriental Museum is an integral part of Durham University and, as such, it continues to be at the heart of University teaching. Using objects from the stored collections allows students to learn by handling original works without curators having to disturb public displays. In 2017, more than 1000 objects from across the museum's collections were used to support Durham University teaching, including many specimens collected by Malcolm MacDonald. The relaunch of Chinese Studies at Durham University in recent years has allowed new generations of students to be inspired by the same beauty that first seduced MacDonald. Today the museum is not tied to a single School but rather serves the whole University. Students studying South East Asian politics, Visual Cultures, Geography or History are accordingly just as likely to work with the Oriental Museum's collections as is a language student.

But why does the title of this essay refer to a 'footballer'? A constant challenge for the Oriental Museum's staff is that another Malcolm MacDonald continues to be celebrated in the North East of England: the legendary Newcastle United and England soccer star. The legacy of a player still remembered by many as 'Supermac' is enduring, and we need take great pains in our tours to explain to visitors that he did not enjoy a secret life as a connoisseur of Asian art! 'Our' Malcolm MacDonald, as museum staff tend to refer to him, deserves to be equally recognised. We hope this book will go some way towards achieving that aim.

Craig Barclay & Rachel Barclay, 2018

A Lifetime of Adventure

'I like Beauty, I love Beauty, I worship Beauty in all its earthly forms'. With these words and the others contained in this book, Malcolm MacDonald transports us into his world. In many ways the world contained within these pages is a vanished one. Through Malcolm's memories we can explore the inter-war antiques market of Europe, the diplomatic scene across Cold War Asia, and the vast cultural changes following the end of empire in Africa. Along the way we encounter a multitude of unique, richly-described characters, from art dealers across southern England to artistic head-hunters in Borneo; from the family of a Prime Minister to landscape painters in Canada; from the Chinese businessmen who made Singapore the success it is today to master silversmiths in Brunei; not to mention a multitude of politicians, diplomats and even King Norodom Sihanouk of Cambodia. This is the world in which Malcolm MacDonald lived and worked, and this book is our gateway into it.

Malcolm John MacDonald was born in the Scottish fishing village of Lossiemouth in 1901. He was the son of James Ramsay MacDonald (more commonly known just as Ramsay) and Margaret Ethel MacDonald (née Gladstone). His family tree included the renowned scientist Lord Kelvin and the equally distinguished statesman William Gladstone. By the time Malcolm was twenty-three years old, his father had entered 10 Downing Street as Britain's first Labour Prime Minister. Ramsay and Malcolm's residence in 'Number Ten' was only short-lived, as by the end of the year Ramsay's government had fallen. Just five years later, in 1929, Ramsay regained the premiership and Malcolm won his first election as a Member of Parliament.

Two events in Malcolm's early adulthood had a defining influence upon the course of his extraordinary life. The first was his father's electoral triumph of 1924, setting Malcolm on the road to his own political career despite a residual dream of becoming a successful author. The second was an Easter vacation in Paris during which the youthful Malcolm – then a scholarship student at Oxford – fell in love for the first time in his life. Malcolm always had an eye for beautiful women. During his final years at Bedales School, as an aspiring writer, Malcolm was placed in charge of organising the school plays. He drew criticism from parents for casting the prettiest girls irrespective of their lack of acting talent.

Yet the lady who captivated the heart of Malcolm in Paris, and retained it ever after, was not of flesh and blood. As you will shortly discover, she was a porcelain shepherdess. Amongst the museums and art markets of the iconic French capital, Malcolm began a lifelong infatuation with beautiful works of art. Before the day was out, he had become a collector.

Whilst some collectors confine themselves to just a single genre, Malcolm amassed an eclectic range of collections during his lifetime. Over the following pages he describes his passion for English porcelain, Queen Anne furniture, Old Master paintings, Chinese ceramics, the craftsmanship of indigenous peoples across the globe, and many more besides. This was the product of his eventful, and at times eccentric, lifetime of adventure. Despite a successful career in British politics from 1929-41, it was a posting to Canada by Winston Churchill which set Malcolm on a new trajectory as one of Britain's most prominent and best travelled Cold War diplomats.

Malcolm's youthful ambitions were to find six lifelong friends, to write six books which would stand the test of time and to compete in the Grand National. A natural, charismatic socialiser, he achieved the first with ease. Many of these friends were not fellow Europeans. Indeed, a case could be made that Malcolm was more comfortable in the company of Canadian and Asian friends than he was with his fellow Scots and Englishmen. Some of his closest friends appear in this book, including the artist Stanley Spencer; the King of Cambodia, Norodom Sihanouk; and Temenggong Koh, the Borneo head-hunter who became Malcolm's second father. Other friends from different periods of Malcolm's life included the playwright and actor Ivor Novello; plentiful distinguished and beautiful actresses of the 1930s; the Canadian painter A. Y. Jackson; the talented Singaporean wildlife photographer Christina Loke; and the communist Chinese diplomats Zhou Enlai and

Chen Yi. These were not empty, political relationships, nor were they the associations of somebody who sought grandeur through the company of the famous. They were Malcolm's genuine personal friends, who shared his love of the arts, appreciated his wit and intellect, and remained in contact with him throughout his life (sometimes to the embarrassment of the British government which he served).

Despite his hopes of a literary career, Malcolm struggled to achieve his second ambition of youth. Unable to score a success with his fiction, his first notable achievement as a writer was to pen a series of articles about the Far East for a coalition of Canadian newspapers in 1929. As a travel-writer as well as an amateur ethnologist and bird-watcher, Malcolm partly achieved his ambition. To date, his published books include *Down North*, *The Birds of Brewery Creek*, *Borneo People*, *Angkor*, *Birds in my Indian Garden*, *Birds in the Sun*, *Treasure of Kenya*, *Peoples and Places*, *Titans and Others*, and *Inside China*. It can be justified that *Borneo People* (an account of the vanishing way of life of the Dayak peoples of Sarawak in the 1950s) and *Angkor* (the first major English-language book about the now famous temple complex) were perhaps a modest literary legacy. He also collaborated with another friend, the pioneering Malaysian Chinese art photographer K. F. Wong, to create visual records of the Borneo peoples with whom he fell in love.

Unsurprisingly, Malcolm's third dream of riding and finishing (although not necessarily winning) the Grand National never came to fruition. The closest he ever came was in owning Billy Carol, a prize-winning racehorse on the Singapore and Malayan circuit who earned Malcolm plenty of money to spend on his collections. As Malcolm reminisced, Billy Carol 'generously allowed me to buy a number of lovely Chinese and Persian carpets and rugs with that money, only asking for sacks full of hay in return'.[1]

After accepting that the life of a novelist was not part of his destiny, the book which Malcolm most wanted to write was his memoirs as a collector. In 1972, his publisher rejected the draft manuscript which he had prepared under the title *The Pleasures and Pains of Collecting*. In those days, there was little academic interest in the history and philosophy of collecting, and Malcolm's editors did not feel there was a market for the book. Fortunately, this has now changed. The history of collecting is now a significant scholarly discipline, and, as the accumulator of one of the most important collections of Chinese ceramics in Britain, Malcolm's story deserves to be told.

This is not to mention the pertinence of Malcolm's successful diplomatic career. Over the course of his twelve years in politics and subsequent four decades as an international negotiator, Malcolm's achievements included helping to pioneer the modern Commonwealth; the championing of racial equality in South East Asia; repairing Anglo-Indian relations after the Suez crisis; ending the Laotian Civil War in 1962; guiding Kenya peacefully to independence; and playing a crucial role in opening up China to the West in the 1970s. Sometimes he made mistakes, and notably proved unable to resolve the conflict in the Palestine Mandate in the 1930s or Rhodesia in the 1960s, but in every appointment in which he served, Malcolm succeeded in leaving behind a positive legacy, be it political or cultural.

In all these achievements, Malcolm's personality and reputation as a collector played a significant part in his diplomatic success. His enthusiasm for learning about different cultures, understanding of the need for cultural as well as political decolonisation, and patronage of modern creative arts to achieve social transformation earned Malcolm the trust and respect not only of the British government but also of key international leaders. Whilst Malcolm was in Beijing as the personal guest of the Chinese government during the Cuban Missile Crisis, the communist premier Zhou Enlai referred to Malcolm as 'the only Imperialist they trusted'.[2] Their conversations about Chinese ceramics played no small part in building this rapport.

Therefore, this book is not only the memoirs of a passionate antiquarian collector and patron of modern artists including the Spencer brothers, John Nash and the Canadian Group of Seven. These reminiscences also cast insight into the making of a successful diplomat. In the world in which we find ourselves – every bit as dangerous (and also exciting) as the somewhat different world which Malcolm describes – this question is just as relevant today as it was during Malcolm's negotiations at the height of the Cold War.

There is a third reason for finally publishing Malcolm's book. After leaving Singapore in 1955, Malcolm placed his collection of Chinese ceramics on loan to support the recently established School of Oriental Studies at the University of Durham. Over a decade later, strapped of cash through what some would regard as reckless spending on beautiful things, he sold them to the museum. Over subsequent years he donated further unique objects from his travels across South East Asia. Today, this institution is the Durham University Oriental Museum: one of the most significant holdings of North African and Asian art in the United Kingdom. Malcolm's collection of ceramics is exceptional in its chronological and typographical breadth. In addition, his collection of local craftsmanship and photographs from Borneo, as well as unique personal gifts such as King Sihanouk's xylophone, make Malcolm's collections at Durham truly special. His strong social conscience and patronage of local art industries in Asia and Africa mean Malcolm was a collector of whom Durham University – of which Malcolm served as Chancellor during the 1970s – can be proud. As well as making Malcolm's thoughts about collecting available to the public for the first time, this book celebrates the legacy of his collections at the Oriental Museum, which are superbly illustrated in the colour plates you will find herein.

It is my hope as editor that you will be inspired to come and visit Malcolm's collections for yourselves, as well as those of many other fascinating individuals including Richard Rutt (Anglican Bishop of Daejeon in South Korea), the Fourth Duke of Northumberland (the accumulator of an internationally significant collection of ancient Egyptian artefacts) and the businessmen and philanthropist Gerard Arnhold. Perhaps you have done so already; in which case, be prepared for a whirlwind tour of Europe, Canada, Asia and Africa, as Malcolm reveals the origins of many of his most treasured pieces over the course of this book.

Before I hand over to Malcolm, I beg leave to further introduce the man behind the collections, as well as to relate some of the stories which – due to the rejection received from his publishers – Malcolm never got around to including in this book. He left behind a number of rough notes on how he wished *The Pleasures and Pains of Collecting* to be finished, as well as suggestions for illustrations. From these I have tried to put together this book the way Malcolm would have wished it to appear.

The Making of a Collector

As Malcolm relates in this book, his epiphany moment as a collector and art connoisseur was in Paris at around the age of twenty. Over the following years, his expanding interest in English ceramics, furniture and paintings was inspired by his father's own collecting impulses, admiring the great artworks in the Prime Minister's country residence at Chequers, and through conversations with the many art dealers he befriended.

Following his entry into Parliament in 1929, Malcolm was able to afford even greater indulgence, and became a friend and patron of living artists including Paul Nash, Gilbert Spencer and Stanley Spencer, as well as beginning to decorate his Tudor farmhouse with some Old Masters. In this he benefitted from the Great Depression which haunted the 1930s, dropping the prices of artworks which he would otherwise have been unable to afford. Rapid promotion from junior minister to senior Cabinet positions certainly helped the comparatively young Malcolm in becoming a satisfied connoisseur, although at first he refused a pay rise due to concern for national finances.

During the same decade, Malcolm continued to pursue beauty through several friendships with eminent actors and actresses. He would leave Parliament late in the evening and await his theatrical friends in their dressing rooms before heading off to dinner with the likes of Ivor Novello, Dorothy Dickson, Beatrice Lillie, Noel Coward, Laurence Olivier and Vivien Leigh. Perhaps today the tabloids would have erupted over Malcolm's visits to their dressing rooms; but those were different times. When preparing this manuscript, Malcolm noted down that 'one of the things one collects is people. I have made a fine collection through the last sixty years, of very many different types: Frenchmen, Americans, Indians, Chinese, Head-hunters, Eskimos, African tribesmen'.[3] Perhaps to this list could be added 'thespians'.

Back in 1924, Malcolm had departed the Old World as a member of an Oxford University debating team. Touring the United States, Canada, Australia and New Zealand, he discovered a love of travel but did not indulge in the artistic passions which his visit to Paris had recently aroused. The only collecting to which he succumbed was the collecting of people. In this he certainly made some unique acquisitions. Whilst in Los Angeles, Malcolm was befriended by a Lord Charles Conyngham who claimed to be an acquaintance of Ramsay MacDonald. Lord Charles was courting a rich, substantially older, American oil baron's widow, and introduced Malcolm to her as the son of his old friend, the Prime Minister. After Lord Charles made a minor *faux pas* in confusing the nickname of an Oxford College for its Cambridge counterpart, Malcolm's suspicions were aroused. With the help of the British Consul-General he proved that the man he had met was not the real Lord Charles but a confidence trickster, and only narrowly prevented what would have been an entirely mercenary and unhappy marriage.

Also on his travels of 1924-25, Malcolm visited the Fiji Islands, where he enjoyed meeting the grandson of the warlord King Cakabau. Malcolm was also introduced to a chief of over one hundred years of age named Ratu Akuri, who reminisced about the bygone days when his people had regularly enjoyed banqueting upon what they referred to as 'long pig'. Thus Malcolm discovered second hand that Europeans made poor fare, having too much salt in their flesh (probably because they were mostly sailors).

Meeting this veteran warrior in Fiji was Malcolm's first encounter with non-Western cultures. It started his lifelong fascination with meeting and understanding peoples across the globe. However, it was Malcolm's next trip outside Europe, in 1929, that introduced him to the peoples and artworks of East Asia. The year 1929 was a defining moment in Malcolm's life as a collector. Not only did his greater income as an MP enable greater spending, but it was also the year in which he first discovered what would become his greatest collecting passion: Chinese ceramics.

Malcolm was in Kyoto, Japan, for an international conference, for which he, as a young Member of Parliament, was acting as a secretary. On this occasion he befriended John D. Rockefeller III, and they together made the acquaintance of a number of geishas at the Ichiriki Tea House. One evening Malcolm risked scandal by escorting an entourage of trainee geishas back to his plush hotel. There he taught them how to use an elevator for the first time in their lives, and playfully woke up all his neighbours to introduce them to his three Japanese friends. Fortunately for Malcolm's reputation, he returned all three young ladies to the Tea House after harmlessly indulging their wishes for repeated elevator trips.

Exploring the beautiful scenery of ancient Kyoto, Malcolm came across the antiques establishment of the Yamanaka Brothers. Unlike the vendors with whom he was familiar in England, the Brothers' premises was not a single shop but an elegant Japanese garden, interspersed with several themed pavilions selling all manner of Asian antiques. Malcolm became enchanted by the Chinese ceramics on display, particularly beautiful Tang dynasty figures which depicted solemn, thoughtful court officials just as magnificently as they captured the lifelike movement of prancing horses or haughty camels. Unfortunately, such treasures were beyond his present price range. In this book you can read some of his impressions, as Malcolm recalls two of the five pieces he was able to buy: a pair of Ming dynasty lion shaped candleholders, now in the Durham University Oriental Museum and illustrated in plate 5.

What Malcolm does not describe in *The Pleasures and Pains of Collecting* is how he was equally entranced by the people, architecture and history of Japan and the Far East. After the conference, he continued his journey through Korea to China, where he became the guest of the British Minister in Beijing, Sir Miles Lampson. Sir Miles showed Malcolm round the Summer Palace and he also made excursions to the Temple of Heaven, Forbidden City, Ming Tombs and – of course – the Great Wall. Completely awe-struck by these majestic monuments of Imperial China, Malcolm began a lifelong admiration for Chinese civilisation and the people who had built it.

On the train to Nanjing, Malcolm jotted down a letter to his sister Ishbel in which he reflected upon his travels in the Orient. He wrote enthusiastically that 'I had always thought that old Japanese pictures could not possible be a fair representation of Japanese nature, that the trees could not be so delicate and grotesque, nor the hills so humpy and green, nor the animals so fantastic, nor the temples so dream-like, nor its people so gay in appearance and costume, nor Fuji even so perfect in symmetry, as Japanese painters made all these things. But it was a really delightful shock to find, even before we had left Yokohama, that the Japanese artists have exaggerated and distorted nothing at all'. Even more pleasingly, 'the way in which they have retained their old courtesy, unselfishness and modesty in the midst of the turmoil of the invasion of Western ideas and customs is remarkable'.[4]

Chinese antiques from the Yamanaka Brothers were not Malcolm's only indulgence in Japan. He also bought many examples of Japanese craftsmanship. As he told Ishbel, 'Kyoto's shops are the most tempting that I ever set foot in, and I did not resist temptation, as prices were reasonable. So I am bringing a good many treasures home; silks, lacquer, damascene, colour prints and even oil-paper umbrellas'.[5]

Despite this first introduction to the Orient in 1929, it was not until Malcolm was stationed as a diplomat in Singapore from 1946 that he seriously began collecting artworks from that region. One of the reasons for this hiatus was simply the unavailability of affordable Chinese ceramics back in London at this time. Another was Malcolm's own consciousness of his lack of knowledge about Asian art. For Malcolm, collecting was just as much about gaining knowledge as it was about acquiring objects.

After arriving in Singapore in 1946, Malcolm found himself in the midst of countless opportunities to expand both his understanding and his ownership of Oriental art. In this book, he describes learning about Chinese ceramics from knowledgeable connoisseurs including the pre-eminent Singapore businessman Dato S. Q. Wong, as well as friendly dealers in Hong Kong such as T. Y. King or Eddie Chow. Malcolm had only a passing acquaintance with King when the latter emigrated from Shanghai to Hong Kong in 1949, worried that his business would have less opportunity to flourish in communist China as it would in capitalist, British, Hong Kong. Needing capital to re-establish himself, King was willing to sell choice pieces for a fraction of their usual cost. Malcolm bought a particularly fine bowl which had belonged to the Chinese imperial court and a lovely Tang dynasty figure of a Turfan man (plate 1), cementing a friendship which would prove equally beneficial for King and himself. Over the course of many years Malcolm would frequently pay over-the-odds for pieces which he particularly desired.

At first, Malcolm's collecting was inspired mainly by his love of beauty, and he prioritised the types of ceramics which he had the most aesthetic admiration for. Although availability and prices sometimes limited his ambitions, he acquired a large collection of Chinese export wares (predominantly from the Ming and Qing dynasties) and he particularly liked domestic wares from the Song and Yuan dynasties. After deciding to place his collection of domestic wares on loan to the Oriental Museum, he began collecting pieces which he found less beautiful in order to fill the gaps in his collection. His collecting became inspired by a desire to create an excellent teaching collection, as well as a love of beauty.

Another leading authority from whom Malcolm learned a great deal about art and antiques was the King of Laos. The ancient royal capital, Luang Prabang, was one of his favourite cities in Asia. Describing his frequent visits during the 1940s and 1950s, Malcolm wrote that 'those trips were like journeys not only through hundreds of miles in space but also hundreds of years in time'.[6] He befriended the King of Laos, who was a renowned authority of certain aspects of South East Asian antiques. On one occasion Malcolm bought a Burmese Karen rain drum from an antiques dealer in Luang Prabang and promptly took it to the King to have its authenticity verified. At other times, he enjoyed learning about Buddhist faith and practices from the Laotian Crown Prince. This understanding gave Malcolm a deeper appreciation of Buddhist art.

Consequently, when Malcolm departed South East Asia for India in 1955, he was entirely baffled by its culture. As he relates in chapter fifteen, he did not fall in instant love with its art and architecture. At first he mainly collected pieces which were recognisable to him because of their Buddhist origins, such as the ancient Gandharan Bodhisattva head illustrated in plate 29. Yet as Malcolm learned more about Indian history and Hindu beliefs, he came to better understand and better love their unique art-forms. One of the few Indian artefacts from his collections to survive in the Oriental Museum superbly encapsulates the political crossroads of India in the 1950s, torn between an ancient and proud history, its contemporary emergence as an independent nation and the strong ties with Britain which Malcolm helped to maintain through the Commonwealth. This is a beautiful wooden walking stick, topped with an end of polished ivory carved into the shape of a lion's head – the iconic symbol of the British Empire (plate 30).

As a collector of art and antiques, Malcolm's activities were shaped just as much by his interactions with the many friends he made around the world as they were by his pursuit of beauty and knowledge. Throughout his postings to Canada, Asia and Africa, Malcolm wished to repay local peoples for their kindness and hospitality through leaving behind a cultural legacy. He explains in this book how he supported new art museums in Malaya and Singapore to encourage young people to appreciate their cultural heritage. Similarly, he extended patronage to up-and-coming creators of beauty in the hope of producing future masterpieces for later generations to enjoy. In India, he particularly admired and collected the modernist painter M. F. Husain; these pictures can today be seen in the University of Malaya Art Gallery and National University of Singapore. A devout believer in the social power of art, in Singapore, Malaysia and Kenya Malcolm hoped to use material culture to build new, post-colonial national identities. A man ahead of his time, he was an early proponent of what future historians would term cultural decolonisation.

Malcolm's social conscience extended to engaging in debate surrounding the ethics of collecting. When on a visit to China in 1971, he gave his moral support to new Chinese laws to prevent the export of artistic treasures to foreign connoisseurs. Perhaps there was some hypocrisy in this, but it must be remembered that Malcolm was buying pieces from the 1940s to 1960s, and that these had already left China – centuries before in the case of Swatow ware ceramics intended for the export market, and others more recently following the relocation of dealers such as T. Y. King. His Chinese friends were most pleased by Malcolm's support, whereas the British Foreign Office felt somewhat embarrassed. The record of British appropriation of antiquities from around the world perhaps hung more heavily on their national conscience than Malcolm's own collecting did upon his.

Whilst many collectors were focused solely on preserving the past, Malcolm was equally committed to securing the future. Perhaps this was the result of his upbringing as the son of Britain's first Labour Prime Minister. Malcolm shared his father's hopes of achieving social progress through democratic socialism. As well as helping to support museums in South East Asia, he was keen for his collection of domestic ware Chinese ceramics to inspire budding scholars back home in England. He loaned and eventually sold this collection to the Oriental Museum in Durham. Throughout his career, Malcolm took his public responsibilities seriously. Whilst serving as Chancellor of Durham University in the 1970s, he would travel around on economy class public transport – just as he had done as a Cabinet minister in the 1930s – in order to reduce the burden upon the tax payer.

The Making of a Diplomat

Malcolm never expected to spend over three decades of his life as a diplomat. After abandoning his hopes of a literary career, he set his sights on the arena of British politics. At first unsure if this was the right direction, he refused the Labour Party's offer of a safe seat and consequently lost his first general election in the Conservative stronghold of Bassetlaw in 1923. During his father's first electoral victory in 1924, Malcolm was debating in North America, so his sister Ishbel contested Bassetlaw as his proxy, again unsuccessfully. Five years later, as Ramsay returned to Downing Street as Prime Minister, Malcolm finally won Bassetlaw for Labour.

Despite his relative youthfulness (for a politician), Malcolm's energy, charm and talent brought him rapid promotion. One of his first tasks as an MP was to attend the Kyoto conference which enticed him into the world of Chinese ceramics. Over the next few years, he pushed the Statute of Westminster through Parliament, thus creating the basis for the modern British Commonwealth, acted as a secret envoy to Mahatma Gandhi, and toured Australia and New Zealand as chair of an interdepartmental migration committee. He quickly achieved Cabinet status, serving Prime Ministers Stanley Baldwin and Neville Chamberlain as Colonial Secretary (1935, 1938-40) and Dominions Secretary (1935-39). He was tasked with communicating with the Dominions during momentous events including the King's Abdication and the Munich Crisis. Upon reaching an agreement with Hitler, Chamberlain telephoned Malcolm to inform him of 'peace in our time'; unbeknownst to the Prime Minister, Malcolm's attentions on the other end of the line were somewhat distracted by the innocent antics of his actress friend Beatrice Lillie.

At the start of the Second World War, Winston Churchill moved Malcolm over to the Ministry of Health. This was a vital job which put Malcolm at the heart of Britain's air raid precautions and civil defence. Like Churchill, Malcolm preferred to watch the London blitz from the open air rather than seeking cover in a shelter. He would travel to bomb sites and watch the emergency services' response, looking for ways to improve protocols and potentially save more lives.

Then Churchill decided to send government ministers to key allies abroad. Whilst Lord Halifax, formerly Foreign Secretary, went to the United States, Malcolm was despatched to Canada. With his experience in conducting negotiations with the Dominions, Malcolm was the obvious choice. Yet he did not expect this posting would be more than a temporary pause in his political career. In fact, it proved to be the start of an even more successful calling as a diplomat.

Whilst in Canada during the Second World War, Malcolm's primary duty was to ensure co-ordination of the Anglo-Canadian war effort. He needed to represent Britain's interests, and also to support the Canadian government in bringing about its own war mobilisation. This sometimes entailed expeditions to the Canadian Arctic, where he helped the Canadians survey sites for potential new airfields, and also reported back to the British Cabinet on domestic opinion in Canada. Malcolm was able to assuage any doubts that the indigenous populations of Canada – the First Nations and the Arctic peoples – would prove lacklustre in contributing to the war effort. He also fell in love, enjoying a whirlwind romance with his future wife Audrey on the ski-slopes. Audrey Rowley was a beautiful war widow, and the two married in December 1946. They had one daughter, Fiona, and Malcolm also gained two step-children.

During his time in Canada, Malcolm proved the qualities which made him so effective as a diplomat and architect of decolonisation: an easy-going manner, genuine fascination with local culture, and disdain for archaic pomp. He refused a knighthood when posted to Singapore in 1946. The government worried this would make it harder for high status people to respect him; Malcolm reasoned that not having a title would make it easier to win the respect of the ordinary people, and in the world of decolonisation and the global Cold War, this was more important.

For two years Malcolm served as Governor General, overseeing the individual governments in the British colonies of Malaya, Singapore, Sarawak and North Borneo as well as the semi-independent protectorate of Brunei. His old friend from Beijing, Sir Miles Lampson (now Lord Killearn), was his Foreign Office counterpart, keeping track of all the British Embassies in South East Asia. Their families enjoyed spending time together, and both Miles and Malcolm became avid devotees of the Singapore antiques scene. Then in 1948, the British government decided one man could do both jobs, and Malcolm became

Commissioner General for South East Asia. He lived in Johore, Malaya, in what was once a grand Sultan's palace called Bukit Serene, which seemed to symbolise the high status but nebulous substance of his appointment. Commuting to work each day in Singapore, Malcolm had no executive powers. His job was to coordinate the activities of British Governors, Ambassadors, military chiefs and even spies throughout South East Asia. The vague nature of this brief gave him opportunity to devise his own, unique role.

Malcolm's diplomatic style was entirely unconventional. Dubbed 'the shirt-sleeve diplomat' by the British press, he disdained formality, saw little point in protocol, and loathed racial segregation.[7] To break up boring meetings he would walk on his hands, usually to his guests' delight. He did everything in his power to promote racial equality in Malaya and Singapore, leading through example by getting out of his palace and spending time talking to ordinary local people. Whether meeting wealthy Chinese businessmen or Malay labourers, Malcolm was his typically relaxed, interested and amicable self. It is little wonder that he won more friends amongst Singapore's Asian populations than its somewhat more conservative expatriate community.

Nowhere was this more clear than in Malcolm's relationships with the indigenous Dayak peoples of Borneo. Borneo, particularly Sarawak, became his favourite bolt-hole. Ruled personally by the British Brooke family (the 'White Rajahs') until 1946, Sarawak was now a government colony, and Malcolm's help was needed in explaining this distinction to its inhabitants.

Whereas other travellers would be forced to wait for the next ferry, Malcolm's status meant he could order the Royal Air Force to provide him a flying boat for his frequent visits to the jungle interior. Landing in Kuching, he would travel upriver and spend days – sometimes weeks – living with and learning from the many different Dayak peoples. Sometimes the British government were driven into a panic during Malcolm's elopements when they found themselves totally unable to contact him. Yet his expeditions – which he wrote about in *Borneo People* – were a necessary part of his diplomatic brief. Malcolm had a vision that one day the British colonies of South East Asia would unite into an independent Greater Malaysia. By cultivating the loyalty of the Dayak peoples, Malcolm played a key role in making that happen. Although Singapore chose to leave in 1965, the state of Malaysia which exists today was first conceived of by a number of far-sighted leaders in the 1940s, one of whom was Malcolm MacDonald.

Of all the peoples of Borneo, Malcolm was closest to the Iban and loved reminding his more staid political masters of his friendship with these famous head-hunters. On his first visit, the Iban built a bamboo triumphal arch to greet him, adorned with severed Japanese heads. He soon established a rapport with Paramount Chief Temenggong Koh, in which a shared passion for Chinese ceramics played no small part. Koh was an aged warrior and statesman with a ferocious reputation. Not only had he taken over one hundred heads in his lifetime, but he also became perhaps the world's first flying head-hunter when he took to the skies in a spotter plane to identify targets for British bombers during the latter stages of the Second World War.

Their relationship developed to the extent that Koh adopted Malcolm as his son. Malcolm's natural father, Ramsay, had passed away in 1937, and he embraced this opportunity to gain a new family. He later reflected that 'one of my proud boasts is that I have had two fathers, one of whom was a Prime Minister of Britain and the other a Paramount Chief in Borneo'.[8] The affection between the Scottish diplomat and old head-hunter was entirely sincere, and Malcolm continued to regard Koh's family as his own after the great chief's passing.

Malcolm's popularity with Asian peoples sometimes earned him the antagonism of the European settler community in Singapore. After a spate of highly critical letters in the Singapore press which attacked Malcolm's drives for a fairer, more equal society, Temenggong Koh came to visit his adopted son. Head-hunting was not allowed under British colonial rule, although during the war it had been tacitly encouraged. In this press criticism, Koh saw an opportunity to gain Malcolm's permission for one final head-hunt, and asked his new son whether he and his warriors could go and take the heads of Malcolm's critics. Perhaps unsurprisingly, Malcolm had little choice but to refuse, but relished the irony that his critics were alive and free to speak their minds only as a result of his own magnanimity.

Whenever Malcolm went to visit his Borneo friends he would don his MacDonald tartan kilt 'to show them that they were not the only wild men in the world'.[9] He taught them the Highland Fling in return for their instruction in traditional Dayak dances. Malcolm certainly appreciated the great beauty of Iban ladies, but never succumbed to any temptations he may have felt. In his own words, 'this was perhaps the only respect in which I did not act as one of the old White Rajahs'.[10]

Malcolm's unconventional approach to diplomacy proved vital in preparing Malaya, Borneo and Singapore for eventual independence. Likewise, it helped him create friendships with international statesmen in South East Asia. It was important for Britain to build alignments with independent Asian nations. Malcolm played a critical role in developing a British approach to the Cold War in Asia, believing that it was better for nations like Thailand, Laos and Cambodia to be a neutral buffer zone than to become American client states which would only generate greater international tensions. His frequent visits to these nations helped Malcolm achieve his goals during the turbulent decade of the 1950s.

After many extensions to his appointment as Commissioner General, in 1955 Malcolm was moved to India as British High Commissioner. For the next five years, he worked hard to improve Commonwealth relations, particularly following the 1956 Suez Crisis which threatened to disrupt Anglo-Indian unity. Once again, he proved extremely effective at this.

His reputation as a connoisseur of Asian art and known respect for Asian cultures earned Malcolm the great respect of the British governments which he served. As a result, when civil war broke out in Laos, Malcolm was chosen to be one of two chairmen of an international conference in Geneva which eventually brokered agreement and ended the conflict in 1962. His fellow chairman was a

Soviet diplomat, Georgy Pushkin, who developed a good working relationship with Malcolm. Despite being opposed to communism in Malaya and Singapore, Malcolm got along as easily with communist statesmen as he did with everybody else. During his time in Singapore, India and Geneva, he became very close with certain communist Chinese leaders, which enabled Malcolm to play no small part in bridging the gap between Britain and China during the later years of the Cold War.

Following a string of successful appointments in Asia, Malcolm's final career move was to Africa. In 1963 he arrived in Kenya, charged with overseeing that colony's transition to independence. By working with nationalist leader Jomo Kenyatta and earning the respect of Kenya's people, Malcolm carried out this duty with distinction. He stayed on as High Commissioner until 1966, when he became a roving Special Representative to the Commonwealth nations of East Africa. This was similar to Malcolm's Singapore appointment, and gave him opportunity to meet many new cultures as he tried to defuse complex conflicts including the Rhodesian crisis (which alas proved too intractable even for Malcolm's considerable talents). In 1969 he retired from public service, and his lifetime of achievements across the globe was rewarded by appointment to the Order of Merit, perhaps the pinnacle of the British honours system. He continued to lead an active public life as Chancellor of Durham University and President of the Great Britain-China Centre.

Malcolm and the King

Because of its rejection by Malcolm's publisher, he never got around to entirely finishing *The Pleasures and Pains of Collecting*. One of the stories which he wished to include was his friendship with Norodom Sihanouk.

Sihanouk, born in 1922, was the youthful King of Cambodia when he first met Malcolm towards the end of the 1940s. Although separated in age by two decades, they discovered that they had much in common.

Sihanouk was a committed socialist who was passionate about improving the lives of his subjects. In 1955 he abdicated the throne in order to stand as Prime Minister, believing this to be the most effective way to enact social change. As a former Labour MP and son of Britain's first socialist Prime Minister, Malcolm empathised with Sihanouk's political goals. They also shared a similar vision of an independent, neutral Cambodia. Malcolm was a strong proponent of self-determination and the right for Asian nations to choose their own course. A neutral Cambodia would also serve Britain's interests in preventing escalation of the ongoing conflict in Vietnam.

It is therefore unsurprising that Malcolm and Sihanouk became close colleagues as international statesmen. But their political relationship was mirrored by a strong personal friendship that started with their first meeting. For Malcolm's visit to Cambodia (then still a French colony) as Britain's most senior diplomat in Asia, Sihanouk threw a lavish party with its centrepiece being a performance of the *Royal Corps de Ballet*. Malcolm was awestruck by the brilliance of the costumes, the grace of the dancers and the beauty of the music. Afterwards, Sihanouk showed Malcolm round his private palace, and there they realised that they both shared a passion for collecting. Round Sihanouk's rooms were beautiful artworks from many neighbouring countries, as well as exquisite Khmer sculptures from his homeland. The similarity to Malcolm's own palace at Bukit Serene, its rooms bedecked with an array of artistic treasures, was uncanny.

As well as returning to Cambodia each year for a formal state visit, Malcolm soon began spending time with Sihanouk while off-duty. They enjoyed watching films produced by the King himself (a keen amateur film-maker), dancing to the music of Sihanouk's rag-time band (the King playing the saxophone), and water-skiing. They once invited the Cambodian government to a display of their talents at this sport. At other times they would journey to ancient monuments where Sihanouk fostered Malcolm's great fascination with the Khmer culture. In 1958, Malcolm penned one of the first English-language guides to the temple complex at Angkor Wat, lavishly illustrated with his own photographs as well as those of another Asian friend: the Singaporean Chinese businessman and photographer Loke Wan Tho. During his retirement, Malcolm decided to have one last attempt at a career as a novelist, and wrote a romantic novel which he called *A Khmer Smile*. The novel was never finished, but contains echoes of Malcolm's infectious enthusiasm for the museums and ancient monuments of Cambodia and Thailand.

The friendship between Malcolm and Sihanouk was of immense diplomatic significance during the Geneva conference of 1961-62. As one of the two chairmen, it was Malcolm's duty to bring the three warring Laotian factions to the discussion table. As a neighbour of Laos, Sihanouk was also at the conference. Together with other far-sighted statesmen including the Soviet diplomat Georgy Pushkin, they succeeded. This was certainly helped by Malcolm's existing relationships with everyone concerned.

A military coup overthrew Sihanouk in 1970, causing him to flee into exile in China. Nevertheless, he continued to remain in touch with Malcolm, and the two old friends were reunited when Malcolm visited Beijing in 1971. The Foreign Office was rather embarrassed, worrying that the press may speculate that Britain was plotting a counter-coup with Sihanouk, but accepted that (in the words of one official), 'I doubt if wild horses could prevent Mr. MacDonald from seeing Prince Sihanouk'.[11]

The legacy of this remarkable friendship lives on through two gifts from Sihanouk to Malcolm, now amongst the highlights of the Durham University Oriental Museum. Perhaps the more visually impressive is a xylophone from Sihanouk's own gamelan set, adorned with the royal crest of Cambodia (plate 2). This was a highly personal gift, reminiscent of times spent together listening to the music of such instruments playing to accompany the spectacle of the *Royal Corps de Ballet* (Malcolm kept all these ballet programmes as souvenirs of occasions spent with his friend Sihanouk; they are now at the Palace Green Library in Durham). In addition to the beautiful wooden xylophone, Sihanouk also gave Malcolm a fabulously lavish Bencharong ware ceramic teapot (plate 3). With a design depicting mythical scenes, this was originally a diplomatic gift from the Thai royal family to Sihanouk's forebears, long before he gave it to Malcolm.

A Gift to China

Malcolm's collecting legacy lives on through the museums he supported in Durham, Malaysia, Singapore and Brunei. To this list should be added one more, for Malcolm was one of the few Western collectors to donate an *objet d'art* to communist China during the height of the Cold War.

The setting was Beijing and the time was October 1962. Whilst the rest of the world was awaiting the outcome of the Cuban Missile Crisis with baited breath, Malcolm had slipped behind the 'Bamboo Curtain' into China as the personal guest of its communist government. Such an extraordinary circumstance had its roots in a fortuitous accident. In 1955, the Chinese communist premier Zhou Enlai was travelling to Indonesia when his aircraft developed a fault and was forced to land in Singapore for repairs. Malcolm eagerly seized the opportunity to meet Zhou for the very first time. During his time in Delhi in the later 1950s, Malcolm often encountered Zhou and his deputy, the future foreign minister and former army commander Marshal Chen Yi. He became genial friends with them both. They were much impressed by his enthusiasm for Chinese culture, although Chen Yi joked that Malcolm must be a very big capitalist to own so many Chinese ceramics. Malcolm retorted that it was Chen Yi who was responsible for much of his collection, as Chen had commanded the communist army which captured Shanghai and caused dealers such as T. Y. King to relocate to Hong Kong in 1949.

At the Geneva Conference from 1961-62, Malcolm came to know Chen Yi even better, as they socialised together after hours. To their mutual surprise, they discovered that they shared exactly the same birthday. From that moment on, they referred to one another as their 'twin'. Following the end of the conference, Malcolm's 'twin' invited him to visit China as the personal guest of the communist government. Unfortunately, it appears that Malcolm had misheard Chen, whose birthday is actually nine days after Malcolm's. Either Chen was too polite to correct his 'twin', or saw some diplomatic value in preserving Malcolm's illusion.

Malcolm had previously visited China in 1948, when he had been somewhat distressed by the shocking social failings of Chiang Kai-Shek's Nationalist government. He harboured no bias against the communist government of Chairman Mao, and was indeed favourably impressed by some of their social policies. As a democratic socialist, he could sympathise with some of their goals. As a collector, he was pleased to see restoration work being started on some of China's most iconic historic monuments: the same monuments which had helped inspire him to begin collecting Chinese ceramics back in 1929.

His visit of 1962 enabled Malcolm to have important political talks with both Zhou Enlai and Chen Yi, although he never met Chairman Mao. Perhaps this was because Zhou was more candid in his talks with Malcolm than any other Western diplomat would have expected, due to the personal respect which had developed between them.

As a token of their friendship and a way of repaying Zhou and Chen for their hospitality, Malcolm gave them a cheque for £100 with which to buy a particularly fine ceramic for the Palace Museum in Beijing. Although this would have been a small sum of money in Western markets, it was a much more valuable sum in China at the time. His friends were able to purchase a large Song dynasty celadon bowl from a private collector in Shanghai.

Malcolm visited China three more times: in 1971, 1975 and 1979. The first of these trips transpired when he was asked to narrate a BBC television documentary about the Chinese collections at the British Museum. Malcolm wanted to film some scenes in China, and asked the Chinese government if this would be possible. With China in the midst of the turbulent Cultural Revolution, they were unwilling to allow access to a Western film crew, but Zhou Enlai hoped that Malcolm would come and visit as his guest. Malcolm seized the opportunity, and the Foreign Office plied him with a great many questions to discover the answers to, ranging from the health of Chairman Mao to whether certain purged leaders were executed or still alive. Even more importantly, Malcolm was tasked with making a vital intervention in the stalled Anglo-Chinese negotiations to establish diplomatic relations. Malcolm was instrumental in brokering a compromise, and as a result, the fellow collector Sir John Addis became Britain's first Ambassador to communist China.

In return for Malcolm's earlier generosity, Wu Chung-chao, the Director of the Palace Museum (within the Forbidden City), gave Malcolm a rare catalogue of their ceramics collections. On his next visit, the two men renewed their acquaintance and Wu gave him the gift of a Ming dynasty blue-and-white bowl. Not for the first time, Malcolm's dual lives as a diplomat and a collector became inseparable. His reputation as a connoisseur led to Malcolm leading two cultural delegations to China in 1975 and 1979.

*

Throughout Malcolm's adventurous lifetime he was both a diplomat and a collector. Being a collector helped to make him a successful diplomat. Malcolm's reputation was an effective ice-breaker, contributing to the friendships he developed with Temenggong Koh, Norodom Sihanouk, Zhou Enlai and Chen Yi. Conversely, being a diplomat gave him opportunities to add unique items to his collections, such as Sihanouk's xylophone.

Without further ado, it is now my privilege to hand over to Malcolm as he recounts the many pleasures, and unfortunately a few pains, brought about by his sixty years as an art collector. This book is intended as a testament of Malcolm's remarkable life, and also as a celebration of his lasting legacy through the superb collections he donated and sold to the Oriental Museum in Durham. I hope that the colour plates inspire you to return to this wonderful museum, or perhaps to visit it for the first time, and make up your own minds as to which objects represent the highlights of Malcolm's collections. Malcolm himself regarded the Dingware bowl illustrated in plate 15 as the pinnacle of his collection of Chinese ceramics. Personally I prefer Sihanouk's gifts because of their artistic beauty and remarkable personal history. That is one of the real pleasures of collecting: the freedom it gives to personal preference. For, as Malcolm fully understood, there is not one universal conception of beauty. Beauty is subjective. It has different meanings across cultures, and indeed differs from individual to individual. Malcolm MacDonald spent a lifetime in pursuit of his own perception of beauty: a perception that changed as he came into contact with new people and places across the world. Perhaps you may see greater beauty in his Brunei silverwork than in his Chinese ceramics; perhaps you may prefer his Indian stone sculptures to his Sarawak wood-carvings. Or perhaps, like Malcolm, you'll fall in love with all of them. I now leave it to the man himself to help you decide.

Alexander Nicholas Shaw, 2018

1. Palace Green Library, Malcolm MacDonald Papers 121/1/322, *Constant Surprise* (draft A), c. 1978, p. 579.
2. Palace Green Library, Malcolm MacDonald Papers 76/14/22, Note by Malcolm on conversations with Zhou Enlai, undated
3. Palace Green Library, Malcolm MacDonald Papers 108/1/14, Undated note by Malcolm.
4. Palace Green Library, Malcolm MacDonald Papers 123/4/84, Letter from Malcolm to Ishbel MacDonald, 19 November 1929.
5. Palace Green Library, Malcolm MacDonald Papers 123/4/84-85, Letter from Malcolm to Ishbel MacDonald, 19 November 1929.
6. Palace Green Library, Malcolm MacDonald Papers 121/1/375, *Constant Surprise* (draft A), c. 1978, p. 381.
7. The National Archives, CO 1030/193, 'The Shirt-Sleeve Diplomat', *The Daily Mail*, 16 May 1955.
8. Palace Green Library, Malcolm MacDonald Papers 121/1/322, *Constant Surprise* (draft A), c. 1978, p. 328.
9. Palace Green Library, Malcolm MacDonald Papers 135/1/21, BBC Script, 'Our Man Anywhere: A Profile of Malcolm MacDonald', transmitted 17 June 1969.
10. Palace Green Library, Malcolm MacDonald Papers 121/1/320, *Constant Surprise* (draft A), c. 1978, p. 326.
11. The National Archives, FCO 21/855, Minute by J. A. L. Morgan, 3 September 1971.

The Pleasures and Pains of Collecting

Chapter 1. Temptation

'I love Paris in the springtime', chanted a popular song in my youth. I caught my first sight of the historic French capital at exactly that season fifty years ago. The sun shone from a clear blue sky, fresh green leaves covered every avenue of trees, and gay flowers bloomed in all the parks. A sense of newly revived life, of joyous youth filled the air. This mood affected the people in the streets. Smiles hovered on their lips, laughter twinkled in their eyes, and boys and girls held hands fondly as they strolled along the pavements. Occasionally mature couples gave more adult expression to their mutual regard.

Aged twenty, I was naturally susceptible to this pervading temper. A shy, unsophisticated undergraduate from Oxford, I went to spend an Easter holiday in Paris to learn to speak *un petit peu de Francais.* Of course I had been warned against certain aspects of life in the gracious and cultured but naughty city, and was on my guard. Nevertheless, I fell head-over-heels in love.

I never knew the maiden's name, and cannot now remember clearly her face or figure, except that she was seductively pretty. She loitered in a gallery in the Musée Cluny, which is not a place that one visits for romance or in search of anything that goes by the name of love. This made her presence all the more unexpected, and enticing. She had evidently been waiting there a long time; and when I glanced at her, and she glanced back I gained an impression that she was waiting especially for me.

As I say, I cannot now recollect her face; but I do recall that it had features which would never grow old, being blessed with sweet rosy cheeks, bright eyes and a smiling mouth. I confess that I promptly desired to possess her. I would have liked to buy her, but knew that the Musée Cluny was not the sort of house where such females can be acquired for money. I should mention two other things about her. First, she was a virtual prisoner, and second she was a pygmy. Locked in a glass show-case, she stood only eight inches high. My enchantress was a Dresden porcelain shepherdess made in the early eighteenth century when the famous Meissen factory reached the height of its creative powers.

I could therefore only stare at her, and she stared back. Within a few moments she did a miraculous thing to me. That tiny midget – partly because she was also a little minx – awoke in me a hitherto slumbering passion, stirring into life an appreciation of works of beauty made by man, a love of the Arts. She lit a spark inside me that morning which later leapt into flame, and afterwards became many flames – indeed, a brightly burning, unquenchable succession of fires which have illumined my path wherever I wandered round the world during the subsequent half century.

She kindled something else in me, less to my credit – an acquisitive instinct. I felt then and there a desire, which had never accosted me before, to own an *objet d'art*. At the time it was a very limited desire, a mere longing to acquire one Dresden shepherdess. I felt no similar possessive attraction towards any other treasure in the museum, although its galleries were filled with precious creations of various kinds from many different regions of the civilised world. They made no similar appeal to a callow Oxford undergraduate on holiday in Paris.

So strongly did I feel the urge to purchase a figurine like the damsel in the show-case that I expressed my wish to a friend who accompanied me to the museum. A kindly middle-aged Frenchman, he lived in Paris and knew the city well.

He remarked that he did not think it impossible for me to realise my ambition, explaining that at that moment in the Place de la République an annual Easter Fair was being held where one might chance upon such a curio on an open-air stall.

We hastened to the Place de la République and wandered in the sunshine among a seething crowd of buyers and sellers. Sure enough, after a while we spied amidst the stock of a dealer in antique bric-a-brac a pair of porcelain figures not unworthy of comparison with the maid in the museum. One of them represented a shepherd boy playing a flute and the other a shepherdess dancing to his music. The couple had not quite the same classical refinement as the museum's model; but my eyes had not then learned the discrimination in such matters which they afterwards acquired by a long process of trial and error. In any case both pieces bore the persuasive Meissen mark of crossed swords drawn in blue beneath their glaze.

Nervously I asked the stall-owner the price for the pair. My heart sank when he mentioned a sum in French francs which was equivalent to thirty English shillings. Being an almost penniless student, I possessed little enough cash to pay for my board and lodging throughout ten days in Paris, let alone to indulge in extra, unnecessary expenses. Indeed, at that time my father could not have afforded to send me to university at all if some strange mental aberration on the part of the examiners in a college had not admitted me as a subsidised scholar.

I asked the merchant whether the two Meissen figures could be parted, so that I might take one away whilst he kept the other; but he replied that they were inseparable.

My sympathetic French companion saw the look of disappointment in my eyes. He enquired whether I could afford fifteen shillings.

When I replied 'Yes', he made a proposal. Asserting – whether truthfully or not I never knew – that his wife was fond of bits and pieces of china, he suggested that if I would like to buy one of the pair, he would take the other as a gift for her.

I jumped at the offer, and we closed the deal. Considerately, my friend asked me which of the two I would prefer. I felt no inclination towards the flute-playing male, and would not have wished to buy him in any case. I bagged the shepherdess.

Experts in England who examined her later told me that although her vintage was not of the early 1700s she had been made at a much sought-after period in the latter half of that century. As a collector I was blessed with beginner's luck.

Recollection of the incident prompts me to offer a comment. I do not think I shall be taking gross liberties with the truth if I suggest that one element stimulating my initial attraction towards *objets d'art* on that memorable occasion was the shepherdess' feminine appeal. I did not feel similarly charmed by the male Dresden figure, although he was probably just as desirable a ceramic specimen as his girl friend. So, to put it bluntly, my introduction to the Arts was induced in part by my youthful admiration for the fair sex.

I am not qualified to expand on that thought, and to weave a theory around it; so I shall merely observe that I suspect that in the cases of innumerable other people an original impulse towards falling in love with artistic beauty is their emotional inclination to fall in love with human beauty. Here, as in so many other surprising places, sex rears its allegedly ugly head.

We know that the most powerful inspiration prompting the development of noble schools of art throughout the ages in various regions around the world has been religion. Many sublime traditions of painting, sculpture, architecture and other such works made by different races were born and bred as acts of worship of their local gods. For example, Seton Lloyd wrote in an authoritative book, *The Art of the Ancient Near East*, concerning one of the cradles of Man's civilisation, that 'in the whole of the Ancient Near East art was inseparable from religion, and without it would have found little inspiration'. The same can be said of numerous historical schools of art scattered across the six inhabited continents and the seven seas. Yet was there sometimes another elemental stimulant? I have not made erudite researches into the subject, and may be expressing a foolish, superficial opinion; but I should not be surprised if a secondary inspiration for the creation by artists (and the appreciation by connoisseurs) of works of beauty was the potent emotion of love between men and women. Just as in many circumstances the urge was an act of worship of a superhuman god, so in others it might have been a conscious or unconscious act of worship of human goddesses.

Chapter 2. Fall

When I returned from Paris to resume my student career at Oxford, the little shepherdess accompanied me. She took up her quarters in my study in Queen's College. The room happened to be a charming, elegantly panelled eighteenth century chamber, so perhaps not unnaturally she appeared very much at home there since in spite of her youthful looks she was a child of the same epoch. She posed, forever dancing, on the mantelpiece, and from that central, elevated situation presided over all the goings-on in my apartment.

That was in 1922. After two score years and ten she still retains a uniquely honoured place in my now sumptuous collection of works of art. No sum of money, however fabulous, could induce me to part with her. Except for my brief encounter with her seductive prototype in the Musée Cluny, she was my first love; and although my eyes have roved a great deal since then, and my taste has shifted many times, and my heart has proved fickle where beguiling pieces of ceramic, sculpture, painting and other artful creations are concerned, I still approve of my initial choice. To that extent I have remained faithful to her. With advancing years I myself – displaying white hair, wrinkled skin and other signs of approaching senility – have altered in appearance beyond recognition, and many other features in the world have greatly transformed; yet she looks precisely the same as she did when I picked her up in Paris so long ago. She still wears her wide-brimmed hat at a lightsome angle, still beams her girlish smile, still displays the same comely figure in a close-fitting bodice, and still holds her skirt wide as she raises one foot in the air to jig to the apparently unforgettable music of her flute-playing partner who disappeared half a century ago. How, in the evening of my days, I envy her immortality!

That her charm has survived all the tests of time says a lot for her. I cannot pay the same compliment to a few other Dresden shepherdesses whom I temporarily adopted not long after my return from France. For about a year I remained partial to such creatures, and with what I assumed to be faultless judgement gradually acquired four more of them. Later I discovered that although two of these were tolerable simulacrums of the genuine article, the others were less worthy, and that none of them had even been anywhere near Dresden. Fortunately my eyes had by then been distracted elsewhere, my spare cash was being devoted to the acquisition of other types of china, and so I had not amassed an embarrassingly large harem of those false wenches.

The fact is that my taste had begun to tire of them, to change – to grow perhaps a little less adolescent. Apart from the circumstance that numerous such figurines assembled on a mantelpiece would appear monotonous – a dozen, two dozen or more of them parading rather like a procession of tin Amazonian soldiers – I began instinctively to suspect that they belonged to a somewhat decadent style of art. Many of them were too decoratively rococo and over-sentimental. This is not to say that I spurned such objects altogether, for one of my faults is a strong tendency to sentimentality. But when I did, just occasionally, afterwards feel tempted by their kind, I transferred my affection to more naïve products like the figures made in the famous English porcelain factory at Bow. I preferred these to their rivals produced by the kilns at Chelsea, partly because they seemed to me more simply graceful, and partly because they were less expensive! Nevertheless, I enjoyed some of the Chelsea craftsmen's studies of animals such as dogs, sheep and wild boars; and when I got married many years later my first present to my bride was a charming Chelsea leopard.

Perhaps the real reason for my switch from the products of Dresden to those of English factories was merely an inbred insular British prejudice. We are all to a considerable extent slaves of heredity: deeply rooted in our make-up lies the native taste of countless generations of ancestors. Environment also plays its part; we are inclined at first to like best what we are most accustomed to see. Possibly for this reason I never again felt much attraction towards any of the celebrated Continental pottery and porcelains, although my liking for English ceramics waxed steadily, and has never waned since. The masterpieces of Delft, Meissen, Sevres and other European factories held few charms for me, whilst those of Bow, Worcester and Staffordshire made an irresistible appeal. The same became true later concerning other types of artistic works, as I shall mention in due course.

In my early years as a collector I was therefore disposed to choose English, or sometimes Scottish, samples of art to the exclusion of any foreign products. Within that insular field, however, my inclinations began to roam. For several years after my fateful jaunt to Paris my fancy remained faithful to ceramics, but it shifted from beguiling china figurines to pleasant teapots, dishes, cups and other articles, and also from chic aristocratic porcelains into the more plebeian realms of pottery. I never fell heavily for nineteenth century Staffordshire statuettes except for an occasional attractive hound, spaniel or kilted Highlander. Instead I leaped straight to the products of the same accomplished region in the previous century, when the art of the English potter (it seemed to me then, and still seems to me now) reached for several decades its summit of achievement. My strongest passion was for white salt glaze wares, both the earlier monochrome pieces adorned with slip or moulded designs and the later specimens decorated with coloured enamels.

My attraction to the enamelled examples was perhaps a first tentative sign of a break-away from narrow, patriotic British prejudice, because I liked not only pieces that appealed to Scottish Jacobite sentiment by bearing friendly remarks about Bonnie Prince Charlie, or to Anglo-Hanoverian loyalty by depicting King George III's portrait, but also those with exotic representations of Chinese mandarins strolling in Oriental gardens. Yet perhaps that was only an extended expression of my British heritage, for those scenes of Old Cathay were samples of the Chinoiserie which pleased English lords and ladies in the mid-eighteenth century, and which remained for a while a rage not only in ceramics but also furniture, wall-papers, other forms of interior decoration, and even occasionally architecture – as was shown by the erection of the Royal Pavilion in Brighton. So this, too, could be an aspect of my ancestral inheritance – a hangover from a quirk in my wine-snipping English or whisky-swilling Scottish forebears' otherwise impeccably British aesthetic taste when an artistic nip of Chinese Maotai intoxicated them.

I became increasingly fond of certain types of English eighteenth century pottery, and through the next dozen years amassed over a hundred varied pieces of it. To make the collection comprehensively representative I included in it several examples of earlier slipware, English Delft and Elers style wares; but my real loves, on which I spent almost all my available cash, were white salt glazed stoneware and lead -glazed earthenware of various coloured types such as the agate, tortoiseshell and related styles made by Astbury, Whieldon and other master craftsmen. Among my acquisitions were charming human and animal figures devised by the accomplished two Ralph Woods, father and son. To give the collection an end as well as a beginning I gathered not only a few examples of black Jackfield and coloured Pratt pieces, but also choice bits of Josiah Wedgwood's blue, green and black jasper wares designed in the neo-classical manner which he made fashionable in the last quarter of the eighteenth century. They were trim, decorative and dignified – yet I was not so attracted by them as by the earlier output of Staffordshire's kilns. Those Wedgwood pieces were too formal for my taste, and perhaps their imitative touch of an alien Graeco-Roman style was uncongenial to my still mainly insular eye. I was more pleased by the freer, more casual, more racily English forms and decorations, such as the same Wedgwood's pots in the forms of pineapples and cauliflowers, some of which I added to my treasures.

Above all I liked every type of salt glaze made between about 1740 and 1765. This still seems to me to be the high water mark of the English potters' achievement, at any rate so far as articles for domestic use are concerned. White salt glazed stoneware began to be turned out soon after fine samples of imported Chinese porcelain became popular in England, and before the means of manufacturing hard-paste as distinct from soft-paste china was generally known in Europe. As every student of the subject knows, it had been discovered for the first time on that continent in 1709 by Böttger of Meissen; but for years he and his artisans kept their secret with jealous professional care, and produced the then locally unprecedented true porcelain which gave the Royal Dresden factory its flying start over all rivals in the Western hemisphere. Only about three decades later did the know-how get revealed to other manufacturers and stimulate the competition between many famous centres in Europe and Britain which thrived from the mid-century onwards.

Prior to that some potters in England set themselves the task of imitating the delicate Chinese teapots, cream jugs, cups, saucers and other objects which were capturing the fancy of their British customers in an effort to regain the favour of those patrons. Gradually they achieved pottery almost as thin-bodied, white-grounded and gaily enamelled as Qing dynasty porcelains. This ambition to emulate Chinese Imperial wares is part of the explanation of the evolution of English salt glaze from its early, delightfully natural native beginnings round about 1720 to the more sophisticated and frequently Orientalised products of thirty to forty years later. In both technique and artistry the output was enchanting. Unfortunately I could never afford to buy an example of the supremely pleasing 'pew groups', but I did secure pieces of almost every other type.

However, most schools of art, both great and small, have their period of rise and triumph followed by decline and fall, and salt glaze proved no exception to this rule. The once fresh style of its pieces wearied around 1770, slipping into decadence. Moreover, by then the skill of craftsmen in England making true porcelain was highly developed, and the factories at Bow, Chelsea, Derby, Worcester and other places were satisfying the demands of clients for elegant tea, coffee and dinner sets.

My rather fanatical fondness for ceramics led me to start gathering flowers in other fields besides those of the eighteenth century Staffordshire potteries. I picked blossoms of various, usually later types such as cream-coloured Leeds pieces, pink, copper and gold lusterware, and Spode transfer-print specimens. Then I skipped into the realm of true porcelain, going for Worcester articles of the Dr. Wall (or, as it is now called, First) Period from 1751 to 1783. Except for some decorative Bow figures and two or three Chelsea objects, I never indulged in the works of other factories as gems for exhibition in my show-cabinets. Yet early Worcester pieces did tempt me in a big way; and, as usual in my art collecting, I followed Oscar Wilde's advice that 'there is only one thing to do with temptation, and that is to fall for it'.

The gorgeousness of the blue-scale, powder-blue and similar backgrounds with their panels or richly painted flowers, fruits, animals and human figures first excited me, appealing to a vulgar streak in my taste which favoured extravagant display. But I also admired white-ground pieces on which simpler sketches were brushed or transfer-printed. In addition I bought specimens with Chinoiserie decoration similar to that of my salt glaze wares; and later (after my financial income improved) indulged now and then in apple-green, pale yellow, scarlet and other aristocratic types. I steadily gathered quite a formidable collection of more than eighty pieces of Dr. Wall Worcester.

Chapter 3. A New Love

For several years my chief and almost exclusive interest as a collector remained English pottery and porcelain. There were several reasons for this restriction. First and foremost, my financial resources were severely limited. In the initial years I was still an impecunious undergraduate at Oxford; after that I spent eleven months making my first journey round the world (at other people's expense); and on my return to England I occupied myself for about a year scribbling a novel which proved to be so bad that it was rejected first by one publisher, then by another, and finally – on my re-reading the tale – by the author himself. With remarkably tolerant kindness my father recognised my ambition to become a man of letters, and throughout those barren twelve months continued supporting me with pocket money as well as free board and lodging. This was typical of his understanding, friendly nature. At the close of the fiasco I took a job at a small salary in a publishing firm. Occasionally I also ventured into free-lance journalism, scribbling articles for the popular weekly called *Answers* on topics of absorbing current interests such as 'Has jazz come to stay?' From 1923 onwards I was also nursing as Labour candidate a remotely promising Parliamentary constituency. My income during those years was therefore moderate, permitting only infrequent acquisitions of a teapot, a sauce boat, a pair of candlesticks or some other ceramic loot.

Another reason for my restricted collecting was my sparse requirements. Being a bachelor with no need for a home of my own, I lived in my father's house. Depending on the vagaries of British politics at changing periods through the 1920s, this was mostly his private house in Hampstead, but sometimes the Prime Minister's residence at 10 Downing Street, with occasional visits to Chequers thrown in. In all those lodgings I had amply furnished rooms with sufficient chairs to sit on, a table to write at, bookshelves to support the few books I was beginning to gather, and other conveniences. So any inclination in me to venture beyond collecting ceramics, and to buy furniture, paintings or other gracious things remained unawakened. Lying dormant, its slumber was scarcely disturbed by even an occasional dream.

However, on one earlier occasion I had strayed tentatively into another field of arts. This was soon after my fateful encounter with the Dresden shepherdess in Paris. Her arrival on the mantelpiece of my Oxford college room introduced an attractive touch of decoration to the place, and made me realise that its rather stately but bare panelled walls should be adorned with at least one picture. My thoughts leapt back to certain engravings which in my childhood used to hang in a Buckinghamshire cottage that my parents rented as a weekend family retreat. My father was a keen student of British history, and a particular admirer of the Parliamentarians who opposed King Charles I during the constitutional quarrels and civil war in the seventeenth century. Among his heroes were John Hampden, Henry Ireton, Oliver Cromwell and their associates, and a collection of portraits of them engraved by Houbraken and other artists hung in our cottage rooms. In my impressionable boyhood I gazed with awe at them.

Recollecting them nostalgically when I desired a picture for my study in Oxford, I would have liked to buy an engraving of that kind. However, at the time my purse lacked even the few shillings required for one such investment. So instead I cut from an illustrated magazine a reproduction of an old print of the Younger Pitt addressing the House of Commons. It showed Mr. Speaker presiding with bewigged dignity in the chamber whilst Honourable and Right Honourable Members lolled on the government and opposition benches listening to the prodigious statesman's oration. I fitted it into a modern copy of an antique black-and-gold Hogarth frame, and hung it on my sitting-room wall. I felt extremely proud of it.

Incidentally – if I may anticipate for a moment – eighteen months later my pride received a fall. In January 1924 my father began his first period of office as Prime Minister. I was still a student at Oxford, and during the following weekend motored to Chequers to visit him there. I was at once impressed not only by the stately dignity of that Elizabethan mansion, but also by the vast assembly of artistic treasures scattered throughout it. Among them I was delighted to find an original print of the very engraving of the Younger Pitt addressing Parliament, a copy of which hung in my college room. Besides being itself a genuine first impression of the picture, it was displayed in a truly antique Hogarth frame. But what struck me most about it was its situation in Chequers. It hung on a wall beside a wash-basin in a gentleman's lavatory along a back corridor! I could not help comparing this humble setting with the place of honour which its trivial imitation occupied in my college apartment; and I realised that Lord Lee of Fareham – who gave Chequers and all its contents to the nation – had put me in my place as an art connoisseur.

It was a sobering lesson. However, although at first I was humiliated by the position which His Lordship allotted to one of my favourite works of art, on second thoughts I felt cheered that he had given it any place at all in his fabulously distinguished collection. I reckoned that this at least indicated that I had begun to work on a correct line where pictures were concerned. Although I stood insecurely on the bottom rung of a very tall ladder, at any rate I was on the right ladder. So I kept my cheap reproduction of the print on my wall in Oxford, and began to dream of owning one day some genuine antique English engravings which might be worthy to hang in a washroom of a stately home like Chequers.

For years that ambition of course remained unrealised. I continued to concentrate my limited financial resources on purchasing bits and pieces of china and lost interest in any further acquisition of pictures. However, after I left Oxford, and later returned from my first round-the-world trip, and occupied a rather spacious bed-sitting room in my father's Hampstead home – to which he had then retreated as Leader of the Opposition – I wished to hang pictures of my own choice on its walls as fitting companions for my steadily accumulating collection of attractive pots. I decided against Houbraken prints because they were purely black-and-white, whereas I wanted those decorations to show splashes of colour. By chance at about that time I found the very things I vaguely yearned for. One afternoon during a summer holiday at Lossiemouth in Scotland I discovered in a shop in nearby Elgin a portfolio containing several coloured engravings. They were some of the younger William Daniell's delicate aquatints of Scottish scenery. I bought one for ten shillings, carried it home in a state of excitement, contemplated it for several hours, and next morning walked ten miles to and from Elgin to buy two more aquatints, for a pound the pair.

This was another revolutionary occasion in my life. I had definitely passed from exclusive obsession with ceramics as objects worthy of collecting, and broken into the sphere of pictures. Yet for a long time afterwards I did not penetrate far into that most variegated, boundless and rewarding of all artistic worlds. I was stupidly halting and short-sighted in developing an appreciation of fine paintings. For several further years I remained interested only in very minor works like aquatints, mezzotints and lithographs, many of them mere illustrations torn by dealers from engravings in old books. This was partly, of course, because finer works would have been too expensive for me. At one period I did dither on the brink of becoming a devotee of miniatures, such as pretty portraits by the fashionable artist Richard Cosway; but after a while that sentimental inclination faded.

Over the next few years I made quite a good collection of the best Daniell aquatints of Scottish landscapes, with a few of his English and Welsh scenes thrown in. A quarter of a century later I recalled them with pleasure when I went to Delhi as Britain's High Commissioner and saw in the lounges of plutocratic club-houses in Calcutta, Bombay and Madras examples of his and his uncle's splendid aquatints of late eighteenth century India. In the meantime I had sold – at a moment when I badly needed ready cash – most of my British ones, plus a number of Pugin's, Rowlandson's and Stadler's attractive London and Thames Valley scenes engraved in the same technique, which I had also acquired during that period of my initiation into appreciation of pictures. But I still retain a few of Daniell's aquatints.

I have also kept about a score of engaging mezzotints which I bought in those introductory years. Engraved by various masters of that cunning craft, they portray majestic figures of Kings Charles I and Charles II, royal Queens such as Henrietta Maria, beauty queens like some of the Merry Monarch's ravishing girl friends, statesmen like Edmund Burke and Charles James Fox, and other celebrities. They are among the minor works to which I have stayed faithful through all the shifting moods of my connoisseur life, and now adorn the walls of a corridor in my house. There they make me feel that, as an art patron, I do not lag quite so appallingly behind Lord Lee of Fareham as I did once upon a time.

Chapter 4. Widening Horizons

I must revert briefly to Chequers, for that great house played a significant part in my education as a lover of the arts. During my father's first occupancy of the Premiership I spent several weekends there. For me this was an amazing new experience, a glimpse of an opulently cultured way of life which I had never caught before in the modest residences where I had previously lodged. Distributed through Chequers' handsome rooms were innumerable works of fine craftsmanship and art, all arranged as domestic furnishings of a private family home instead of as exhibits in a public museum. They wore an air not only of gracious beauty, but also of personal intimacy which opened my eyes to fresh aspects of their charming characters. However, my visits to Chequers in 1924 were too few for the place to exert any abiding magic over me, because soon after that year's Labour government came into power I left England on the round-the-world tour which I have already mentioned.

It was after my father's return to Downing Street and Chequers on the formation of his second government in 1929 that the grand Elizabethan mansion, with all its splendid contents, cast an abiding spell over me. Probably I was more susceptible then to its fine qualities, partly because I had grown mature in my appreciation of things artistic, and partly because I was now toying with the idea of setting up house on my own, and so was interested in acquiring other types of domestic furnishings besides bits of antique China and old engravings. I became sensitive to the appearance of various kinds of household necessities, keeping an eye open for all sorts of objects which would be useful as well as decorative in my future dwelling.

There is no better place for learning good taste in such things than one of the ancient stately homes of England. In those historic, noble mansions families lived with unsurpassed graciousness not only generation after generation but sometimes century after century, surrounded by excellent furnishings accumulated with loving care by successive owners. Often the inmates were themselves distinguished connoisseurs with discriminating aesthetic judgements on fine pictures, sculptures, furniture, carpets, silver, porcelains and other desirable objects. Their houses thus became small art museums as well as comfortable residences.

Chequers was such a place. It was filled with many admirable examples of the works of English craftsmen from the moment of the present building's main construction early in Good Queen Bess's reign throughout almost four hundred later years. It also contained some relics of notable historic interest, for at one time the lady owner of the place happened to marry a grandson of Oliver Cromwell, who brought Cromwellian heirlooms to his bride's home. Among other treasures in the Tudor long-gallery, for instance, a vivid life-like mask of the great Protector himself, 'warts and all', lay cushioned in a glass case.

Eventually the family's line of descendants died out, the estate came on the market, and Lord and Lady Lee bought it. During the years when they lived there they added works of art of their own choice to its collection – until as a thank-offering for Great Britain's victory in the First World War they presented the palatial residence lock, stock and barrel, chairs, tables and sideboards, carpets, paintings, silver and all its other contents to the nation, to be a weekend retreat where future Prime Ministers could find rest and recreation from their heavy labours in London.

This was the place where my education in the proper appointments of a civilised man's home was considerably developed. During six years I stayed there frequently. Arranged with seeming casualness (but in fact with deliberate design) through its rooms were superb examples of the grand succession of assorted English arts and handicrafts of the Tudor, Stuart and Hanoverian periods. The oak, walnut, mahogany, satinwood and other furnitures; the china, glass and silver table-wares; the porcelain, crystal, gold and other decorative objects; and many engravings, drawings and paintings revealed much of the evolution of British artistic skills through three prosperous, cultured centuries. Other fabrics in the house were foreign, such as Persian rugs, Flemish tapestries and Chinese ceramics, all living congenially together where they had been at home for so long in the peaceful Buckinghamshire countryside.

My study where I worked was a handsomely panelled Tudor parlour. Through the mornings I sat on a high-backed Queen Anne chair writing at a Carolingian table amidst other pleasing period furnishing. At nights I slept in a huge Elizabethan oak four-poster bed in a well-appointed room with windows overlooking an old, yet perennially young, walled rose garden. Naturally such an environment made a deep impression on a susceptible young man with half-formed, eager notions about things artistic.

It guided my acquisitive instincts prudently into the collection of antique furniture. As I have already written, I was now contemplating buying a house of my own. Although still a bachelor with only an occasional hesitant, fleeting inclination to get married, I should not continue living indefinitely as a dependent in my father's house, and was keen to set up my own establishment. In 1929 I had entered the House of Commons, and so gained an income of £400 a year; and in 1931 I became one of His Majesty's junior ministers entitled to a salary of £1,200. At first I refused to accept this ministerial pay because at that time of national economic crisis, when almost everyone else was forced to suffer a reduction in their incomes, I felt it wrong for me to enjoy an increase of emoluments. After the crisis ended, however, I did take the money, and so my income suddenly permitted me to purchase an occasional more expensive *objet d'art* than a teapot or an aquatint.

I wished to choose carefully each and every one of the pleasing objects which would go to the furnishing of a small home. Realising that, if they were all to attain the standard of perfection which I desired, I could not pick them up in a few days, a few weeks, or even a few months, I reconciled myself to taking years to find as well as afford them. Two alternative courses therefore faced me: either I could buy a house immediately, ask a firm like Maples to provide forthwith suites of modern furniture for its rooms, and then progressively banish those inferior pieces, one by one, as I bought better replacements; or else I could first collect gradually my chosen items of furniture, and afterwards secure a house when I owned sufficient chairs, tables, beds, carpets and other requirements to fill it. As there was no urgent need for me to acquire a property, I decided on the latter course.

So I began to buy now and then, as I found leisure to scour antique shops, useful and at the same time attractive bits of furniture. My taste was still robustly and almost exclusively English. For instance, the dignified seats, cupboards and other pieces fashioned around 1700 by renowned cabinet-makers in the Low Countries, and refined French types like those glorying in the titles of 'Louis Quinze' or 'Louis Seize' left me cold, whereas not wholly unrelated English chairs, tables and chests of the same periods captivated me. And although I liked the little touches of Chinoiserie on some salt glaze, Worcester and other ceramics which I owned, I did not care much for Chinese Chippendale chairs, tables or footstools. I felt no objection to occasional extravagances such as rich marquetry decoration on cabinets or bold lion-masks on armchairs, but they had to be of predominantly English character, whatever foreign influence might have contributed to this or that detail of their design.

I started my furniture collecting cautiously. My first acquisition was a simple William-and-Mary oak table with baluster legs and tied feet. I gave £8 for it in a shop in Camberley. Like my original Dresden porcelain shepherdess, it has held ever since a place of special honour among my possessions because it was my first love in the important field of furniture. Also like the shepherdess, it is worthy of favour, for its excellent, unpretentious yet decorative character has stood all the tests of time. If she can be called the mother of the vast family of works of art in my home, it might be named, in Parliamentary jargon, 'the Father of the House'.

My next purchase was a small, walnut-framed mirror made in the memorable reign of Queen Anne, when the triumphs achieved by England's cabinet-makers in their workshops were as fine as the victories gained by her soldiers captained by John Churchill, Duke of Marlborough, on the battlefields of Europe. I think those master craftsmen were in some ways better exponents of their art than any of their predecessors or successors. Their instinct for firm and strong yet gracious forms was often faultless, whether it were exercised in the designing of chairs or tables, tallboys or writing desks, stools or other objects. And no English wood appears more beautiful than the honey-coloured walnut that they frequently employed. If I had to choose which samples I like best in the whole range of products made by Britain's furniture-makers, I would plump for certain Queen Anne pieces. My favourite item in my own collection is a walnut double-chair back settee of that vintage, with nothing more ornate than the graceful curves of its cabriole legs and arms, and a petit-point needlework seat-cover of contemporary date.

I made many pleasant raids, however, into most periods, and over the years captured all sorts of prizes representing different epochs, from a severe oak-and-leather Cromwellian chair to a few flamboyant mid-Victorian bits of nonsense contrived in papier-mâché, gilt and mother-of-pearl inlay.

It is tempting to write at length about the comparative merits of successive distinguished styles of English furniture, but I must express my views only briefly. My taste is catholic. Nevertheless, virtually all the products of William Kent seem to me pompously over-ornate; and although some of Robert Adam's have true charm as well as dignity, most of them also are rather too extravagantly grand for my liking. Of course, they were made to look appropriate in the setting of the palatial rooms with superb neo-classical interior decoration which the Adam brothers designed, and which I admire – but those sumptuous chambers and their contents were made for immensely opulent aristocrats or tycoons, not ordinary mortals like me. Even the great Thomas Chippendale's furniture seem to me in many cases a trifle too ponderous and solemn, although their air of nobility is impressive, especially in large, formal rooms such as I did not aspire to own. I prefer a dining-room furnished predominantly in the style of Hepplewhite, whose chairs and tables, sideboards, sofas and other pieces are lighter, gayer and more charming. Indeed, after certain pieces produced in and around the time of Queen Anne – including some adorned elaborately with tortoiseshell veneer or marquetry – they are, on balance, my favourite type. Sheraton furniture appears to me often too delicate, pretty-pretty and even fragile, whilst many Regency pieces become too frenchified for my unqualified liking. However, these statements are over-simplified, sweeping generalisations which do not by any means always apply to individual products of this or that period. I prefer some Chippendale mirrors, for instance, to those of Hepplewhite, and certain Sheraton china cabinets and bookcases have unsurpassed elegance. Every varied manner has its masterpieces of grace combined with practical utility.

Among others this applies to the earlier output of Tudor and Stuart times. Many of their carved chests have fine as well as robust quality. Their refectory tables, too, are handsome; through the decades I have used one for writing in my study. Yet most of their contemporaries in the forms of cupboards and presses seem to me excessively ponderous. And much as I feel regard for the squirearchial British character shown in Jacobean and Carolingian oak chairs, I can find little use for them except as decorative objects in entrance halls or along corridors.

Nevertheless, ever after my weekends at Chequers I had harboured a snobbish hankering for sleeping in an Elizabethan four-poster bed; and the last bit of important English furniture that I bought, a few days before the Second World War broke out, was a majestic specimen of that breed. I was fortunate to secure it in an Oxford shop for only £40. You could sometimes do that sort of thing in those days.

Chapter 5. Collaborators

It was great fun dropping into antique shops in various parts of Britain in the 1920s and 1930s, inspecting their contents in the hope of finding some breath-taking bargain, and just occasionally realising that hope. Often at weekends or on brief holidays through the dozen years before the outbreak of war in 1939 I toured this or that region of England in company with my friends Godfrey (now Lord) Elton and his wife Dedi. He had been my tutor at Oxford, and she was then his bride from Norway. They were genial kindred spirits to me, partly because we happened to share an enthusiasm for several identical hobbies. Among these were bird watching, studying historic English architecture and collecting old furniture and *objets d'art*. We used to jump into a car and drive for two or three days across, for example, the West country, alternately gazing at ravens, choughs, peregrine falcons and buzzards in Cornwall and Devonshire, visiting the ancient parish churches, abbeys and cathedrals of Dorset and Somerset, invading every antique shop in sight throughout those shires, and ending up with the grand climax of a visit to famous Mallett of Bath. In many ways those escapades were rewarding. One of the secrets of never being bored with life, and usually enjoying every minute of it, is to cultivate half-a-dozen varied recreations, one or another of which can be indulged in at any time in any place according to the mood of the moment.

Among the profits of our expeditions were desirable additions to our respective collections of household furnishings. With an eye to establishing a well-appointed home I was now buying other pleasing things besides tables and chairs, cabinets and mirrors, prints and porcelains. Amidst this or that wayside antiquarian's clutter of goods I would come upon a pair of Sheffield-plate entrée dishes, an incomplete but adequate Spode dinner service, a few odd Waterford wine glasses, a small Crown Derby dessert set, a couple of branching Georgian silver candlesticks, a Chelsea china inkstand and pen-tray, or some other treasure which would look distinguished as well as being useful in a dining or sitting room. During the difficult 1930s in Britain a national economic depression often seemed round the corner – if not actually present – and prices were therefore reasonable for most articles of merchandise. As a result I snapped up many choice bits and pieces at comparatively little cost.

Not all the prices were as modest, however, as that charged to some friends of mine for an early nineteenth century tea-set which they discovered one afternoon in a village junk shop. The place was untidily crammed with all sorts of cast-away household utensils, most of them worthless; but a few items were quite good. In particular the searchers observed, scattered at random here and there among the trash, a cream-jug, sugar-basin, teapot and several cups and saucers all decorated with the same pleasant pink-lustre design. Rescuing them from various nooks and crannies, and re-uniting them as a group, the shoppers found that they formed a small, if incomplete, set. They asked the store's proprietress how much it would cost.

She had apparently refreshed herself a little too heavily at lunch. Eyeing it unsteadily, she hiccoughed and said, 'Threepence wouldn't hurt'.

'Threepence for each piece?' enquired her customers, thinking this an excellent bargain.

The woman hiccoughed again and declared emphatically, as if to stop any argument, 'Threepence for the lot'.

My friends gave her ten shillings in the hope that when she sobered up she would appreciate their refusal to gain too great an advantage from her inebriation, and left the shop exultantly.

Those were the good old days for collectors. I fear they have slipped into the mists of the past.

One of the pleasures of my hunting expeditions was the forming of friendships with some of the most genial antique dealers in the land. Several became favourites of mine – men with a sound knowledge of their trade, who were honest in all their dealings as well as being charming, stimulating personalities.

There was, for example, Mr. Roberts in his emporium on the High Street in Camberley. A typical, unassuming provincial salesman, he was shrewd, intelligence and alert. It was he who sold me the William-and-Mary table that was my first acquisition in the field of old furniture. Afterwards, on periodic visits over years to his showrooms, I bought numerous excellent objects of various kinds.

One day he and I had an argument about a piece of tapestry. I disliked tapestries; at that time they seemed to me rather dark, dreary and even turgid wall decorations for a room. Roberts knew of my aversion, and did not usually broach the topic with me. That morning, however, I had inspected his current stock of goods for an hour without finding anything sufficiently to my taste to buy, and he realised my disappointment. As I was about to leave the premises he asked whether I would like to see a tapestry wall-hanging which he had bought a day or two earlier. He said it had just arrived in his store-room and was not yet on display, but that he would gladly unfurl it if I would like to view it. Adding that he remembered my prejudice against such objects, he asserted that he realised I would probably not wish to buy it, but that I might like to look at it as a curiosity.

I replied that tapestries bored me, and that he should not bother to produce it.

Reluctant to part from him without some mutually advantageous exchange, I returned to a show-case to re-examine an English Delft bowl which had momentarily tempted me. After dithering over it for a further while I resisted it once more, and walked towards the street door. Roberts sensed again my regret that the afternoon had been fruitless.

'I think you might really enjoy seeing that tapestry', he remarked. 'Of course not to buy, but just as an interesting sample of its kind'. Before I could voice again my lack of zeal he added as if casually, 'I bought it very cheap in a country house sale'.

Not to seem indifferent to his success in capturing at little cost an object which he evidently admired, I asked 'How much was it?'

He did not give a direct answer. 'For you,' he said, 'I'll make the price £7. I don't know much about tapestries, but I'm sure it's rather good'.

My Scottish financial instincts were mildly aroused.

'If you're really so keen to show it to me,' I observed, 'let's have a look at it'.

When he unrolled the piece I saw that it was not unduly large, having had its edges cut (presumably for earlier framing) and measuring about 10 by 8 feet. I did not think much of it, but was reluctant to leave the shop without the agreeable exchange which usually marked our meetings – and £7 would not bankrupt me.

'I'll buy it', I said.

Since he could tell me little about its age or place of origin, I asked him to send it to me in London, care of my knowledgeable friend Sir Alec Martin at Christie's, the famous auctioneers. I explained that I would write to Sir Alec asking him to give me an expert opinion on the tapestry.

A few days later I received an answer from Martin. He stated that the tapestry was a good example of late seventeenth century Flemish work, but that its commercial value had unfortunately been spoilt because its floral margin had been cut off. 'I hope you did not pay too much for it', he wrote, 'since it is worth only £175'.

The tapestry has hung in an honoured place in my home ever since!

Another memorable antique dealer was small, shy A. E. Perry who, aided by his jolly, buxom wife, kept a shop on Exhibition Road in South Kensington. He was the friend who, years earlier, had persuaded me to buy my first piece of Staffordshire salt glaze pottery – a simple, slip-decorated bowl and cover made in about 1740 – thus initiating me into one of my most satisfying fields of collecting. He acted not only completely honestly with his customers, but also generously whenever possible. If he bought something inexpensively, he was prepared to sell it inexpensively, at any rate to a favourite client. For him the antique business was a partnership – almost a conspiracy – between a dealer and his regular patrons, all of whom should profit handsomely from his cunning professional knowledge. He was more of an expert than Camberley's Roberts, whose primary line of business was in fact modern furnishings. With Roberts, therefore, antiques were only a side -line about which his expertise was moderate, whereas Perry was a specialist with painstakingly acquired wisdom on English furniture, pottery and porcelain. He displayed his learning with modesty; but it was wide, deep and reliable.

From him I bought one of my most remarkable bargains. An early white Bow porcelain group, it represented a pair of pastoral lovers. One foot on the female figure was chipped, but otherwise the piece was in excellent condition; and Perry must have known it was so rare that he could receive from one of the rich collectors who frequented his shop a much higher price than he asked from me. But I liked it, he had bought it very cheap, and he was eager for me to possess it. So I acquired it for £9. Twenty years later, at a moment in the late 1950s when I needed some ready cash, I sold it (to my sorrow) in an auction for 425 guineas (£446.25). What a pity that I could not have kept it until today, when it would be worth a four figure sum.

I must comment that not all my purchases were advantageous bargains like the tapestry from Roberts and the piece of china from Perry as will become clear later.

Another engaging dealer was old Mr. Williamson of Guildford. His gallery stood half-way up the steep High Street there. Its numerous apartments had an air of grandeur that was not present in Perry's two small, although spick-and-span, rooms in Kensington. Williamson's place gave an impression of its contents being bought only from the aristocracy and sold only to the plutocracy. Its atmosphere was slightly reminiscent of such happy hunting grounds for wealthy connoisseurs as Frank Partridge's showrooms in New Bond Street in London. And its assembly of furniture and carpets was worthy of that comparison.

Williamson allowed nothing except high-class specimens of art to grace his impeccable chambers.

Thus the shop was full of extremely fine pieces of walnut, mahogany, satinwood and other types from all the best periods. Nevertheless, in my opinion the noblest antique in the place was the proprietor himself. Williamson must then have passed man's allotted span of three-score years and ten. His comely head was massive, with smoothly brushed, long white hair crowning a senatorial face. Holding himself primly erect, he was always immaculately dressed in a black jacket, stiff white collar, pearl-stabbed tie, and pin-stripe trousers. When the Eltons and I entered his front showroom he would issue from an office alongside it, beam a genial smile and bend in a low, courtly bow as he declared, 'This is a great honour: I am so privileged to see you'. Then he snapped back to his customary upright posture, as if a ramrod had suddenly been inserted down his spine, and for quite a while we would exchange pleasantries about the latest vagaries of the English weather, current developments in world affairs, matters of concern in national politics, or other topics unconnected with the mundane buying and selling of antique furniture. It was as if we were unaware of his trade, and he was utterly ignorant of our purpose in intruding into his premises.

However, we could not for long restrain our eagerness to examine the array of tallboys, grandfather clocks, settees, escritoires and other phenomena marshalled at silent attention around us like soldiers of a Guards regiment standing on parade for inspection by royalty. Williamson worked in partnership with a similarly aged, twin-like brother who was stone deaf, and who therefore could not take part in our conversations. Throughout our tours of the galleries he hovered, ever grinning, in the background like a friendly ghost. In contrast to Roberts and Perry, Williamson never to my knowledge sold any of his treasures for a modest sum of money. I suspect he would have thought it beneath his dignity to buy anything cheaply, and certainly I believe he would have considered it an insult to his patrons if he offered them anything at a low price. Nevertheless his charges were not unreasonable, being less exorbitant than those in elite emporiums in more fashionable centres than Guildford. A comfortable provincial standard marked his requests and whatever might be the sordid quantity of guineas involved, one received in return works of artistic craftsmanship of only the finest quality. It was a fair exchange.

Other such characters as that trio of gentlemanly dealers could be found in antique shops all over England, Scotland and Wales in those times. I remember with pleasure and gratitude quiet, proficient Mr. Halliday on Oxford's High Street; old-maidish Mr. Godfrey shuffling among his show-cases of Dr. Wall Worcester porcelain in which he specialised, in the same city's St Giles; benign Mr. Bruford in the main street at Exeter; plebeian but cultured Mr. Anderson along a side-lane in Elgin; and several more. They were admirable collaborators in the hobby of discovering choice, lovely antiquities.

Of course, not all the dealers of that period were as reliable as them. I recall another member of the trade in Elgin who kept a shop well stocked with plausible looking examples of ancient furniture. The rascal did an especially good business during the summer months when holiday-makers were dallying on the shores of the Moray Firth. His prices were not too outrageous, and gullible visitors fell to the temptation of buying his clever fakes. Towards the close of each season he held an auction of his still unsold goods, and I recall the advertisement which he inserted in a local newspaper about one of them. After listing the principal Jacobean, Queen Anne, Georgian and other period pieces for sale, it announced that they were 'all more genuine than ever'.

Most of those memorable personalities have now left this world, and I am not sure whether their like still exist in large numbers in the highways and byways of Britain. Certainly some do, such as Mr. Allbrook in South Kensington, from whom I bought excellent pieces of English seventeenth and eighteenth century pottery during the 1950s and early 1960s. However, throughout almost thirty years from 1941 onwards I lived in North America, various parts of Asia and Africa, with only occasional fleeting visits to England; so I lost touch with the new generation of antique dealers in Britain.

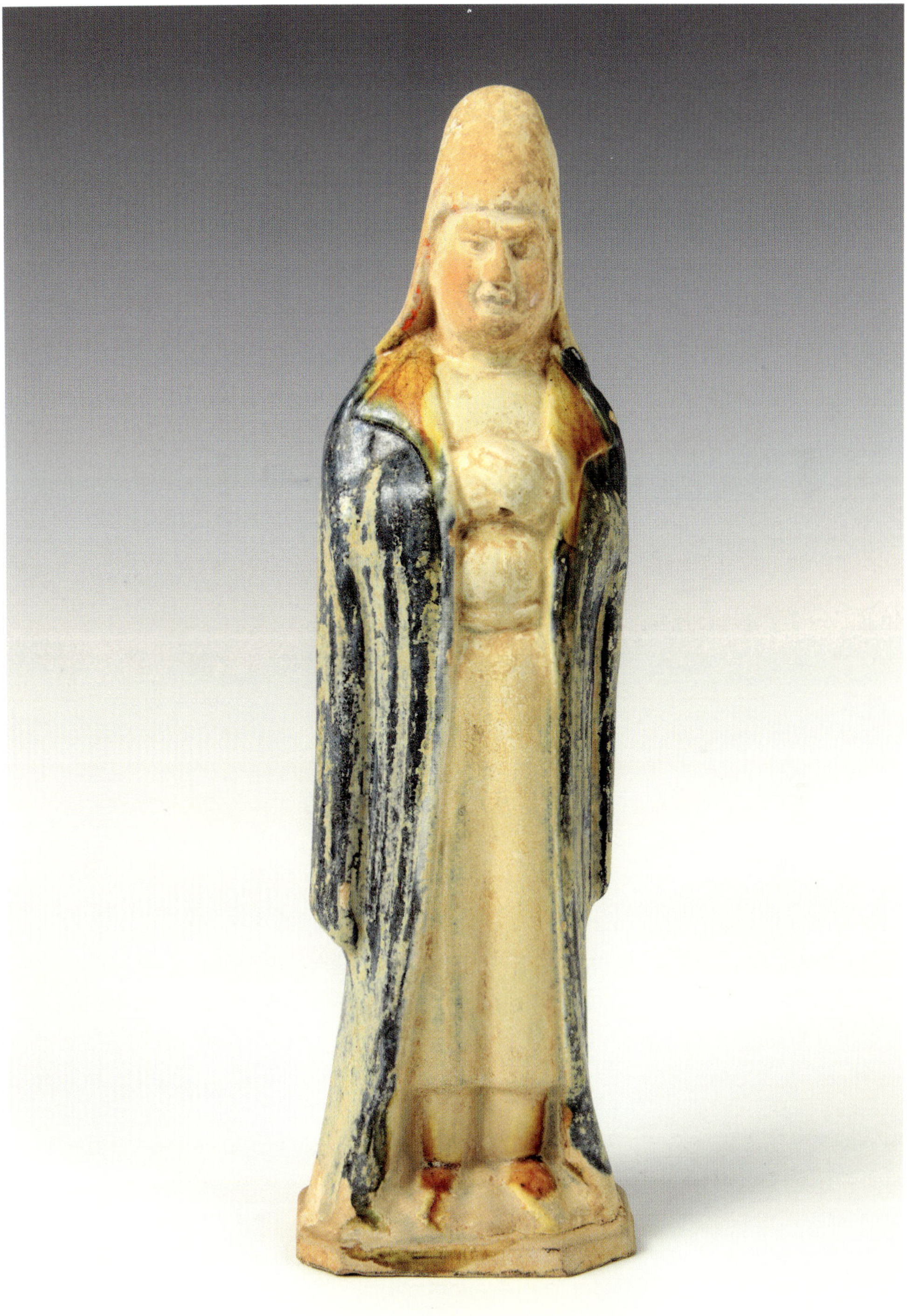

Plate 1

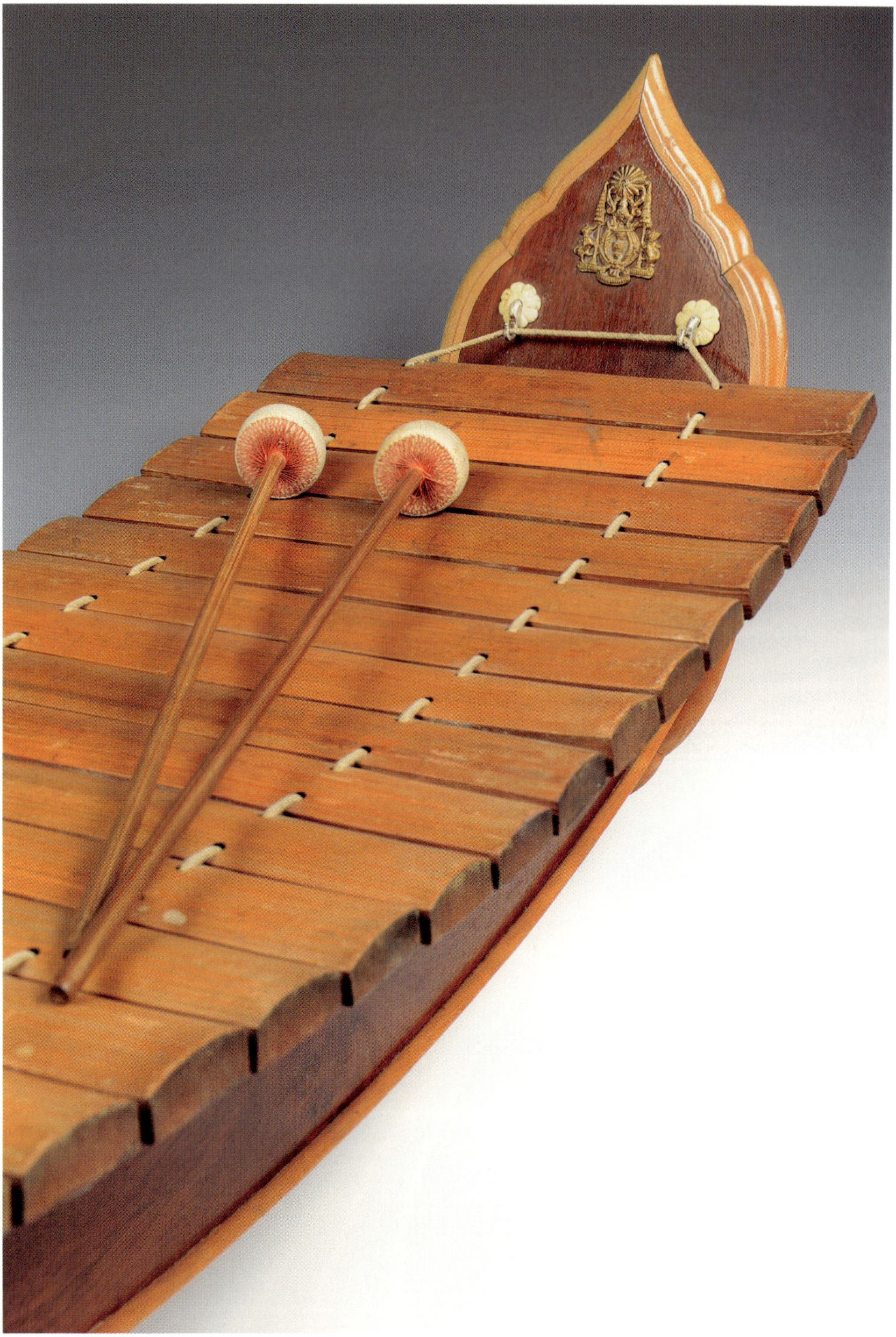

Plate 2

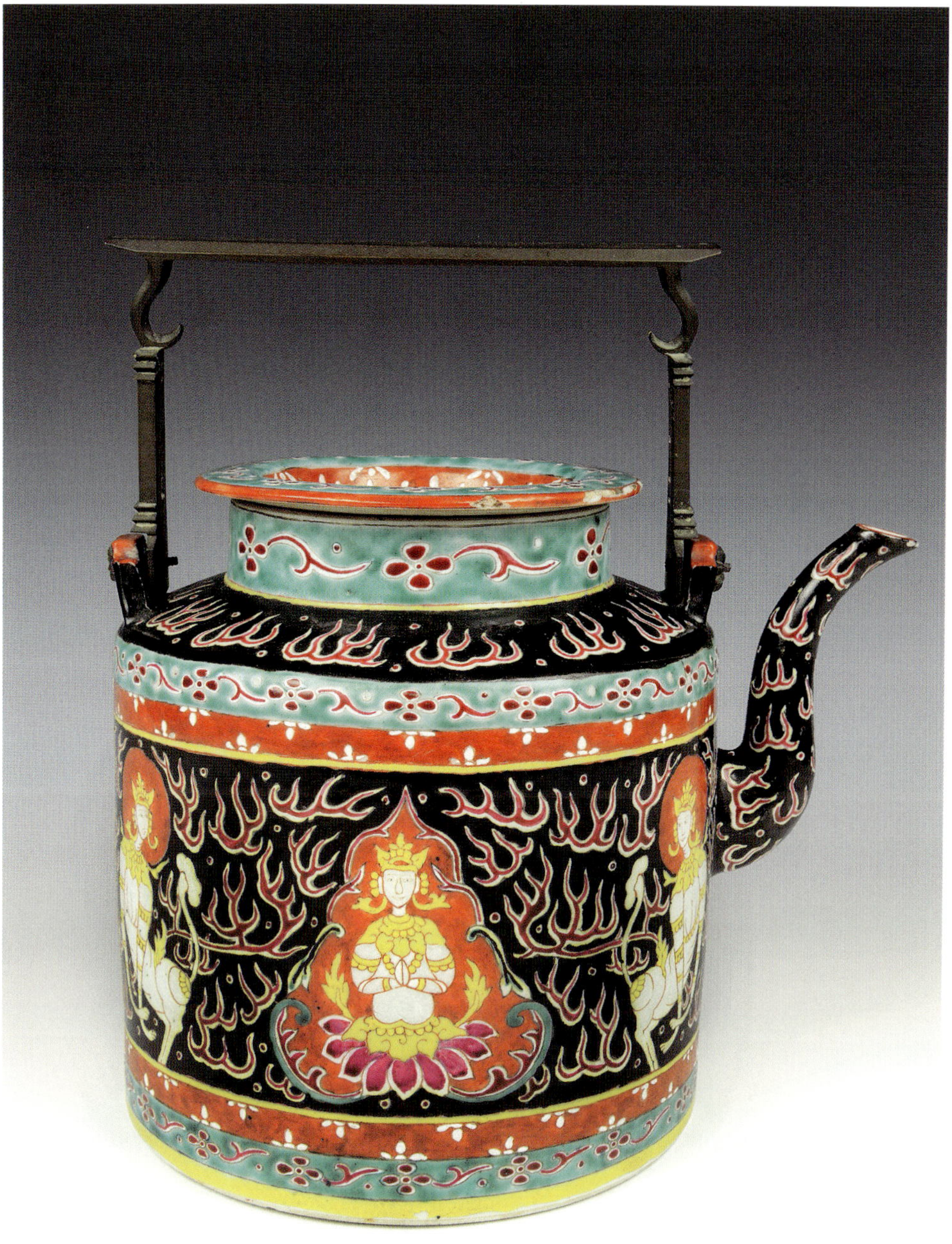

Plate 3

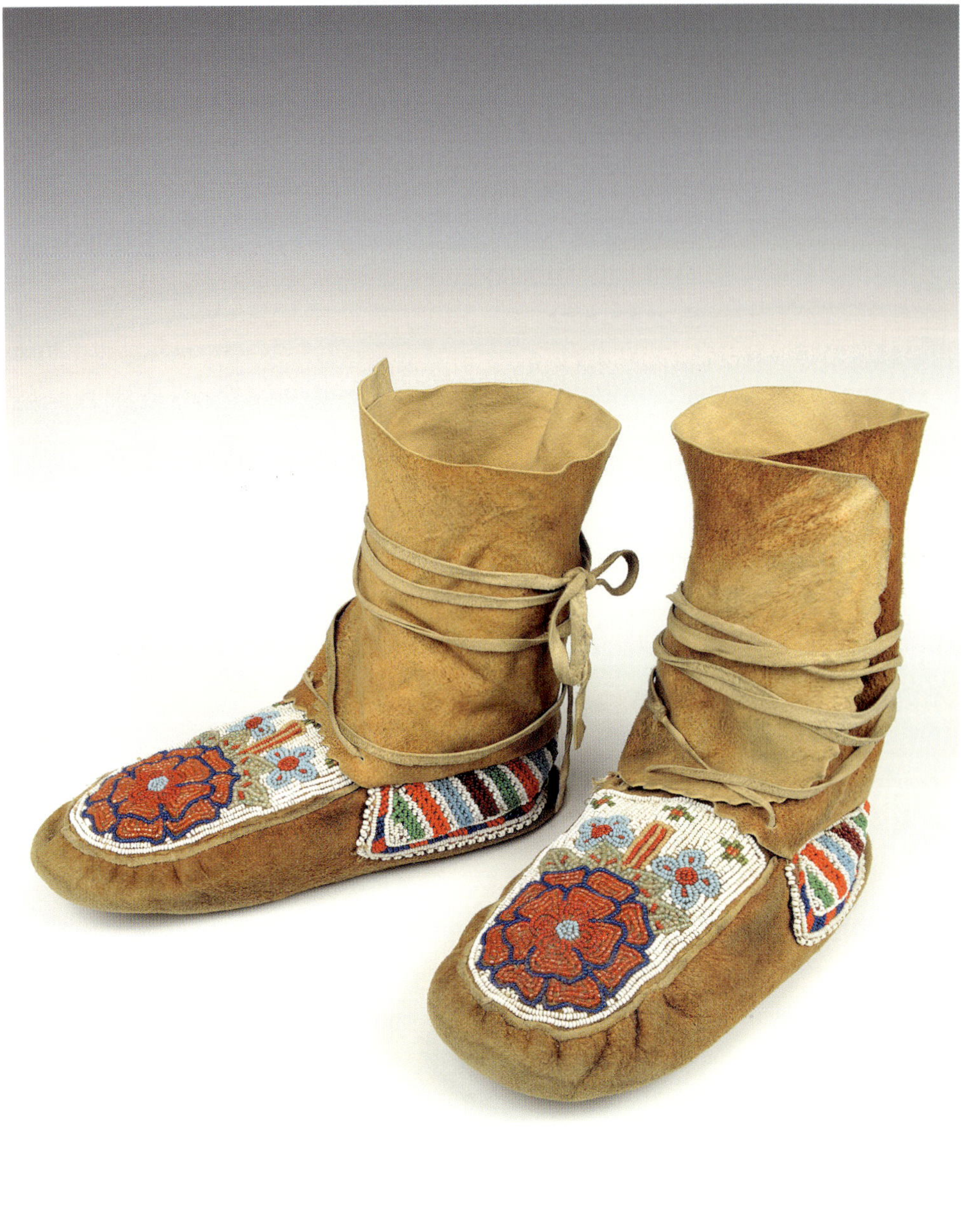

Plate 4

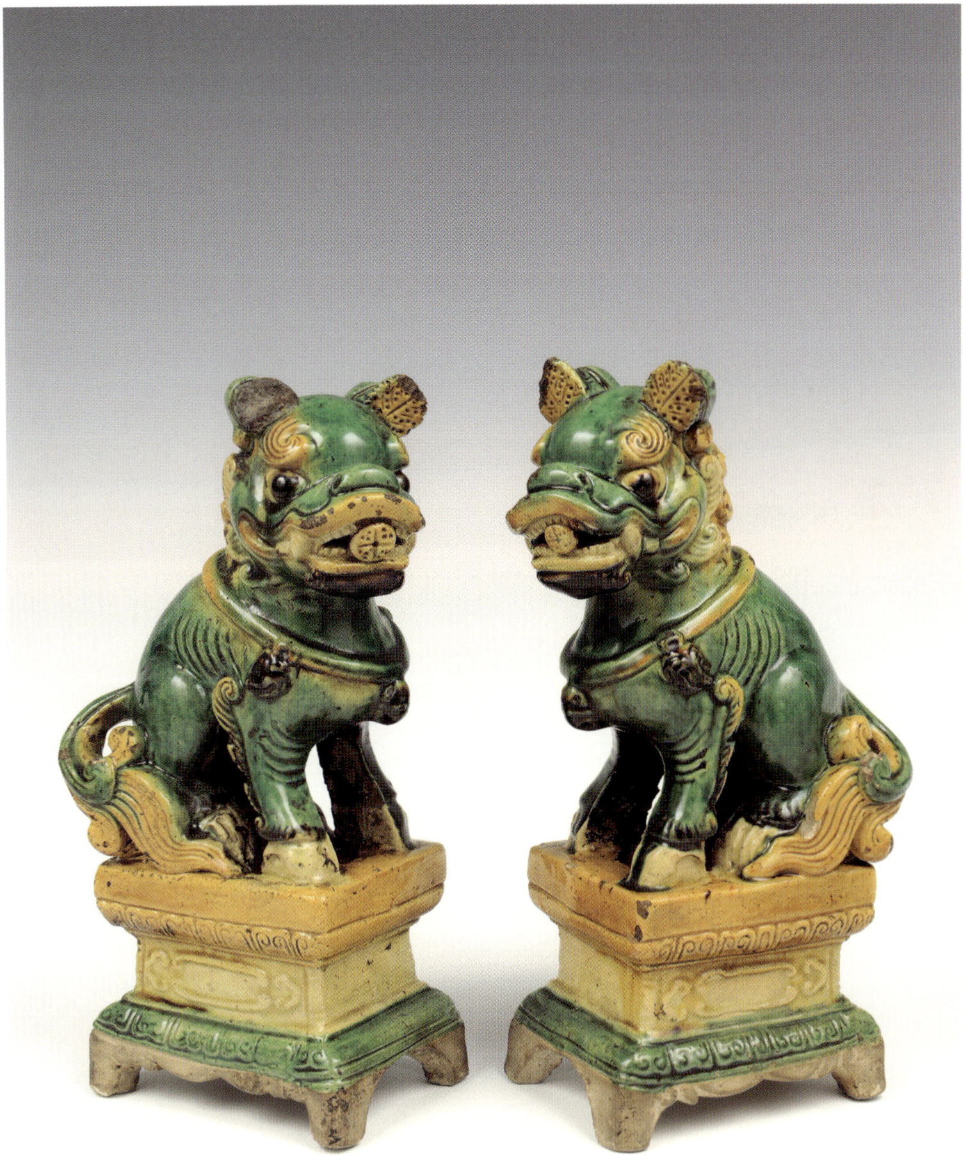

Plate 5

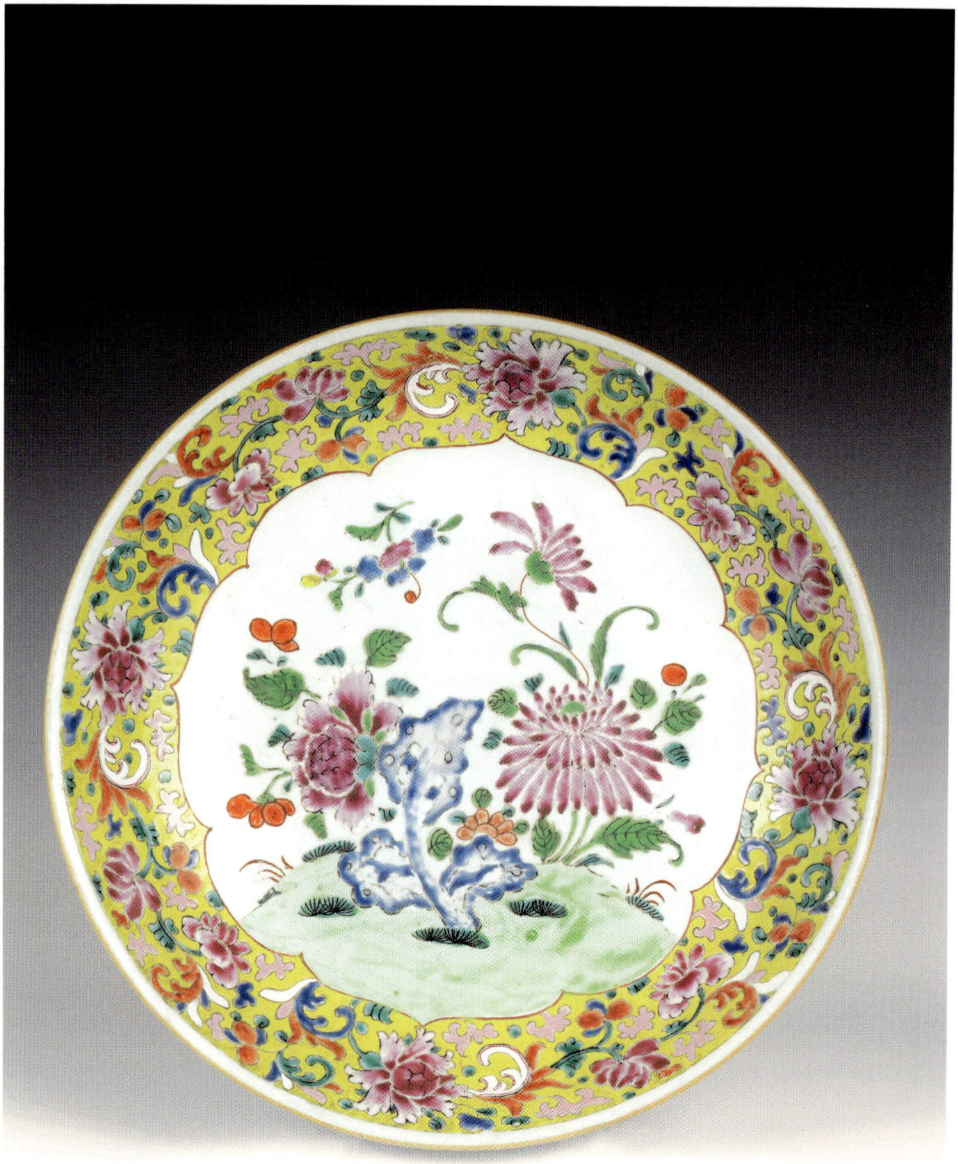

Plate 6

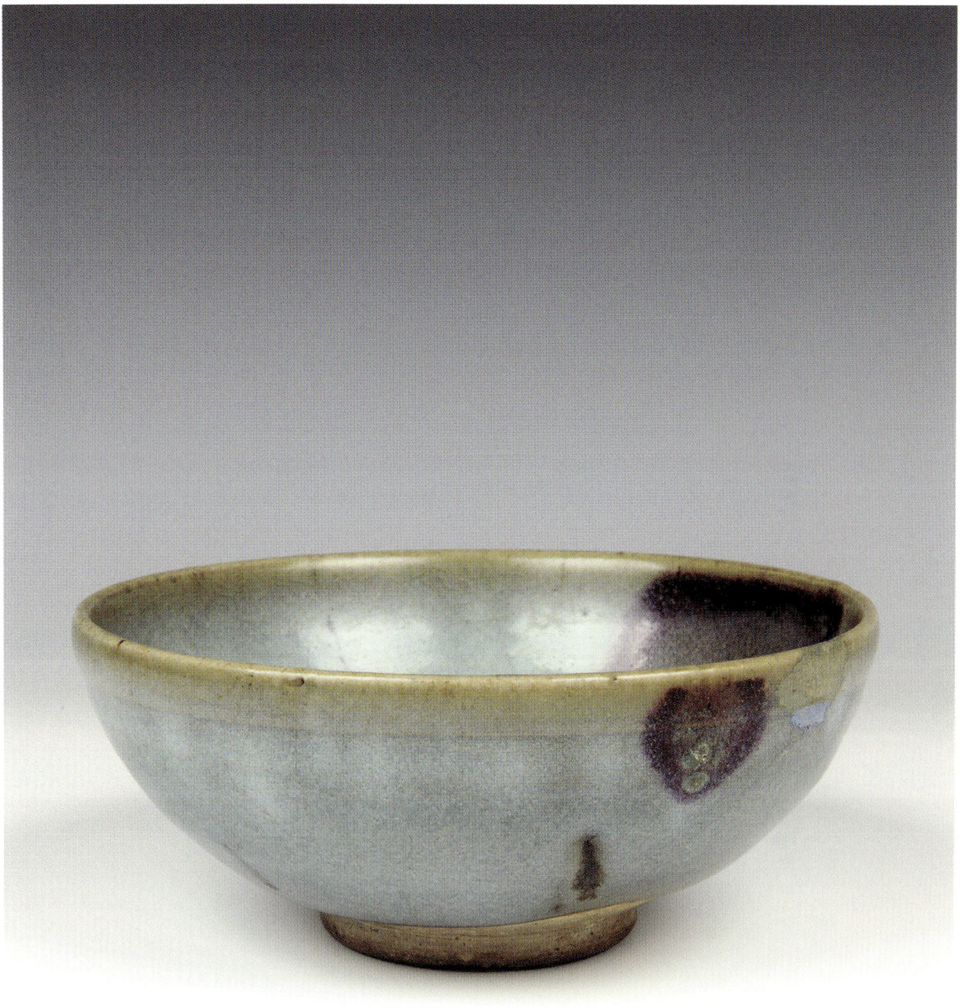

Plate 7

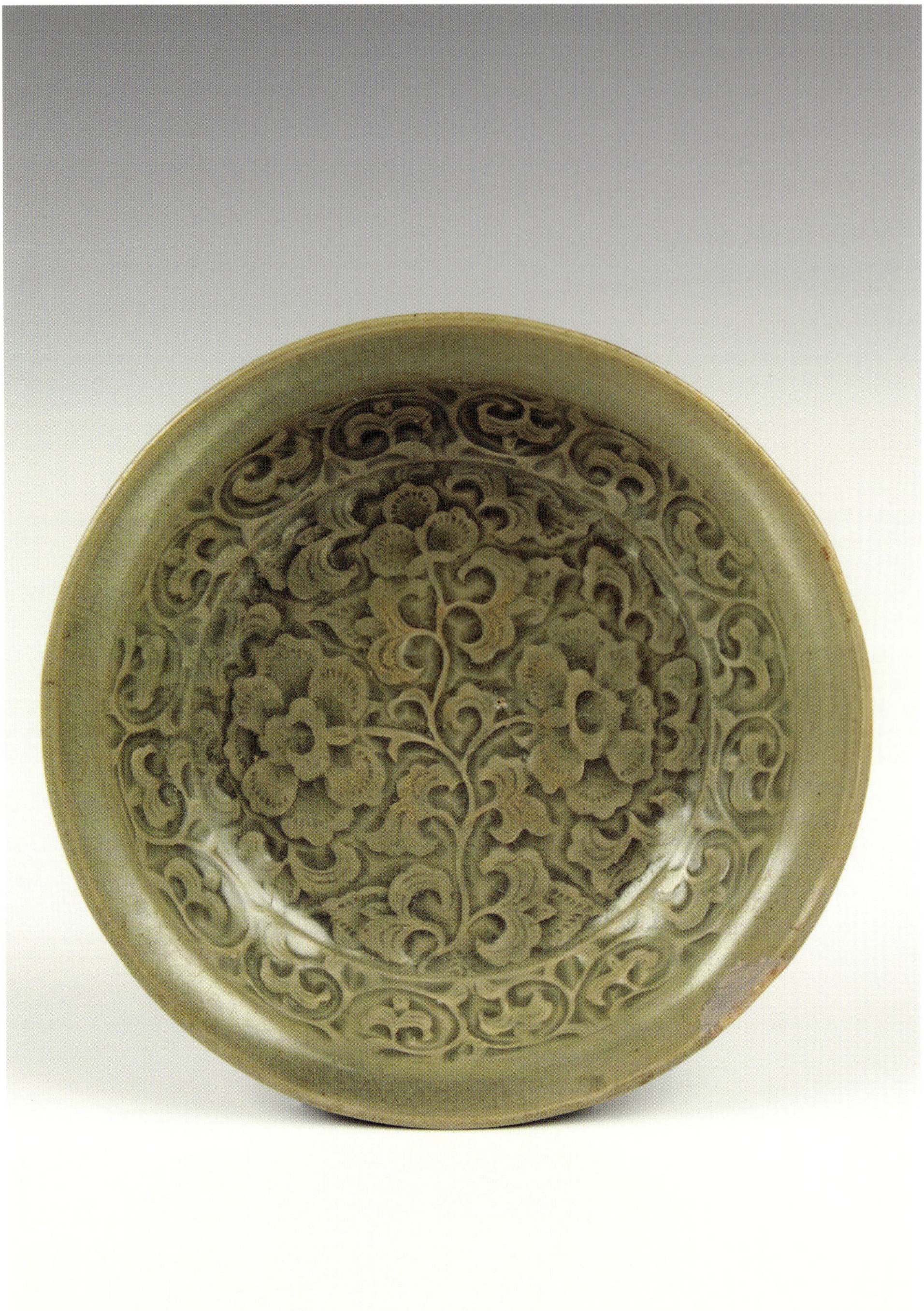

Plate 8

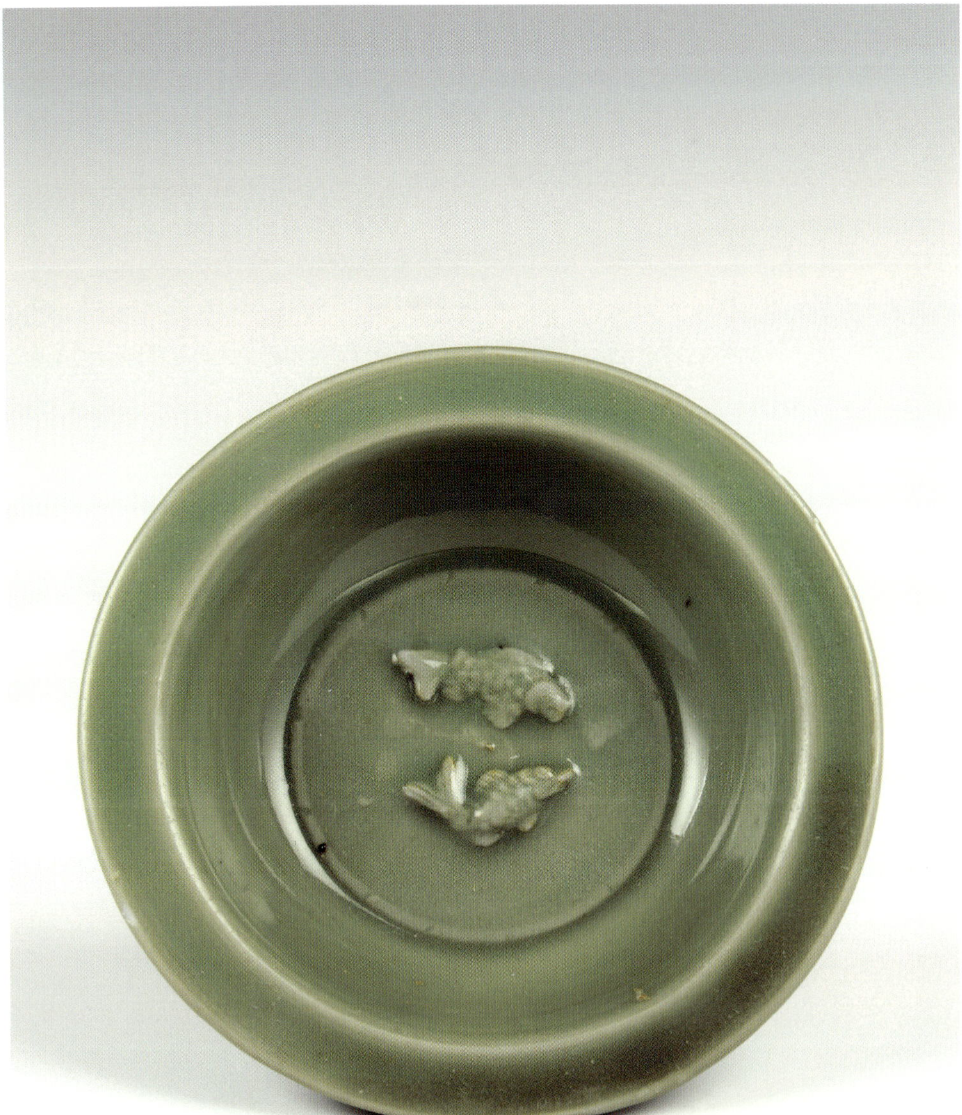

Plate 9

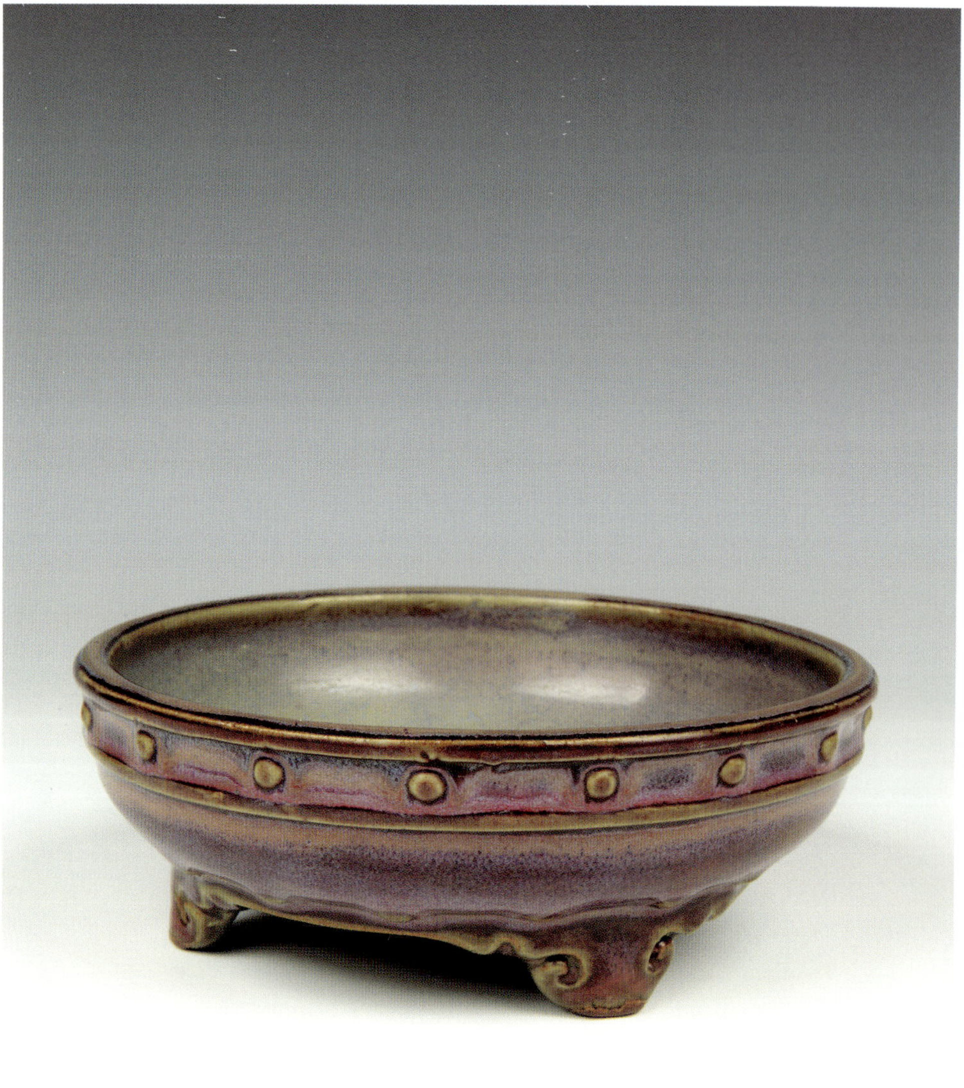

Plate 10

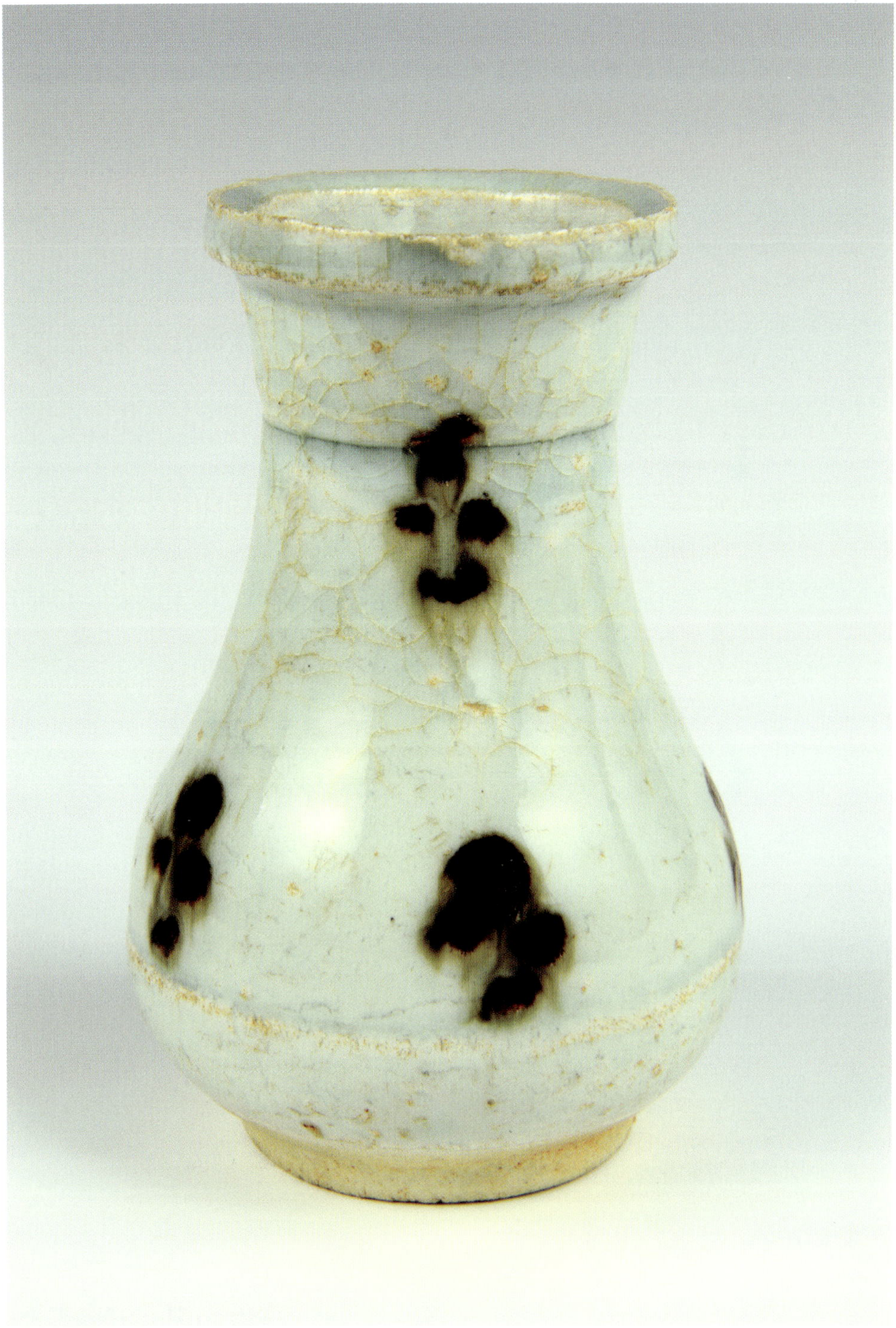

Plate 11

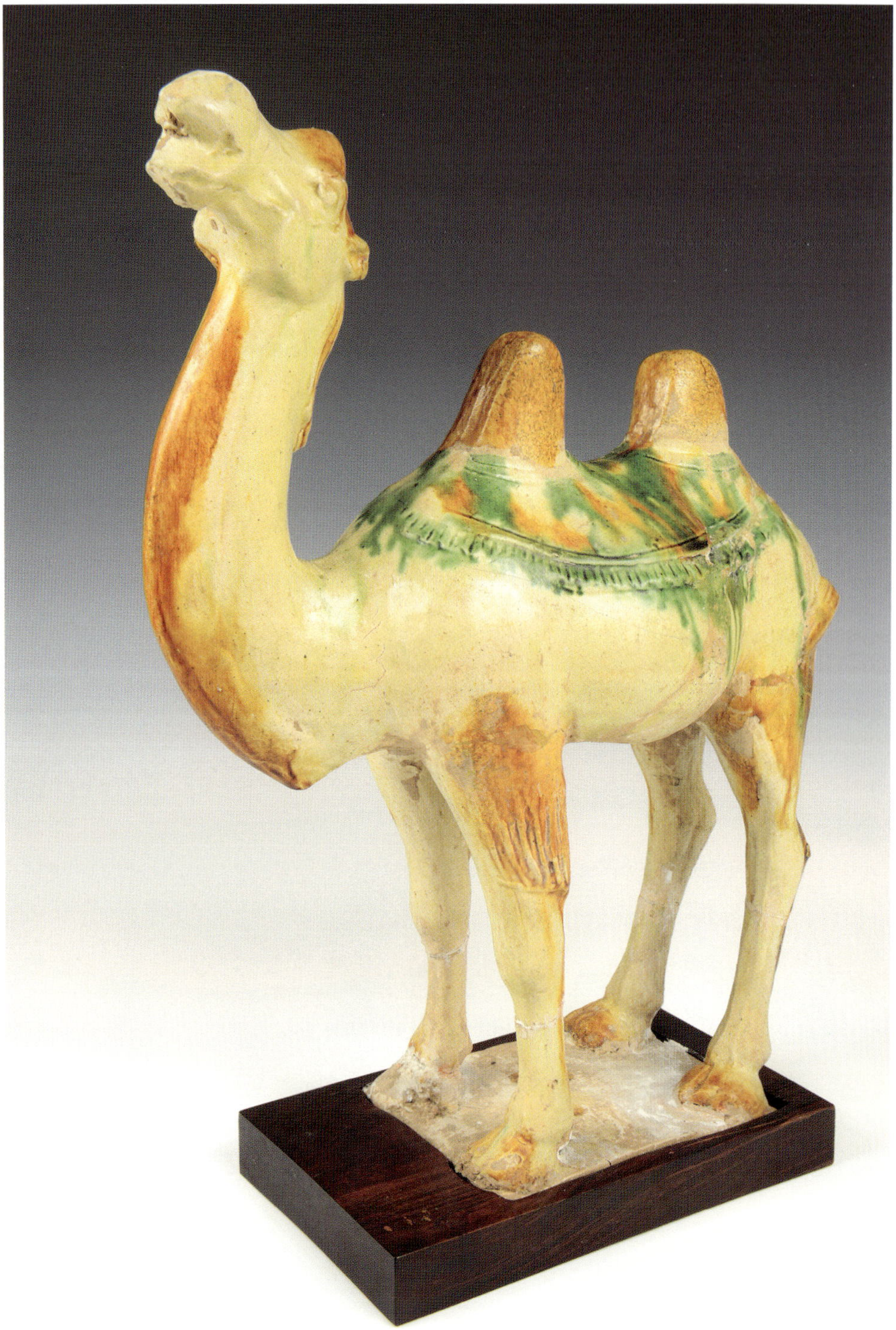

Plate 12

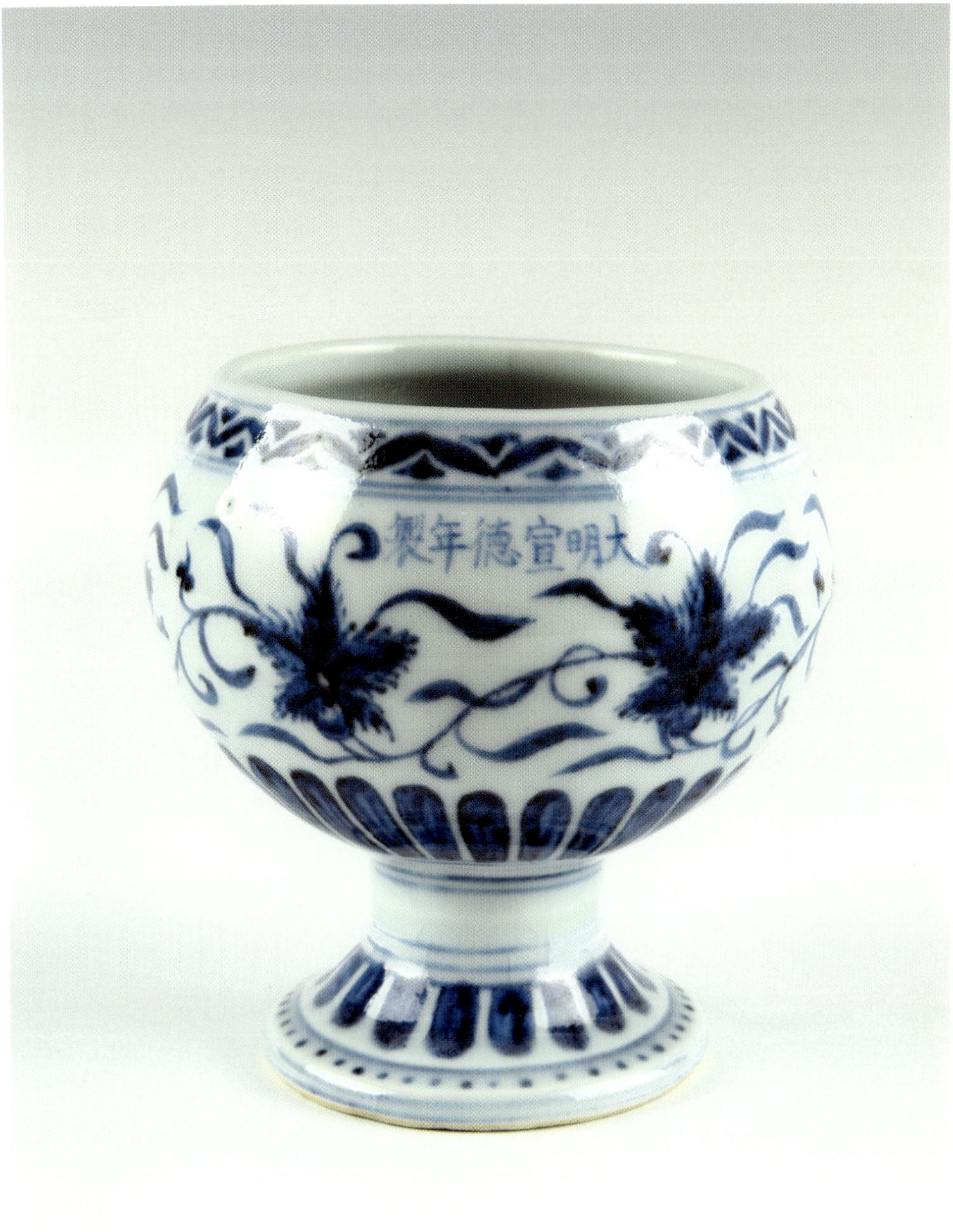

Plate 13

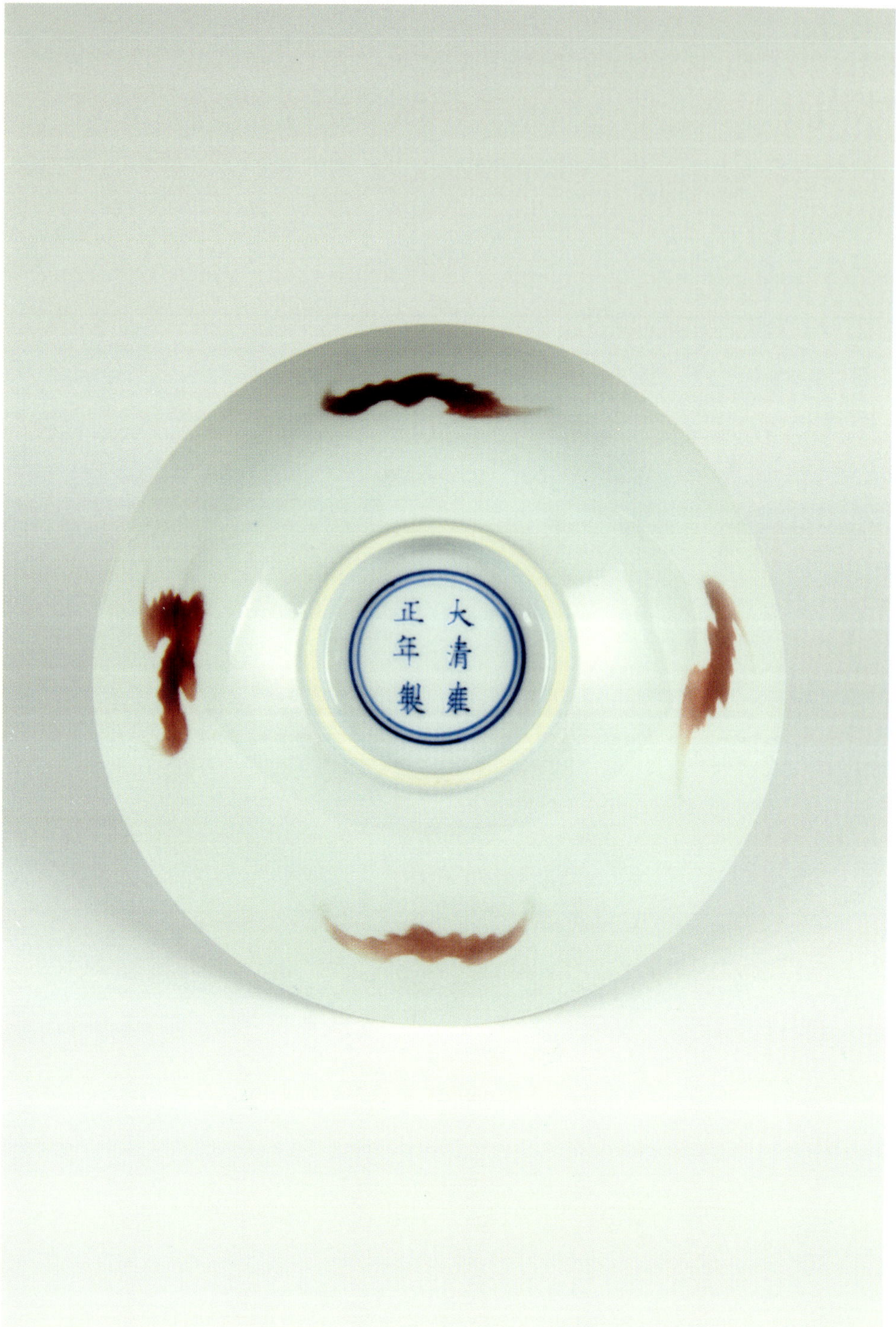

Plate 14

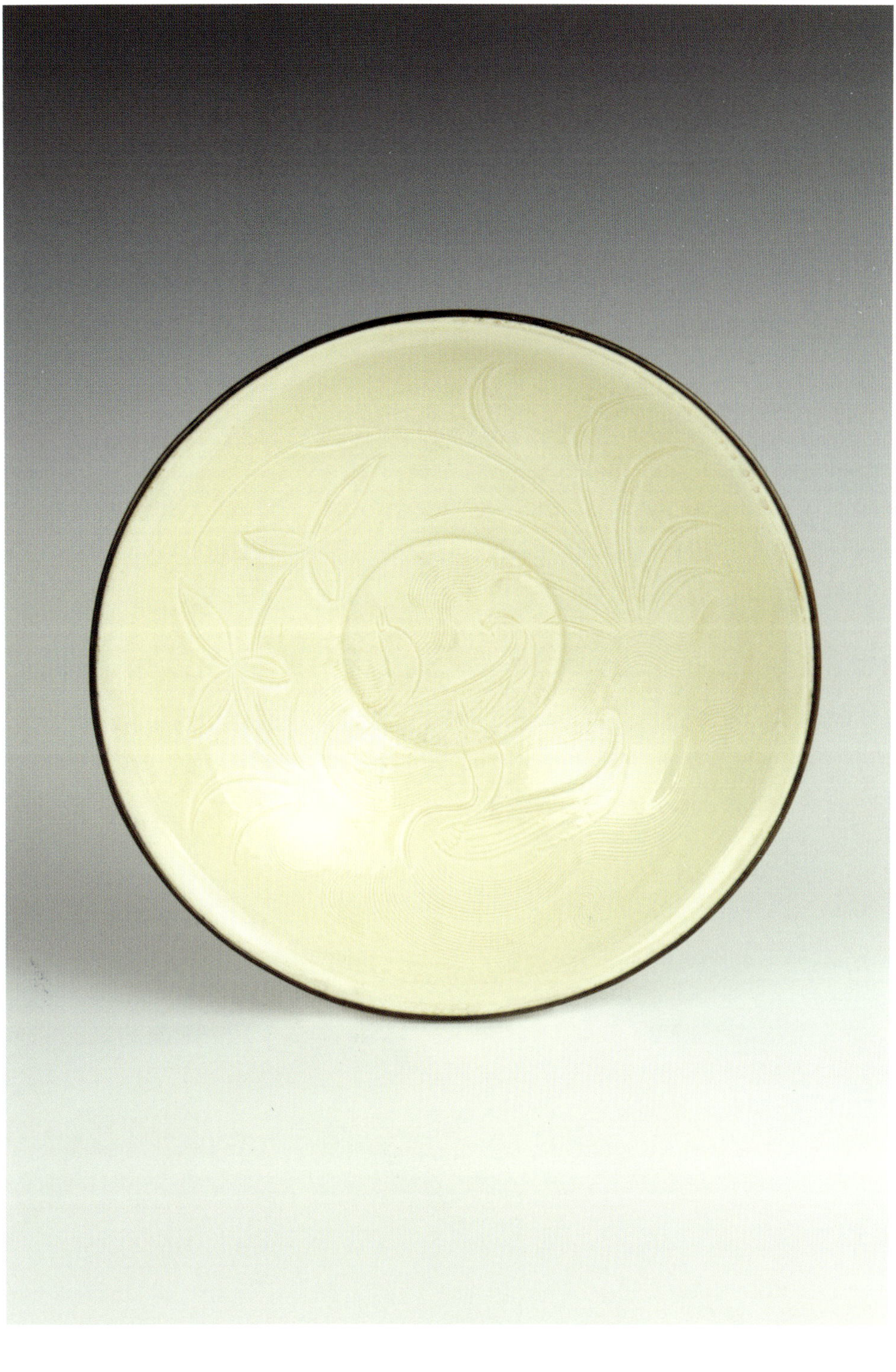

Plate 15

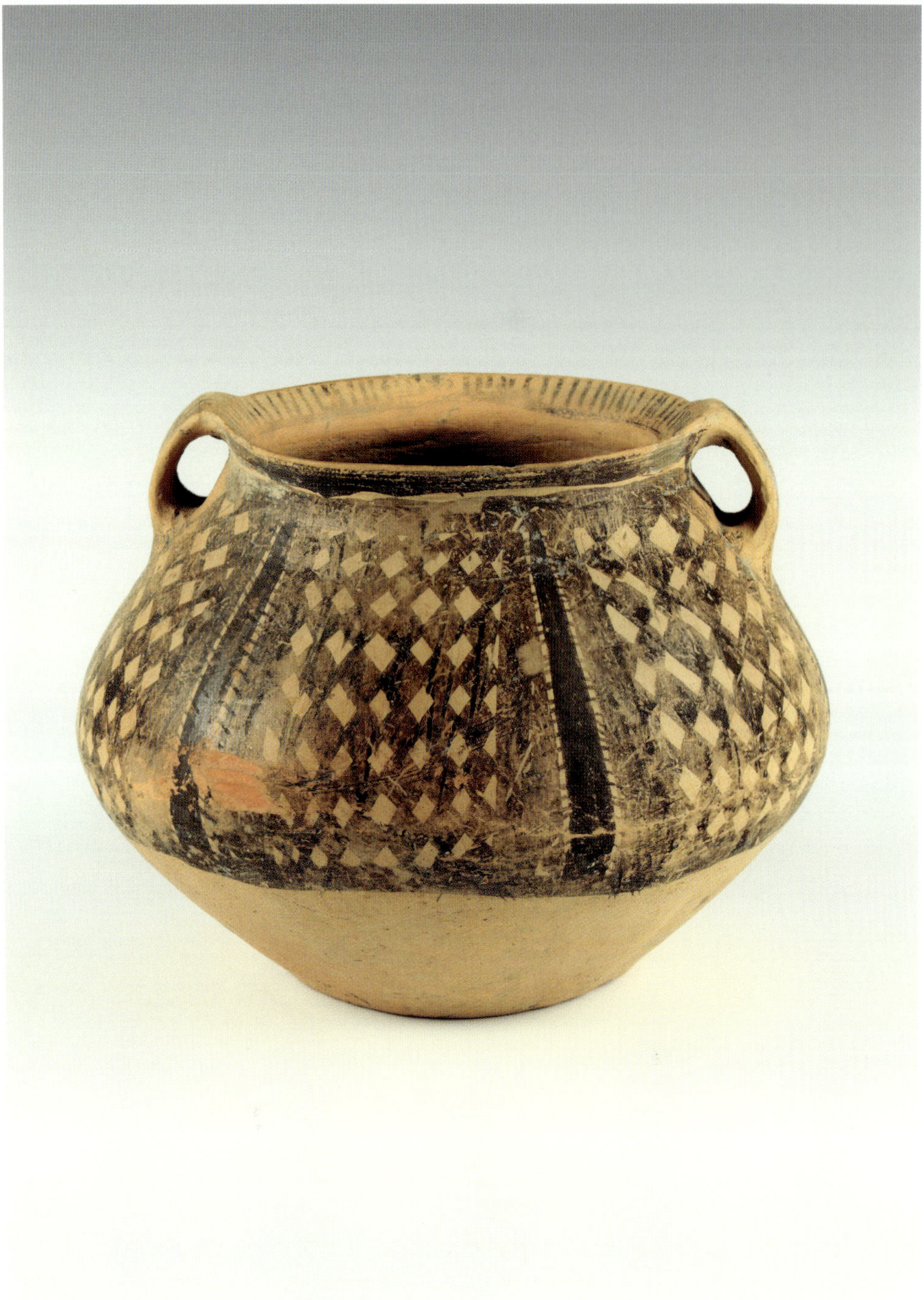

Plate 16

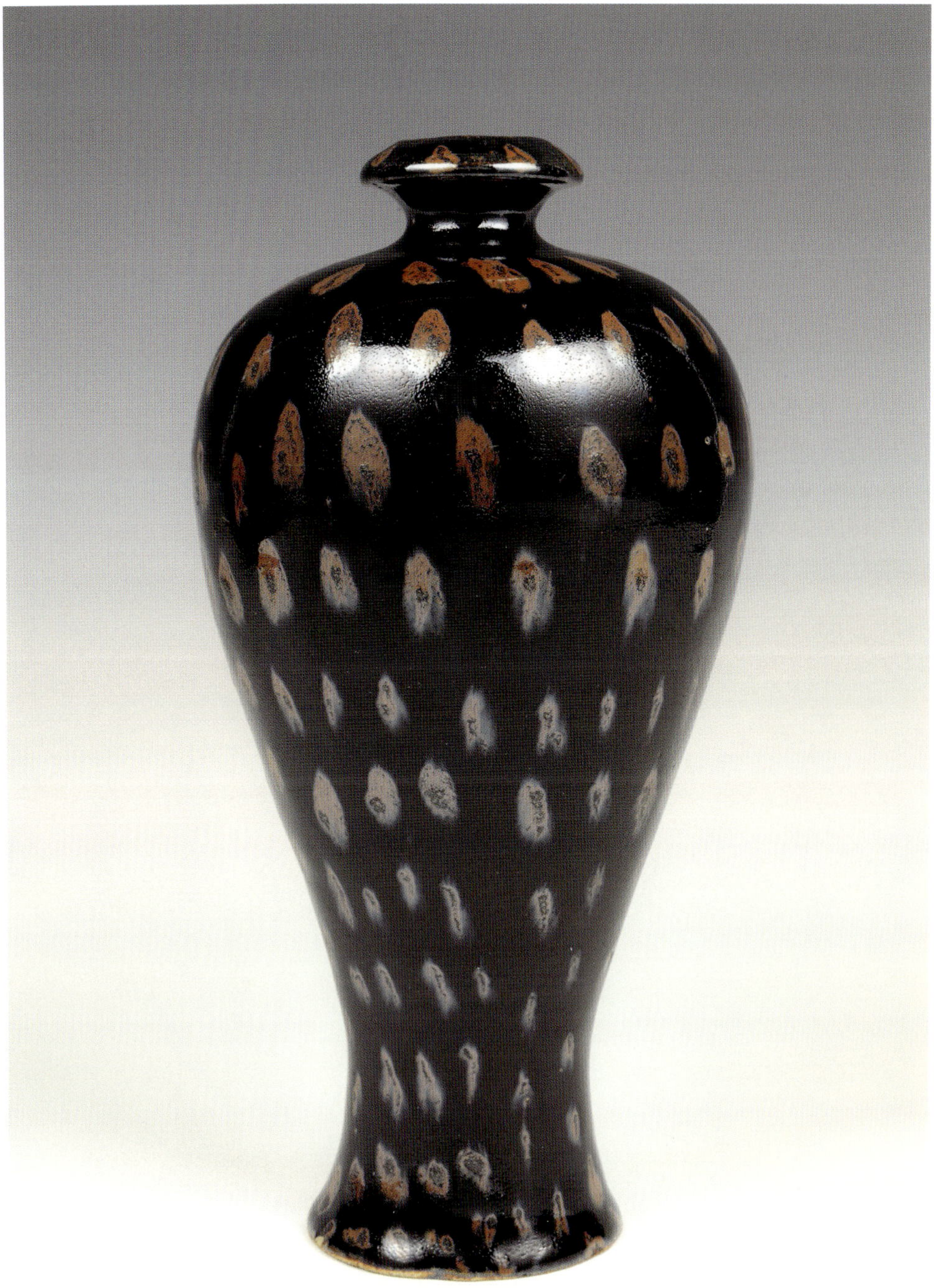

Plate 17

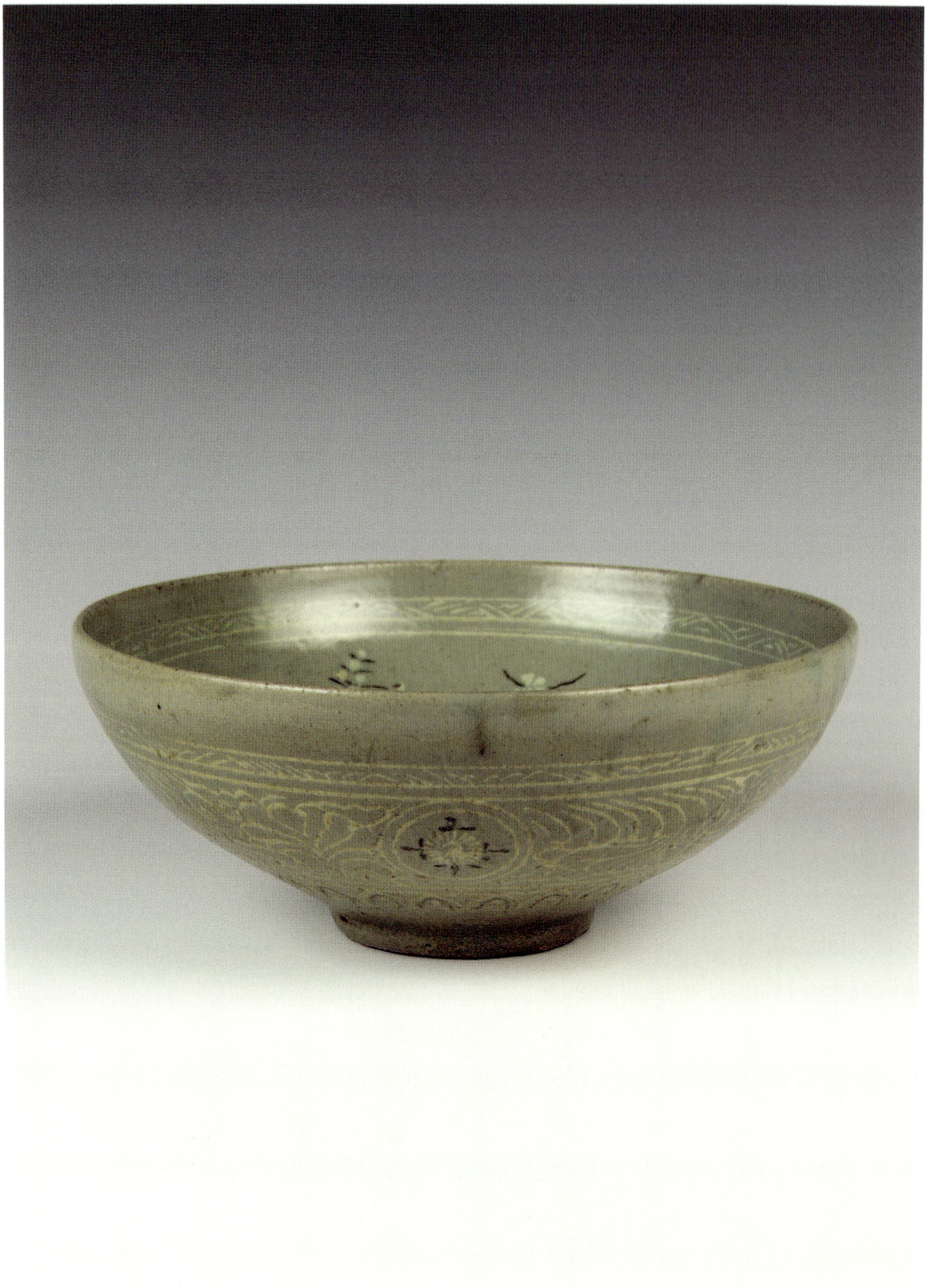

Plate 18

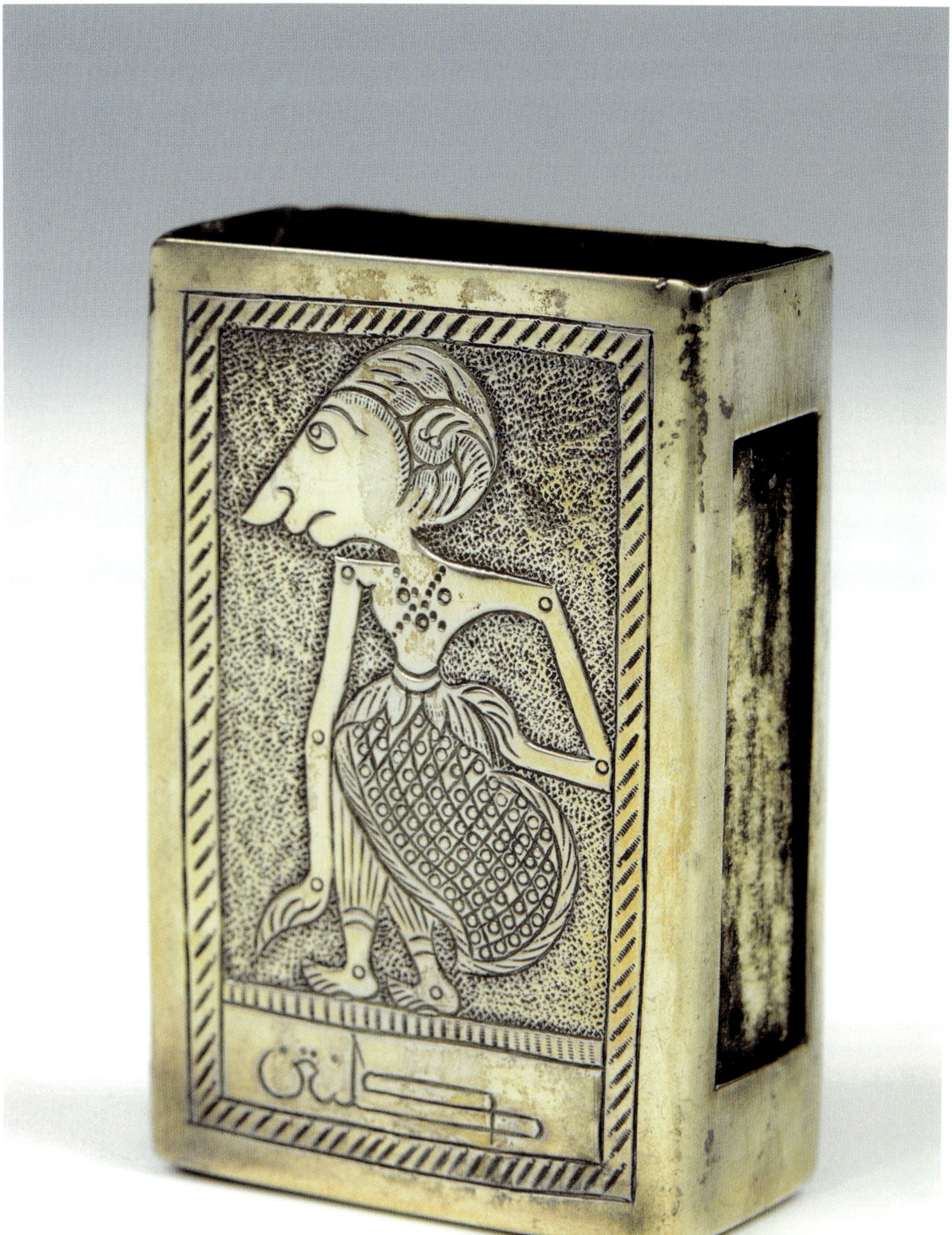

Plate 19

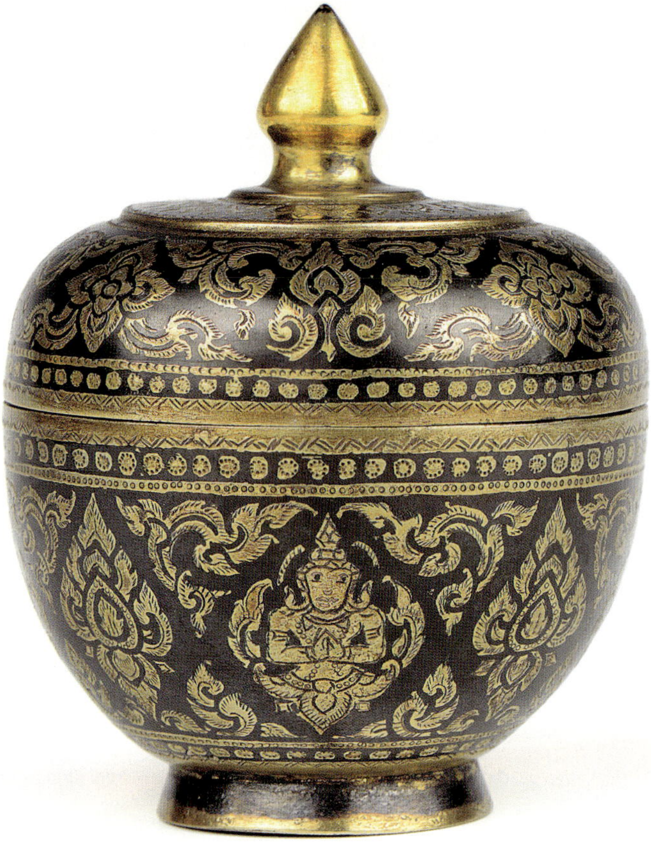

Plate 20

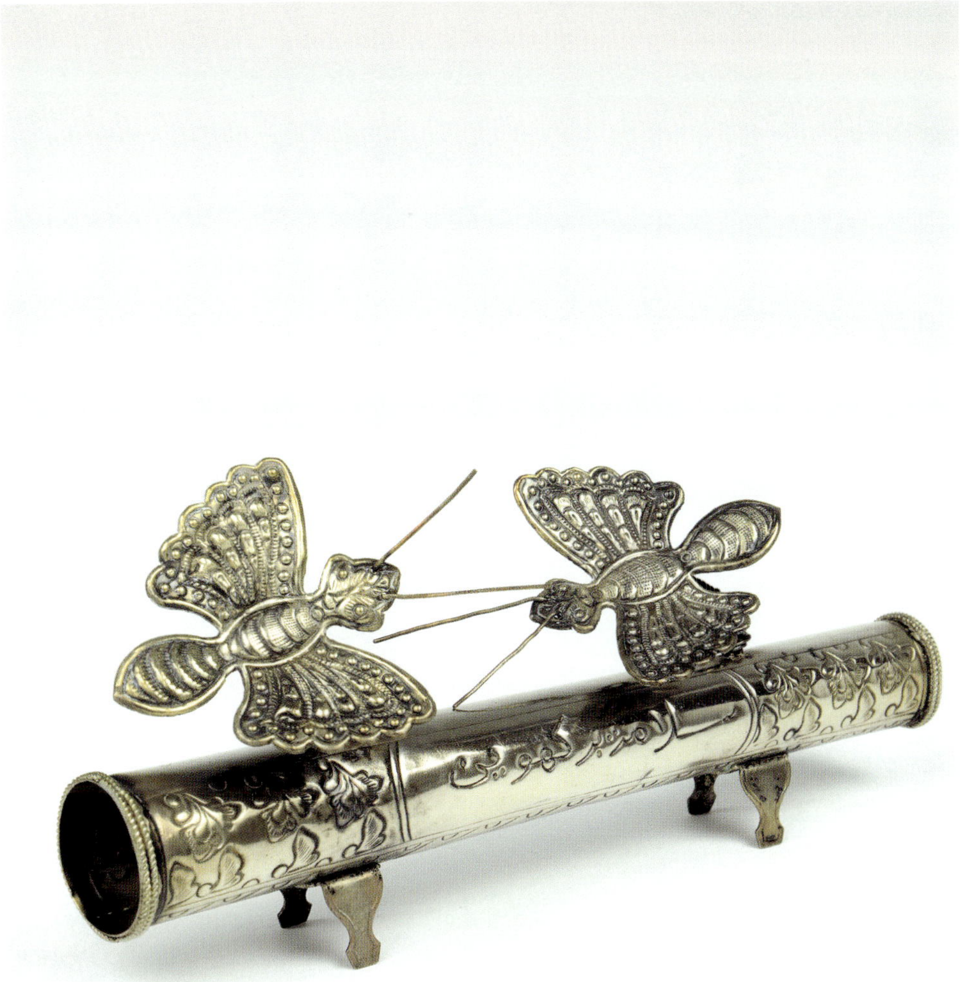

Plate 21

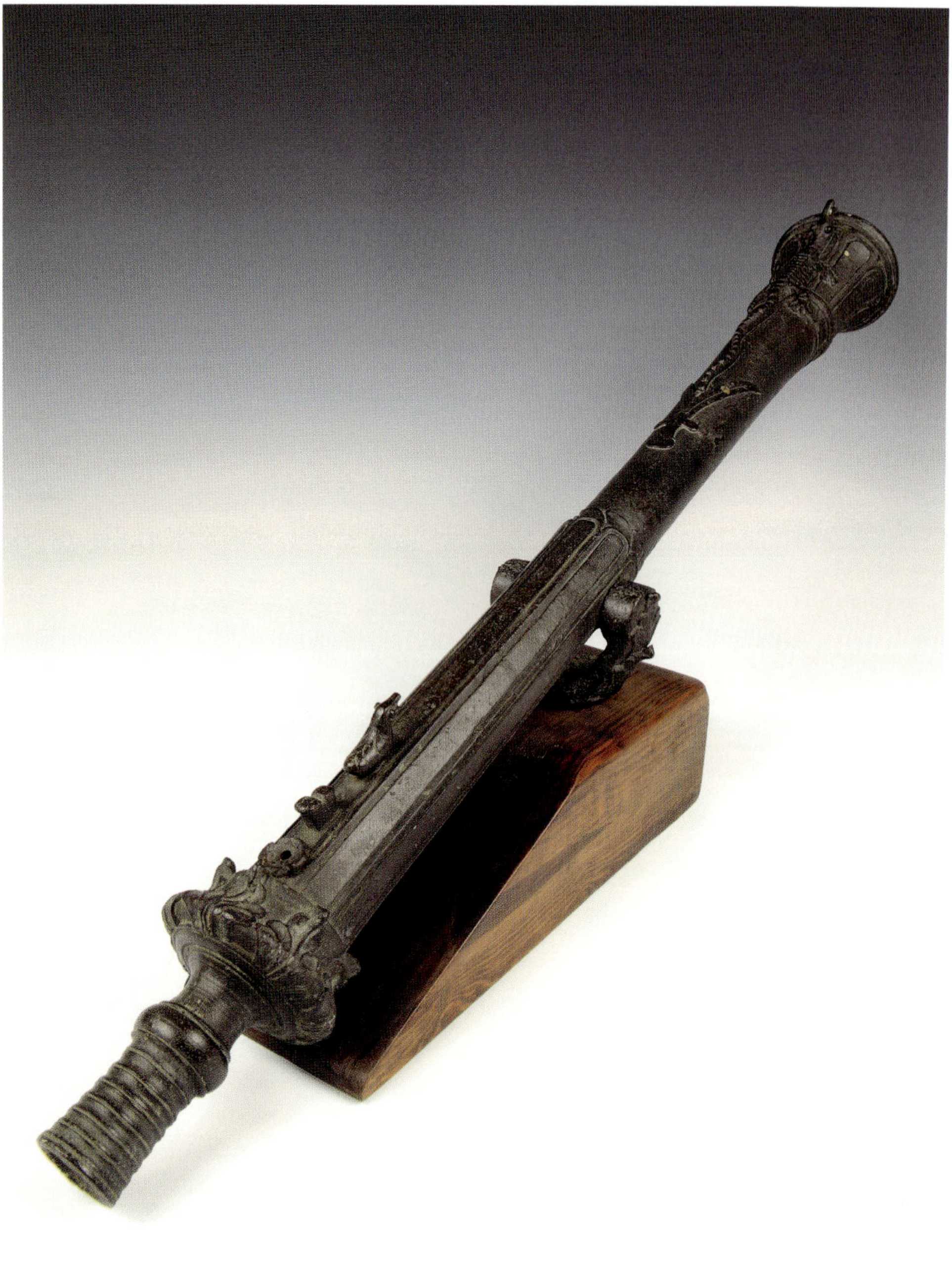

Plate 22

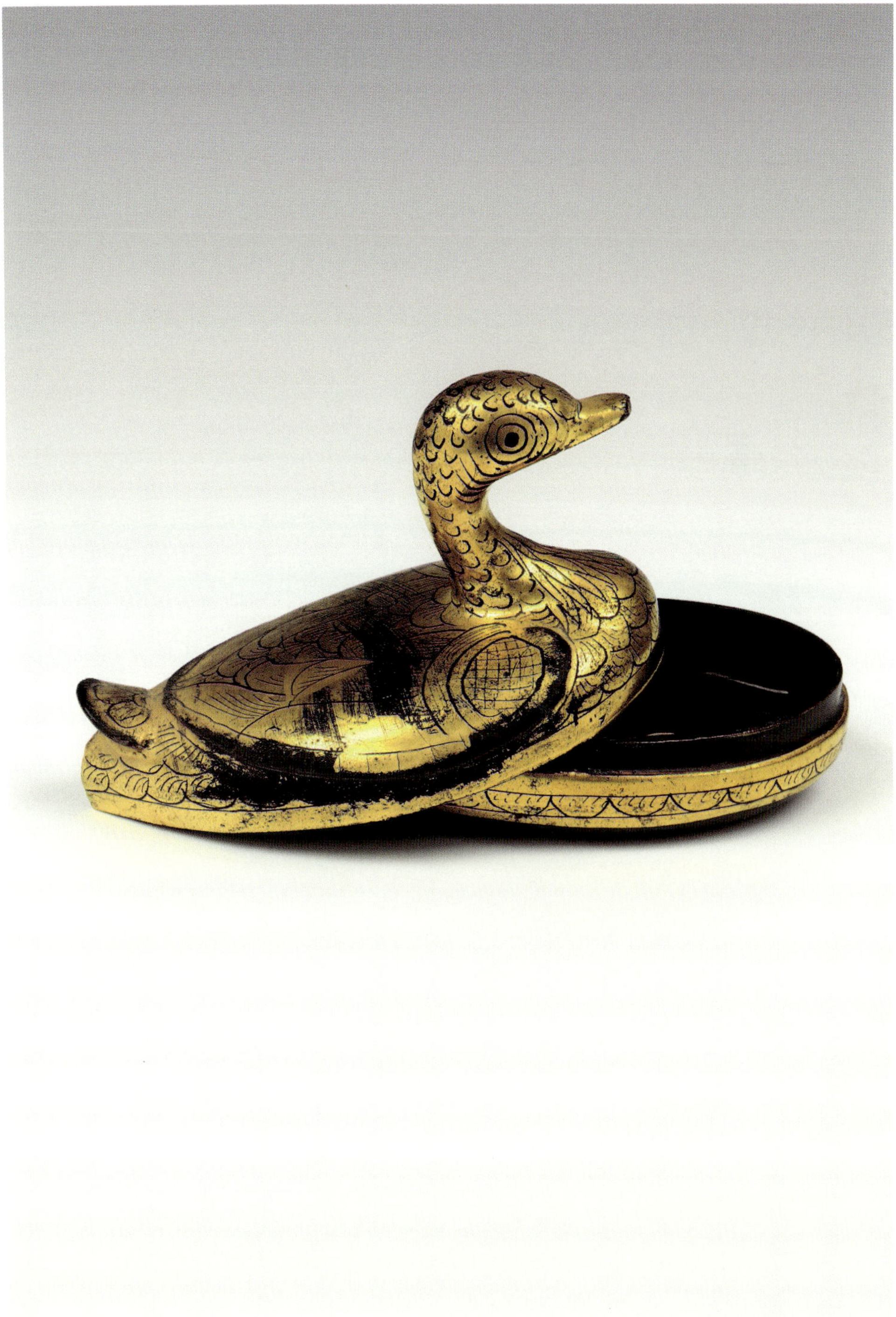

Plate 23

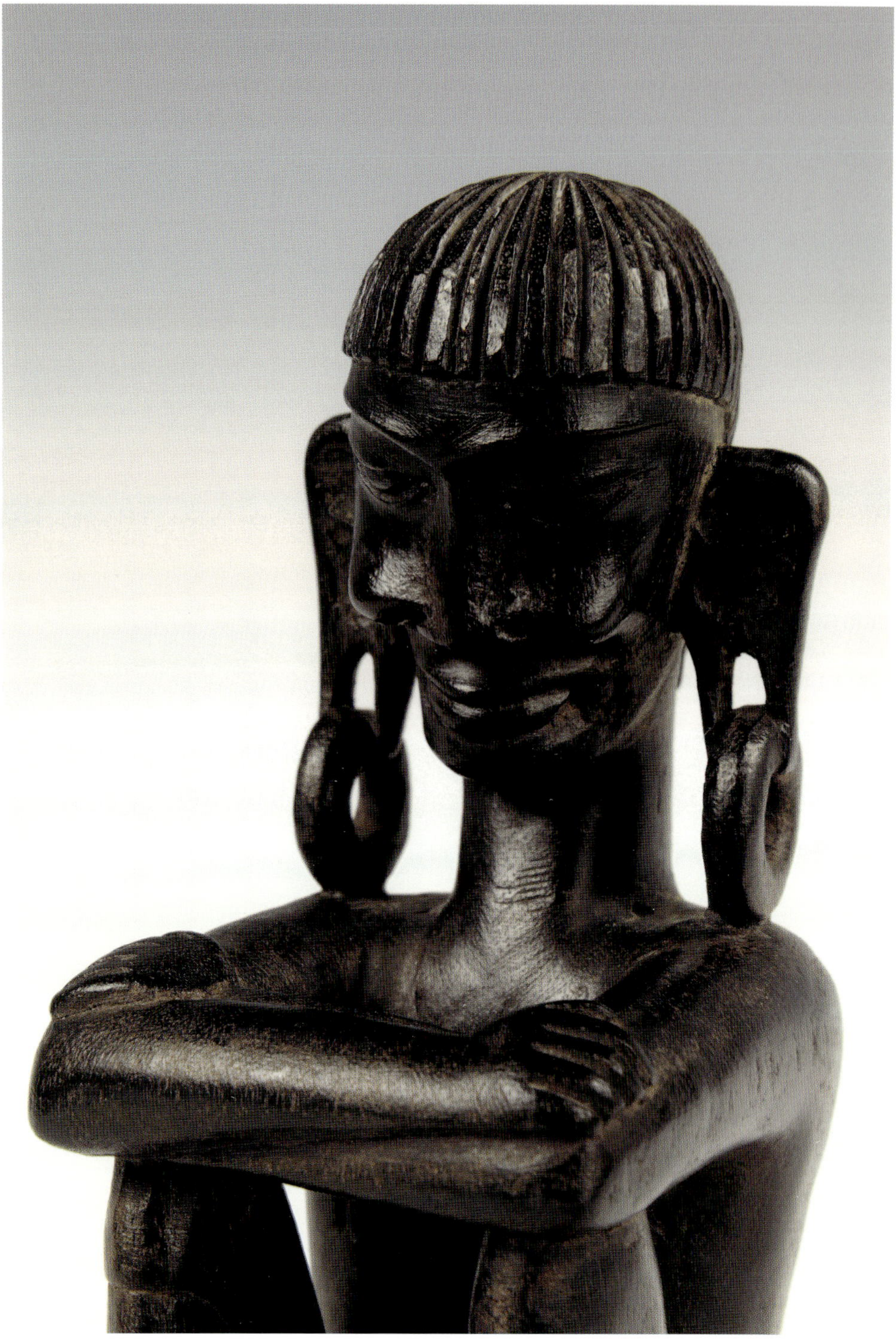

Plate 24

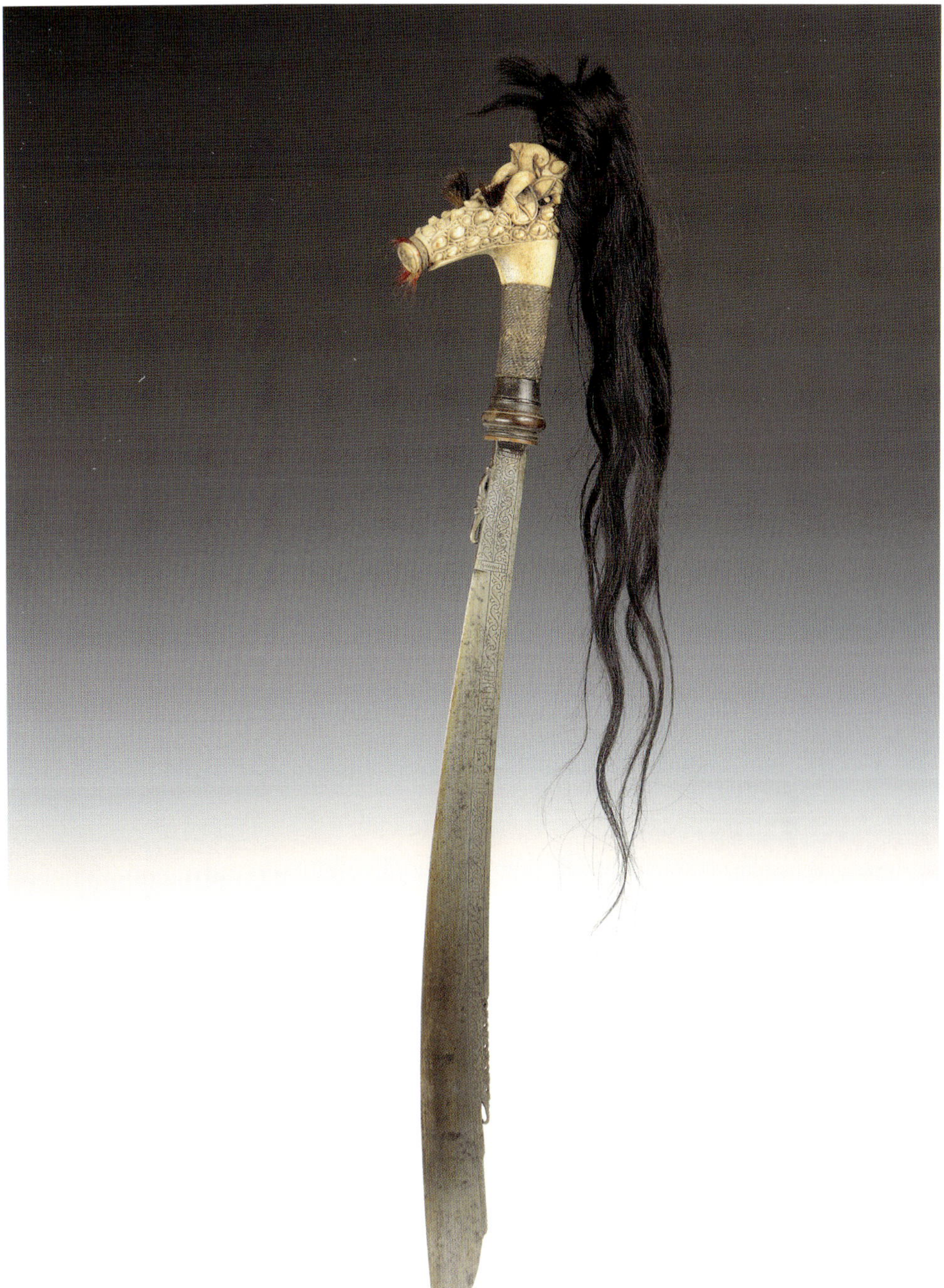

Plate 25

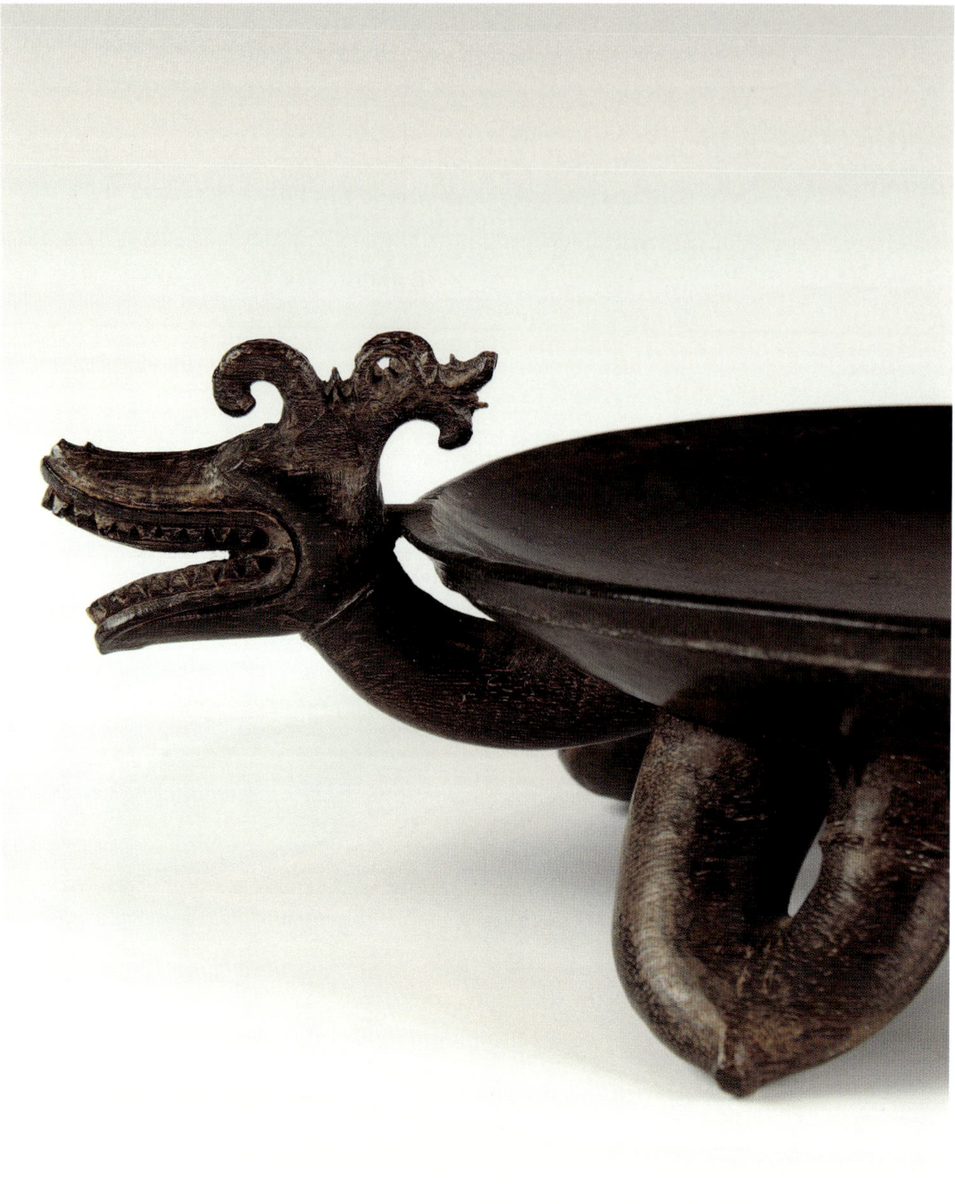

Plate 26

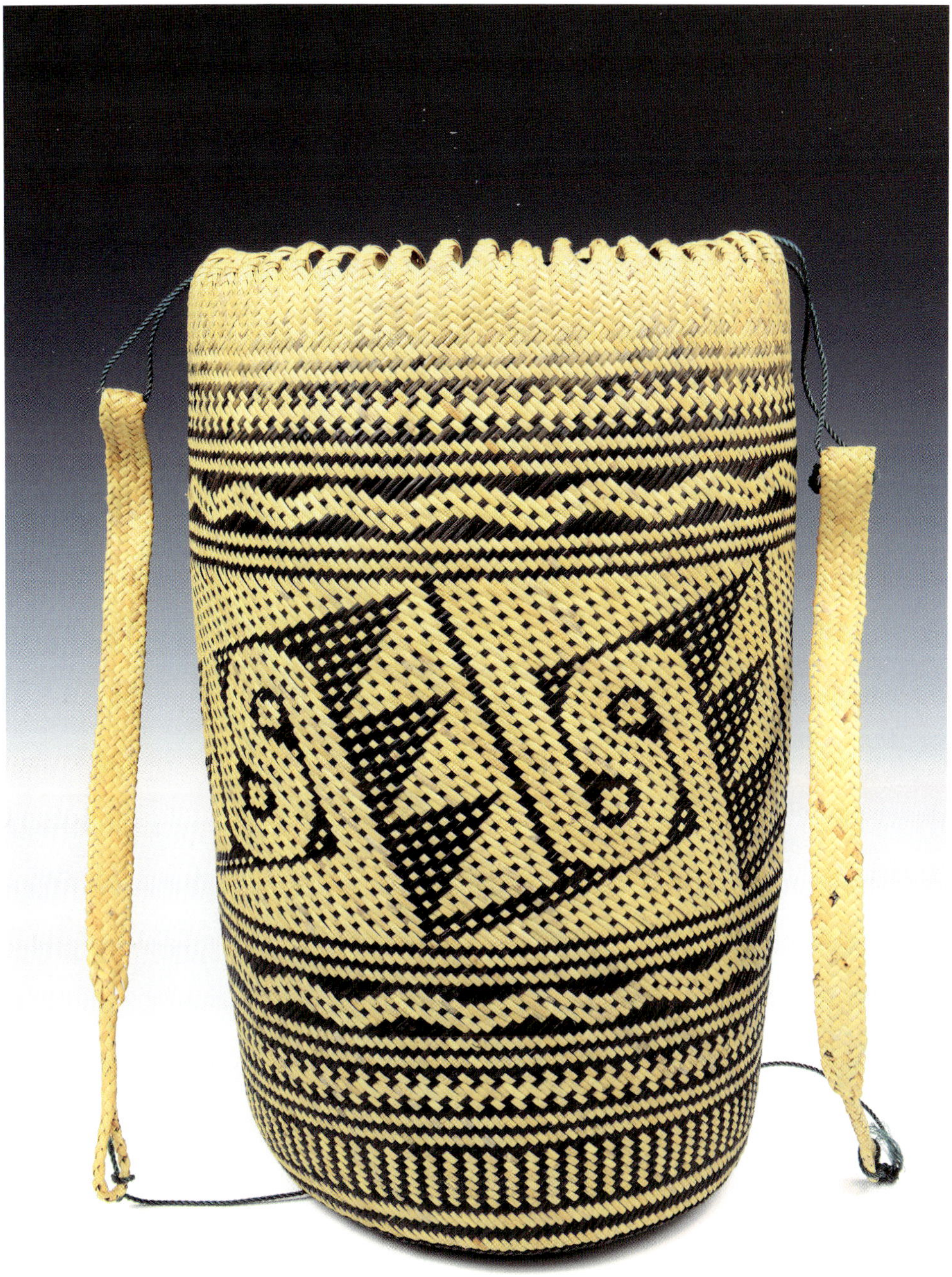

Plate 27

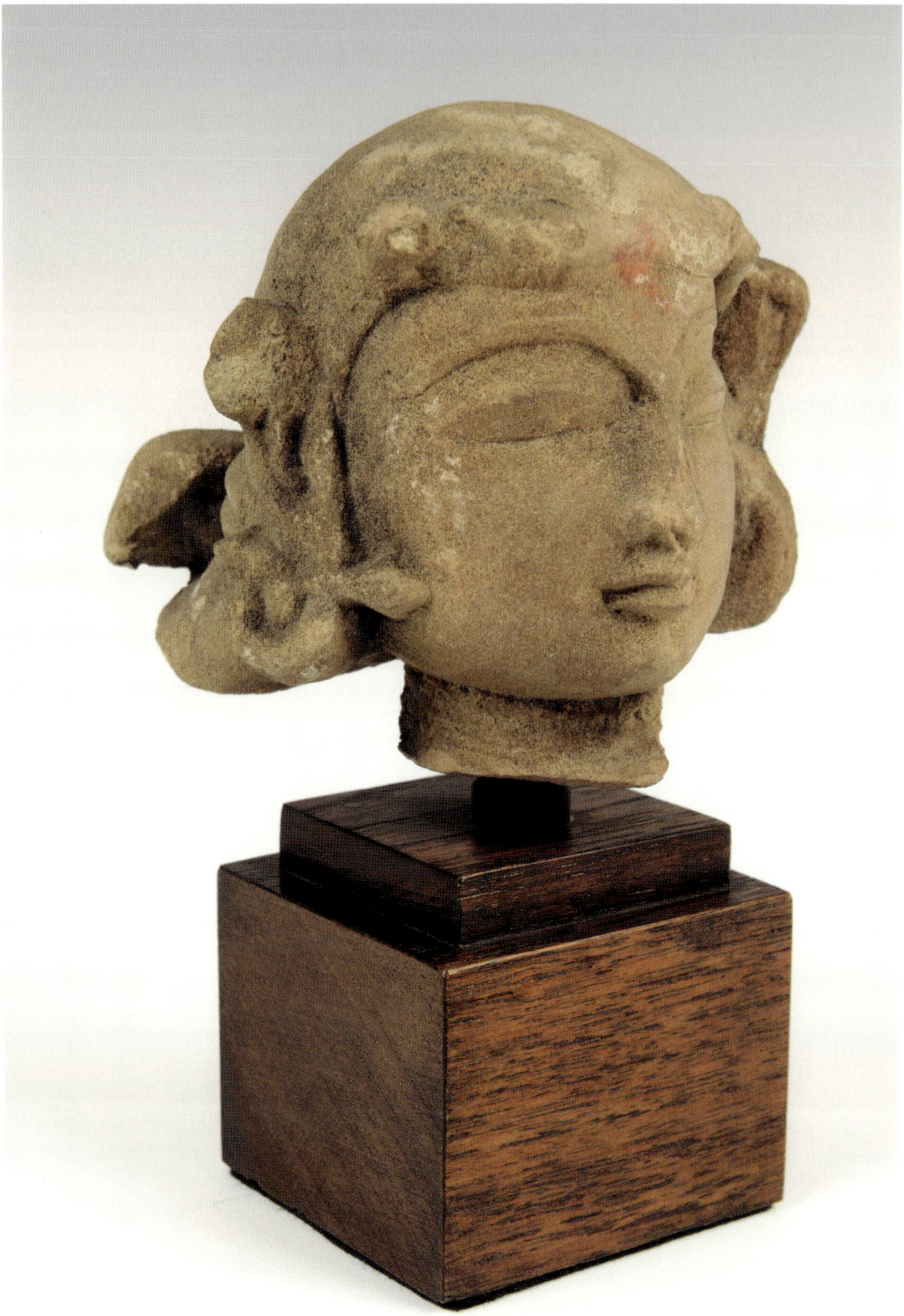

Plate 28

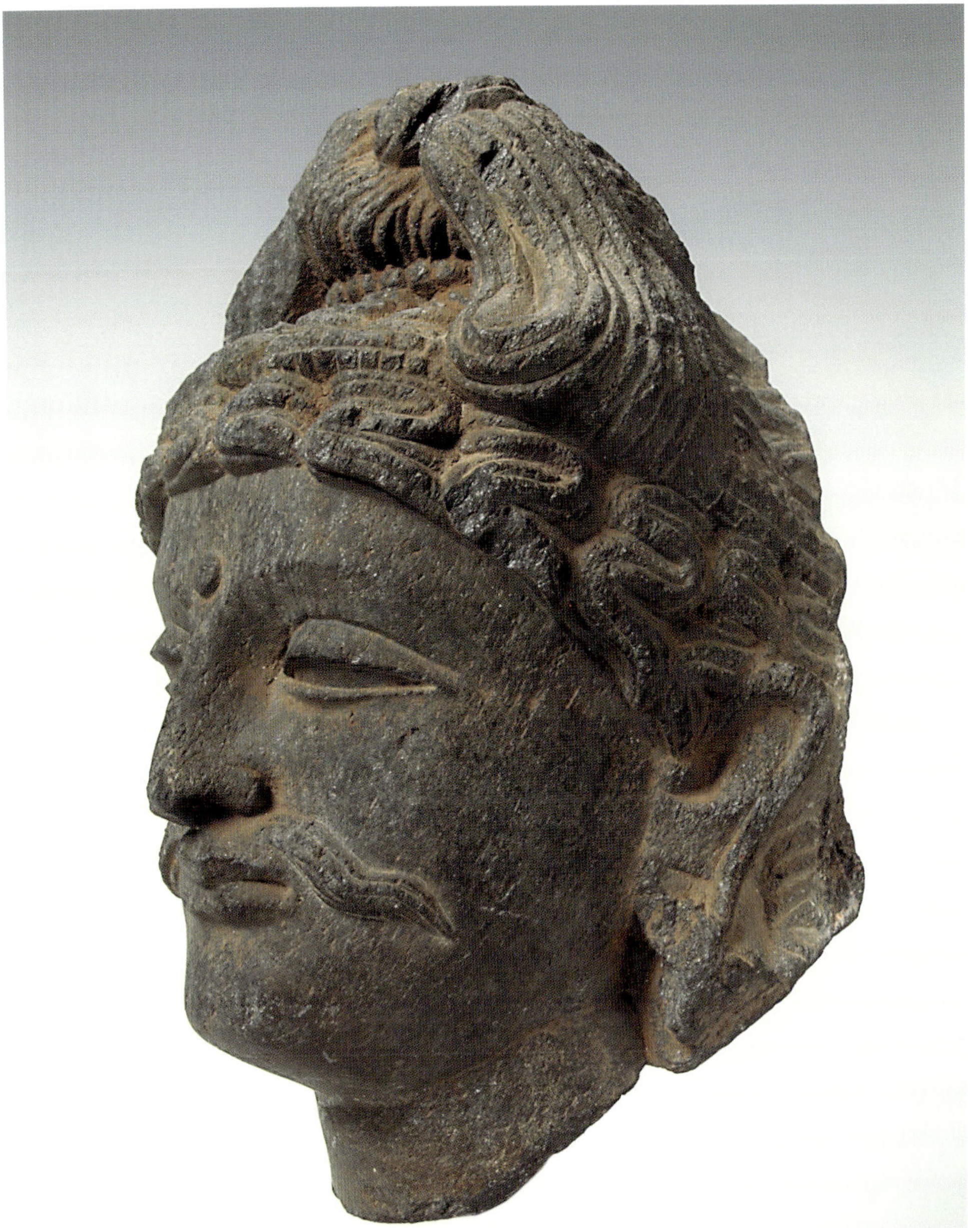

Plate 29

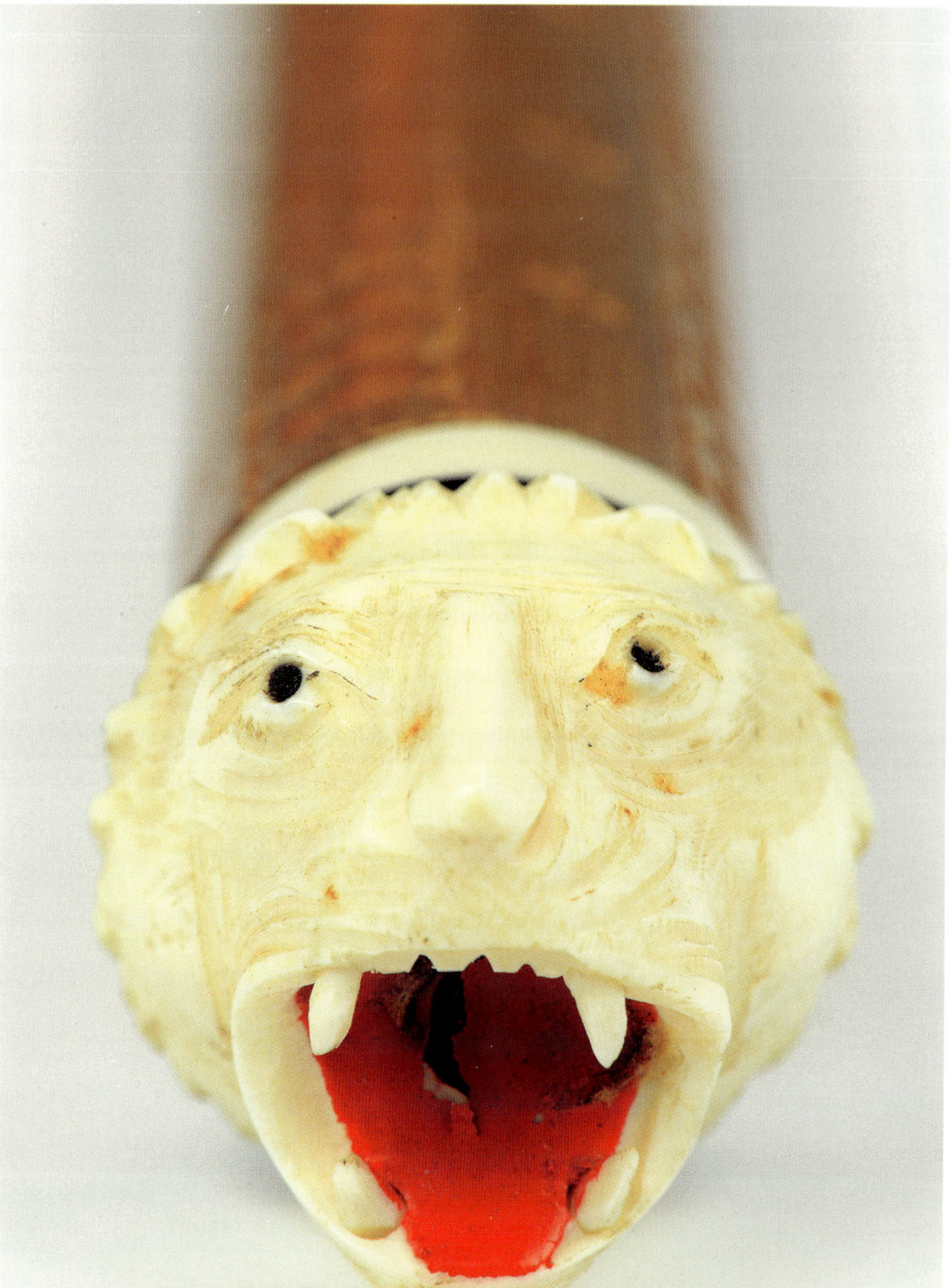

Plate 30

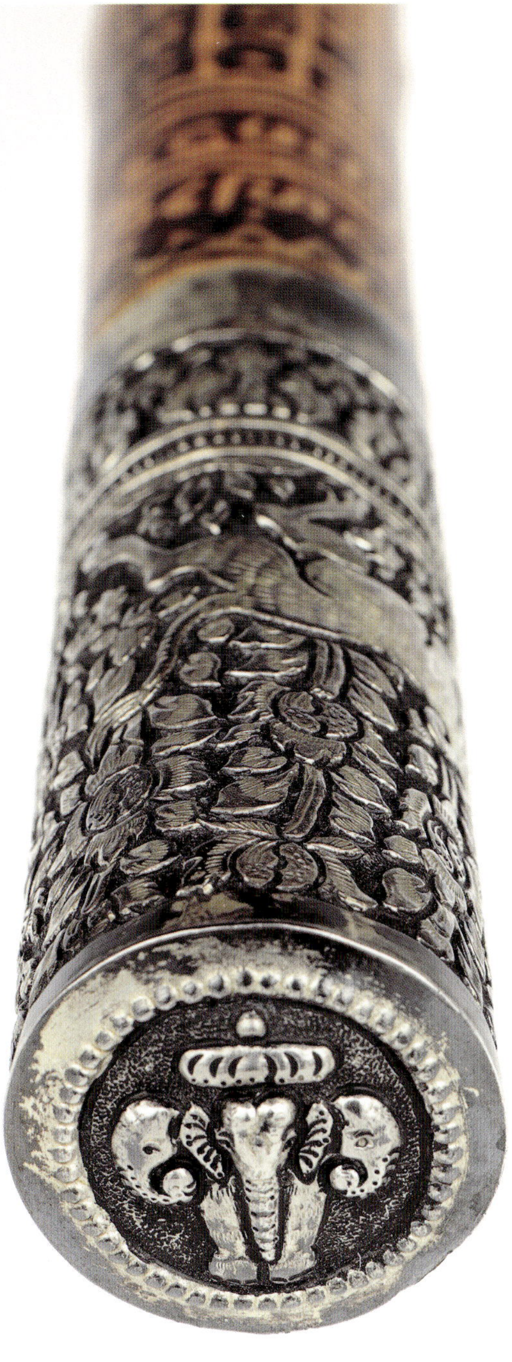

Plate 31

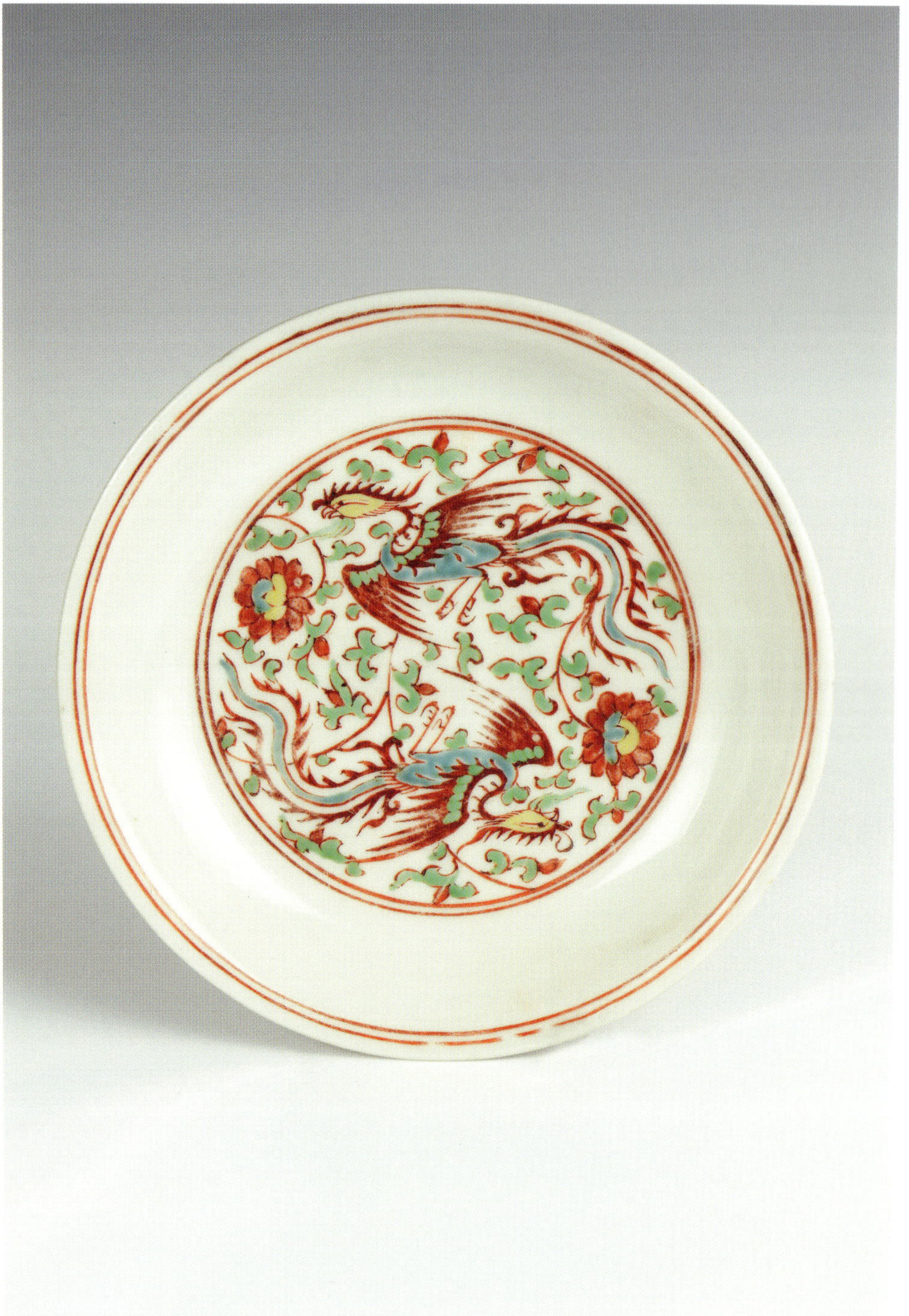

Plate 32

In some important ways during that period circumstances have changed very much for the worse for art collectors. Particularly unfortunate is the tremendous soaring of prices for almost every type of work of art which has occurred. This originally sprang in part from an ominous shift in the motive which impelled many bidders to purchase lovely possessions. After the war some collectors began to be primarily influenced not by the fact that an object was artistically beautiful, but that it was commercially valuable. For them its acquisition was a financial investment, not an aesthetic indulgence. Thousands of their transactions became samples of present day mankind's descent from an interest in ethical and aesthetic values to an obsession with material values. As a result, prices have been inflated to quite unreasonable levels; and in the process perhaps more dealers than used to be the case have got corrupted by a passion for undue financial gain in an occupation which should be chiefly concerned with a just appreciation of gracious arts.

One of the sad results of this is that most young people can no longer afford to collect *objets d'art* as my contemporaries and I could in our youth. It is therefore much more difficult for them to develop their knowledge of, and enthusiasm for, all sorts of beautiful things, since these processes are greatly stimulated by the satisfaction of hunting for and owning at least a few modest bits and pieces. This is a particularly deplorable consequence of what has happened.

Chapter 6. Home Sweet Home

In the summer of 1935 my father resigned the Premiership, and Stanley Baldwin became Prime Minister in his place. I was appointed a Secretary of State in the reconstructed government and my salary suddenly soared to an unexpected height. As a result I could afford to buy many more exquisite objects, and before long would therefore possess sufficient pieces of furniture and other household goods to equip a home.

So I began looking for a suitable property. My ambition was to own a small Queen Anne or early Georgian house with the charmingly dignified external architecture and well-proportioned internal rooms which characterise those dwellings. It should be somewhere in the unspoilt countryside tolerably near London, for my plan was to continue staying in my father's home in Hampstead through each week, and to escape to my own retreat for weekends and holidays – if my busy life as a Cabinet minister ever vouchsafed me a holiday.

The well-known estate agents, Hampton and Sons, kept a look-out for a place for me; and every now and then they produced photographs with typed descriptions of this or that possible answer to my dream. For one reason or another none of them quite satisfied me; and this fruitless state of affairs continued for several months. I felt in no particular hurry, being anxious to secure a truly ideal residence. A main difficulty was that the price for any such gem within easy motoring distance of London was apt to be prohibitive.

One morning when I visited the Hampton office, pored over pictures of some available properties, and again rejected them all, the fellow with whom I discussed the problem remarked, 'It's a pity, sir, you're not interested in a half-timbered Elizabethan manor-house. There's a little beauty on the market'.

He knew from our earlier talks that I was averse to acquiring an example of that type of building. Apart from the fact that half-timbering struck me as rather too sentimentally 'ye olde worlde', I suspected that the floors in a house of that nature would be too uneven, the walls too much out of true line, and the diamond-paned windowpanes too small for furniture and other works of art to stand erect or appear at their best in such surroundings.

So I confirmed to the agent that the abode he mentioned would make no appeal to me.

'It's a poppet, sir', he commented regretfully, 'I know you like beautiful things. Just have a look at a picture of the place – as a museum piece, so to speak'.

He produced a picture of it.

It was certainly a 'poppet': a superb example of Tudor domestic architecture of modest size, with a handsome façade built partly of brick and partly of wood-and-plaster topped by a row of five gables. In front of it, like a fore-court, stood an antique walled garden, whilst at its back were glimpses of an apple orchard.

'You're certainly right to say it's a museum piece', I commented. 'It's perfect of its kind; but I don't fancy it as a place to live in'.

The salesman waxed eloquent. 'It was built in the year 1600', he said, 'and the local squires lived there for the next 150 years. Then the current lord of the manor grew rich, built a larger Georgian mansion in a nearby village, and turned this place into the principal farm on his estate. A magnificent, even older tithe barn goes with it, and there are also the original stables for a carriage and horses, and a gardener's cottage. The property includes a fish-pond and three acres of land surrounded by a broad ditch that used to be its moat. At present the firm of Strutt and Parker farm the estate, and this house has become a liability to them. For a quick sale they're ready to accept only £3000'.

I asked him where the place was, and he answered, 'A few miles beyond Chelmsford in Essex. It's called Hyde Hall'.

The day happened to be a Saturday, and I enquired whether he could arrange for me to go and see the house that afternoon. 'Of course, you understand', I added emphatically, 'that I'm not interested in buying it, but I'd like to see it as a historic sample of architecture'.

I went, I saw, and I was conquered.

That evening I telephoned to my Hampton friend, and bought Hyde Hall.

Chapter 7. Artists

That was in the spring of 1936. A few weeks later all my furniture and other domestic goods were moved into the house; and on the following Saturday I spent my first day and night there.

My tables and chairs and other antiques were now reinforced by a few comfortable modern beds, sofas and armchairs, as well as by gay chintz curtains and other necessities. Among them was Tudor-style rush-matting on the bedroom floors in imitation of those at Chequers. Even so, my collections were not sufficient to provision adequately every room in the place, and I looked forward to continuing my searches for desirable additional pieces to fill some gaps.

Many friends came to spend weekends with me, and they warmly approved of the Elizabethan manor with its tithe barn, cottage, stables, walled garden, fish-pond, apple orchard and moat. Among my frequent guests were three of my artist cronies: John Nash, Stanley Spencer, and the latter's brother, Gilbert. One of the conspicuous omissions in my house was its almost total lack of pictures, for my numerous engravings were too small to look right on its living room walls. I was still an ignoramus where paintings were concerned, with an unperceptive if not completely blind eye regarding them.

I took a decision, and one morning at breakfast announced it to my three painter friends.

'I think it entirely wrong', I said hypocritically, as I cast loving glances at my congestion of antique bric-a-brac, 'for an art patron to buy the works of craftsmen and artists who are dead. Living artists have to earn cash so that they can keep the wolf from their doors and enjoy physical strength to wield paint brushes. So their contemporaries should buy nothing but their pictures. I would utterly despise myself if I spent money filling this house with Michelangelos, Leonardo da Vincis and Rembrandts, or even with Van Goghs, Renoirs and Gauguins. I'll fill it with Stanley Spencers, Gilbert Spencers and John Nashs instead'.

That very weekend we launched this project in a pleasing way. One of the most decorative attachments to Hyde Hall was its gardener, whom I had acquired with the house. He could not claim the same distinguished antiquity as its tithe barn and other amenities, but was nevertheless a glorious veteran aged 84. Named Old Kemp, he had worked on the surrounding farm as a lad more than seventy years earlier in return for a wage of sixpence a week. That was before the introduction into Essex of sophisticated agricultural machinery. One of his vivid memories – which he often recalled at loquacious length – was the day when his then employer ordered him to drive the first mechanical contraption that ever got imported into those fields for reaping and binding. He could manage horses, rakes, hoes and other tame creatures with expert skill, but was frightened by this wild-looking new animal. When he climbed onto its driver's seat he felt terrified of losing his balance as it ambled along, tumbling into its metallic anatomy, and being cut to pieces by its revolving knives. To the end of his life he preferred more ancient implements, and in my day still refused to use a lawn-mower, always cutting the grass with beautiful sweeps of a tall-handled, long-bladed scythe. He looked like Father Time with a few whisps of hair on a mostly bald head, shrewd eyes, a hooked nose, thin lips, and wide white whiskers framing his otherwise clean-shaven face. His countenance was an ideal subject for a portrait.

Following my pompous homily that morning, Gilbert Spencer agreed to make a drawing of Old Kemp, and after breakfast the artist and his model settled in the dining-room. Kemp sat on a Windsor chair even more antique than himself, with a small table at either hand. One of them bore half-a-dozen bottles of beer whilst the other supported a snuff-box, so that he could pose contentedly for hours, sustaining himself with alternate gulps of ale and sniffs of powder. The sittings continued throughout the morning and afternoon, and eventually Gilbert finished the picture. It was a delicate, characterful pencil sketch of the grand octogenarian's head and shoulders.

When it was completed Kemp took his first look at it, and nodded approval.

'I'd like six copies o' that for keeps', he remarked.

Perplexed as to how he thought the artist could make so many, we enquired what he meant. Then we realised that he thought Gilbert had spent the whole day taking a photograph of him! He told us he remembered hearing many years ago of a wonderful new invention called a camera, which took people's portraits and afterwards made reproductions of them by strange processes in a dark room.

I hung the drawing of Kemp in a place of honour in Hyde Hall; and during the next several months it was joined by three other Gilbert Spencer pictures, four water-colours by John Nash, and a pencil sketch plus two oil paintings by Stanley Spencer.

One unrealised project I shall always regret. At a period of crisis in his personal life, Stanley came to stay at Hyde Hall for several weeks. Certain events in his private affairs had plunged him into deep gloom; indeed, into a suicidal mood. He accepted my invitation to escape from devastating circumstances elsewhere by taking refuge in peaceful rural Essex; but he felt so broken that he could not even paint. I joined him in the house at weekends; but the pre-Munich situation was developing in Europe at the time, and I had to stay in London for the rest of each week helping to grapple with the problems that plagued Chamberlain's cabinet through those anxious days. I told Stanley that he could live at Hyde as long as he liked, either by himself or with whatever friends he chose to invite to keep him company. The married couple who were my cook and butler would look after him. And in the hope that his paint brushes would soon come to his rescue, and that reviving use of them would start healing processes in his wounded spirit, I added that he could treat my house as a colossal piece of canvas. Its rooms contained many spaces of empty plaster wall, both large and small; and I said he could choose any one of them he fancied as a site for a Spencer mural.

I myself favoured a particular bit of wall in my study, an oblong stretch measuring about two feet high by six feet long above a mantelpiece over a Tudor fireplace. I suggested that in one of his devout religious moods – which often inspired him – Stanley might paint there a small Annunciation, or some similar Biblical scene.

I was, of course, taking a fabulous risk. Any Friday night on my return to Hyde from a harassing week in London I might be greeted by a grotesquely disturbing work of genius filling a vast wall in the dining-room, the sitting-room or a bedroom. Alternatively I might indeed find that lovely little Annunciation waiting to welcome me.

I think the very suggestion helped Stanley. He promptly felt a sense of impending release, a freedom to start renewing himself by leaping into artistic creation whenever the spirit moved him. He told me several times he was on the verge of commencing to decorate this or that room. However, when he did suddenly one morning feel an urge to lay brush on canvas the sun was shining out of doors, and he hastened instead into the garden to paint a picture of a laburnum tree which had burst into glorious bloom and so was dripping with 'golden rain'. During the following weeks he resumed his sketching with gusto. Each day he put his paint box, brushes, canvas and some sandwiches into a perambulator, wheeled them to a nearby rustic spot, and worked in peace and contentment all day.

But I regret that he never painted that Annunciation. He did try to give me as gifts several of his brilliant pictures, including the famous one of Christ sitting in a wilderness with scorpions as his companions. But I firmly, if reluctantly, resisted the temptation to accept them. Stanley's domestic troubles had landed him in financial straits, and indeed for a few months after his return to London I paid the rent of his lodgings there. He needed money badly, and I urged him to keep all his works for sale. I myself bought at that time a superbly lovely oil painting of magnolias which has been ever since one of my treasured possessions.

Thanks partly to the influence of the Spencers and John Nash I began to develop a discriminating eye for paintings, and before long started to collect important pictures. However, I was not wholly faithful to my promise to buy nothing but the works of living artists.

This was partly my father's fault. He was a great, many-sided man: vivid, sensitive, wise, with a touch of the poet about him, and passionately sincere in everything he did. By nature he was perhaps more of a scientist than anything else. Geology, biology and kindred matters were among his first enthusiasms when he was a poor studious youth living in the remote Scottish village of his birth. His understanding of the evolutionary processes of nature profoundly influenced his later political philosophy of evolutionary rather than revolutionary socialism, which guided the beliefs of the British Labour Party more than any other contribution of thought by an individual leader.

Literature and history were amongst his interests, and he had a strong inclination towards the arts. Music gave him great pleasure, he dabbled a bit in collecting furniture, and then he became attracted by pictures. His knowledge regarding these was never profound; among the graphic arts he groped as an untutored amateur. Occasionally he bought a minor masterpiece of painting. In his choice of them he was guided by two friends of whom he was fond: the scholarly, charming Sir Alec Martin and the exuberant, and in some ways great, Lord Duveen. He liked sitting with that stimulating pair engaged in racy conversation frequently punctuated by His Lordship's guffaws of laughter.

Gradually he gathered almost a score of enviable paintings. With a patriotic bias in favour of Scottish artists, he included in the collection an Allan Ramsay, two David Wilkies, an Alexander Naismith, a Gavin Hamilton, two Patrick Geddeses, and a John Moore which he afterwards presented to the National Gallery of Scotland. He also acquired some good English oils and watercolour. Those gracious pictures hanging on the walls, sometimes in Downing Street and at other times in our Hampstead home, helped to convert me to the superlative beauty of great paintings. And after his death in 1937 they completed my capture, for in his will he left almost all his possessions to my brother, three sisters and myself. In our division of them I chose a Richard Wilson landscape, an Alexander Naismith painting of Edinburgh, a conversation piece by Gavin Hamilton, a portrait by David Wilkie and a Gainsborough water-colour sketch. I became puffed up with pride as their owner, and deeply infected by the bug of possession of fine pictures.

During the next twenty years paintings were the chief additions to my assortment of British works of art, although I sometimes still bought other beautiful objects made by my fellow-countrymen. However, my continuous absence from Britain from 1941 onwards prevented me from accumulating further examples of furniture and other domestic properties to fill an English home, since I no longer occupied an English home. My visits to England became infrequent, and were always made for official consultations in Whitehall which left me little leisure to wander around in search of *objets d'art*. I therefore resolved to make the most of my brief opportunities for that pastime in London by concentrating on viewing the paintings for current sale by my favourite picture shops there: the Tooth gallery in Bruton Street, the Fine Arts Society in Bond Street, and the Leicester Galleries off Leicester Square.

My progress in collecting fine paintings before I went overseas was slow because their prices, even in those uninflated days, often made me hesitate. However, if the cost was at all manageable by either a prudent diminution of my bank balance or a sale of some other artistic possession of which I had grown tired, I seldom hesitated long. In collecting (as in numerous other activities) it is foolish to dither: emphatic, sometimes bold and usually positive decisions are essential. I feel no regrets about anything I ever bought – my only regrets concern certain objects that I did not buy. And since I almost always in the end decided to acquire this or that article about which I temporarily wavered, I have in fact few regrets. Even when a purchase proved afterwards to be a gross mistake because it was a fake or a very inferior piece, I did not deplore the error. One learns from one's mistakes. Indeed, those blunders can teach a person his best, most instructive lessons.

Now and then I fell to the temptation of procuring a painting foreign to the English or Scottish schools. Indeed, twice during the Second World War I bought works by eminent Impressionists. That was a measure of my impudent ambition in those momentous days! The first of them was an early Van Gogh canvas portraying a peasant woman laying her laundry out to dry on a lawn. I paid £1,400 for it in

1940, and managed to keep it through the next two years. Then I could afford to do so no longer, and sold it for £1,750. If I really had to dispose of it, how I wish I could have waited until today!

My second similar treasure was a small female figure painted in oils by August Renoir, for which I gave £400. In a fit of generosity a few years later I presented it to a dear friend and that was the end of my collection of works by the Impressionists.

If I could choose which school of painting among all those that have flourished on any continent in any century I would most like to patronise, I would probably plump for the French Impressionists. Certain others would be hot competitors, such as Italian Renaissance masterpieces, the Flemish primitives, Vermeer's, Rembrandt's or Velasquez's efforts, and Chinese scroll pictures of the Tang or Song dynasties. In some ways all of these are greater than the works of the group of revolutionary geniuses in France at the turn of the nineteenth and twentieth centuries; but the products of earlier artists are generally more aloof from the world of today than the Impressionist creations. Of course, if I were a king with a palace or a tycoon with a castle, I would hanker after grand masterpieces by all the top giants, because then I would own appropriately vast walls on which to display them. Many of them are not suited for exhibition in the intimate rooms of a comparatively small house; and that is another reason why I could content myself with a selection of paintings by Manet and Monet, Degas and Renoir, Cezanne, Van Gogh and their contemporaries. This is probably what I would have done if I were a millionaire. But although I have filled various other highfalutin roles in life, I have never for even five minutes been a millionaire; so I must rest on my sparse, faded laurels as a collector who once upon a time owned one Van Gogh and one Renoir. It is a memory to cherish.

Compared with those and other superlative schools of painters, the British artists must generally take a humbler place. Nevertheless they created beauty in gentle and occasionally brilliant forms representative of the grace of their island and the character of its inhabitants; and some individuals among them are worthy to stand beside most of the European giants. Thomas Gainsborough, John

Constable and in particular J. M. W. Turner are peers of any but the absolute titans.

So, partly because in the late 1930s and the next few decades their pictures cost much less than those of foreign masters whom I have mentioned, I confined myself almost wholly to the British school. For a while I was chiefly attracted by water-colours, a field in which the British genius did seem to me to be pre-eminent. Gradually I gathered quite a respectable company of works by Varley, Cotman, Girtin, Rowlandson, Gainsborough, Constable, Cox, Turner and some other Old Masters, with paintings or drawings also by moderns like Wilson Steer, Augustus John, Gilbert and Stanley Spencer, John and Paul Nash, Felix Topolski and a few more. When I went to live in India a decade later I took a number of these with me, and they made a charming small private art gallery in my house in Delhi. I thought it part of the duty of a British diplomatic representative overseas to show our alien friends good examples of Britain's artistic achievements. However, after those water-colours had hung on my walls there for some years I realised that exposure to India's strong sunlight was endangering their fresh, gentle quality of colours. I took them down, and since I am averse to keeping beautiful aesthetic works hidden away in portfolios, I decided to sell them. In any case, by then I had accumulated so many collections of varied works of art that it seemed sensible to reduce their quantity. So I disposed of nearly all those water-colours.

During the later war years I began to concentrate on buying oil paintings by British artists. Most of my collection of these was acquired, however, after the war, so I shall postpone any further reference to them until a later chapter.

My only acquisitions of British sculpture were two bronze heads of my father made by Jacob Epstein. That famous artist cast the first of them in the 1920s and the second in the 1930s. I recall my initial meeting with him at the time when my father was sitting for the earlier piece.

I went to visit him in his house in Hyde Park Gate, to view the then half-finished work. The front door of the house stood slightly ajar, but since I had not met my host before I thought it would be rude to enter unannounced. I therefore rang the door-bell and waited for someone to invite me in. No-one appeared. I rang the bell several times, with the same negative result. Through the narrowly open door I noticed that the hall floor was covered with thick dust, and a noise of hammering sounded somewhere inside the building. I presumed that plumbers must be doing a job there, and that I had come to the wrong house. This place was evidently unlived-in, being in a state of dirty neglect whilst workmen made repairs to render it habitable.

Before departing, however, I poked my head through the door, peered curiously within, and noticed that the bangings came from the far end of a passage where a large room was so brightly sunlit that it must have a glass roof. Then I saw that in the room's centre stood a colossal, rocklike block of white marble and I came to my senses, realising that it must be a sculptor's studio, and that the noise was made by Epstein's hammer and chisel as he carved. The front door had been deliberately left open for me.

I ventured along the passage and entered the room. Sure enough, I caught sight of my host perched on top of a ladder propped against the massive stone. As soon as he saw me, he stopped his bashings, descended and gave me a friendly greeting.

Near the summit of the marble appeared the faintly carved features of a human face, whilst the rest of the stone was still in the rough state in which it had emerged from a quarry.

Expressing interest, I asked what the sculpture was going to represent.

'I'm not sure yet', replied Epstein. 'It might become a monstrous dictator, or it might be a figure of Christ'. Many months later the second possibility proved to be correct, for the piece developed into his celebrated statue *This is the Man*.

He said, 'Come and tell me your opinion about this', and led me to a slim pole standing about five feet tall with a towel wrapped round some protrusion on its top. Epstein unwound the towel, and revealed a clay bust of my father's head. It was a fine piece of work, with the model's strong, handsome features reproduced with remarkable liveliness.

We studied it from various angles, discussing both its general effect and certain individual details. Epstein occasionally asked me a question about my father's personality, which I answered. I felt very impressed with the head, and he was pleased at my approval of it.

When we finished examining it he led me to another similar pole, also surmounted by a towel. Removing the towel, he displayed a head of George Bernard Shaw. This, too, was a vivacious impression of the playwright, with tousled hair, lively eyes, and a wide open mouth between his fluffy moustache and beard. Epstein explained that he was compelled to show the sage's lips parted because Shaw never stopped talking throughout their sittings – so he never saw his model with the mouth more than momentarily closed.

We stepped to another of the half-a-dozen poles standing around the room, and when its towel was removed I saw a head of Lord Beaverbrook. It seemed to me not only an astonishingly good likeness, but also a mischievous one. There was a naughty look in Max Beaverbrook's eyes.

I asked Epstein about this, and he answered that the effect was true to nature. He explained that the press lord refused to come and sit quietly, doing nothing whilst the sculptor modelled his head. He insisted on continuing his own work during their sessions; and so he brought with him a pretty young female secretary to whom he dictated memoranda all the time. Epstein added that sometimes His Lordship bullied the girl whilst he looked at her desirously out of the corners of his eyes.

Afterwards we unwrapped several other busts of celebrities stuck on the top of poles. I felt almost as if I were being conducted round a prison yard during the French Revolution, inspecting the heads of distinguished victims who had been decapitated by the guillotine.

Incidentally, several year later some friends persuaded me to sit for my own head to be similarly executed by a struggling young sculptor of great ability called Loris Rey. The result was a brilliant bronze bust which got finished shortly before the outbreak of war. I bought it; but Loris kept it for exhibition in his studio as a temptation to other possible models to invest their money in a work by him. One night in the middle of an air-raid the place received a direct hit by a bomb and everything in it, including my head, was smashed to smithereens.

Chapter 8. War

I enjoyed the pleasure of living at Hyde Hall for only about three years. As soon as war broke out in 1939 I lent the house to the government so that it could perform some national service; and it became a home for about a dozen fragile old men and women evacuated from the East End of London. I was so busy that I never got leisure to store away my art treasures from its rooms; and for the next several years they and Hyde's aged residents lived with mutual acceptability together. Throughout that period none of them came to any harm.

For the first twenty months of the war I lived in my father's house in Hampstead, which I continued to occupy after his death. I had furnished it also with many fine pieces of furniture and other attractive objects. During the Battle of Britain they taught me a good lesson.

Sometimes a wrong relationship grows up between a connoisseur and his collection of works of art. Instead of him possessing them, they come to possess him! Unqualified devotion to them turns him into their slave – as a miser is a slave to his hoard of accumulated money. An over ardent devotee of paintings, sculptures, silverware, porcelains and other lovely things can become so emotionally subservient to them that they monopolise his whole attachment, abrogating to themselves his entire affection, and robbing him of freedom to enjoy other pleasures in life. I have seen that happen to certain fanatical collectors.

Fortunately it never happened to me. Perhaps this was partly because I am too much of an amateur, too superficial a scholar, too flibberty-jibbet an art connoisseur to become so deeply involved. But an experience during the Battle of Britain also taught me that there are more precious attachments in life than ownership of even the most beautiful artistic works ever made by man.

By the time that war broke out I had accumulated considerable, quite valuable, collections of English furniture, water-colour paintings, ceramics and other *objets d'art*. Many of these adorned my Hampstead home. They were all more or less delicate, and so could be smashed by falling bombs in a blitz. My hundreds of fine pieces of antique English pottery and porcelain, for example, were displayed in cabinets distributed through the house – perilously exposed to possible enemy attack. As soon as war was declared I therefore removed all the best china, pictures, furniture and other objects from the living rooms, and stored them safely away in a large cellar-like basement.

During the following months of 'phoney' war, free from air raids, I greatly missed the pleasing sight of them. Often I thought to myself, 'Why do I allow that tyrant Hitler to deprive me of the joy of contemplating beautiful things? This is a surrender to his will. I should fetch everything up from the basement, arrange the rooms charmingly as in the days of peace, and defy the scoundrel'. So during the Parliamentary summer recess in 1940 I got leisure one weekend to restore all my distinguished possessions to their accustomed places. Amidst the tribulations of life in besieged Britain they became a delightful consolation, giving me more pleasure than ever before.

A few weeks later the Battle of Britain began, and from then onwards bombs rained down on London nearly every night. But I now felt so unwilling to make any concession to our Nazi foes that I left my precious Worcester teapots, cream-jugs, cups and saucers, Hepplewhite chairs, tables and side boards, Gainsborough, Cotman, Girtin and other paintings, and the rest of my artistic gems exposed through the rooms, all cocking a collective snook at Hitler.

Four months earlier I had become Minister of Health in Winston Churchill's government, and so was responsible for the operation of such Civil Defence provisions as the emergency hospital services, the public air-raid shelters, the food-and-rest centres for people bombed out of their homes, and various related organisations for protecting the well-being of our populations. Every evening therefore, as soon as the air-raid sirens began to shriek and bombs started tumbling in the streets, I hastened to some borough where a raid was likely to occur, to see for myself how our plans were working on the ground. I could then observe with my own eyes any mistakes that we might be making, discuss problems with the local authorities, and initiate the next day in

Whitehall any changes in our policy which seemed desirable before fresh loads of bombs fell from the skies the following night. In the small hours of the morning I returned home to Hampstead for a brief sleep.

Then it was that I learned that ownership of beautiful paintings and other works of art – however precious and lovely they might be – was of less importance than certain more priceless possessions which I could claim. When dawn broke a few hours later, and I opened my eyes and wondered what havoc the latest air-raid had wrought, I did not hasten through the rooms to discover what breakages my art treasures might have suffered. For a while I gave them no thought; my anxieties lay elsewhere. I wanted to know at once whether my dear friend Diana was still alive in her flat in Kensington, whether George and Sarah continued hale and hearty in their home at Westminster, and whether the Smith children with their parents had survived the night in their Anderson shelter in Chelsea. First I telephoned them in turn, to make sure that they remained in the land of the living. Their affectionate friendships were my most precious possessions, and none of my other personal concerns seemed to matter. Of course, certain national and international causes mattered a great deal; they were of supreme importance to the continued well-being of Humanity. But no other private interests were of extreme account. If my entire collection of fine art objects had lain in ruins, I would have felt regret – but no heart-break. I realised then that I would willingly sacrifice them all to save a hair of Diana's head, or to preserve the lives of George, Sarah and several other favourite buddies. The safety, happiness and love of chosen friends was what mattered most.

As it happened, none of my *objets d'art* suffered any damage. Although bombs sometimes fell near enough to my house to shatter this or that window pane, its indoor contents remained unharmed throughout the war. I was naturally glad. However, when I did lose many of them later (as I shall describe in due course) I remembered that wartime lesson and took the disasters philosophically.

No doubt if I had owned a work of art of supremely rare, superlative aesthetic beauty I would have felt differently about it. If Leonardo's painting of Mona Lisa, or one of Michelangelo's sculptured

Pietàs, or the exquisite bust of Queen Nefertiti, or a Chinese fresco of immortal fame had belonged to me, I would not have left it exposed to run all the risks of those nights of terror. But I never had to consider that prospect.

Chapter 9. Canada

Churchill soon initiated his policy of sending certain of his ministerial colleagues overseas to represent the British government in the capitals of important Allied or Associated Powers. In April 1941 he asked me to go to Canada as our High Commissioner. I felt deeply distressed at being torn away from my comrades undergoing exhilarating experiences in the front line of the Battle of Britain, although there would be some compensation on the other side of the Atlantic in the form of assisting in mobilising the vital aid of many kinds which the Canadians were sending to the beleaguered islanders.

Another sorrow for me at being transferred from England was the loss of opportunities to glimpse the works of art which still remained on view in London's public galleries and museums. All the most superb paintings, sculptures and other treasures in the National Gallery, the British Museum, the Tate Gallery and other such places had of course been banished to safety in remote, unbombable corners of the British Isles; but agreeable minor works were still on display, helping to sustain the morale of countless people in besieged Britain who gained comfort from seeing them. Occasionally in moments when I could escape briefly from almost ceaseless official duties I had gone to gaze at them, seeking refreshment and inspiration from their serene beauty.

Indeed, the delight that I invariably received from contemplating the graphic arts was an essential element in my make-up, and even during the earlier, calmer days of peace I frequently felt a need to satisfy it. I did this partly by enjoying the contents of my own collections, since my parliamentary and governmental work so filled every day with a succession of engagements that it was difficult to snatch time to visit public exhibitions. Yet periodically my yearning to see classically beautiful works became such a hunger that I could not deny it. The desire received no satisfaction from contemplating day after day the somewhat plain faces of politicians sitting on the Government and Opposition benches in the House of Commons. So I used then to ask my private secretary to telephone my host or hostess at a luncheon party to which I was committed, and to make some plausible excuse why I suddenly could not attend it whilst I slipped away for an hour in one or another of the great art galleries. Instead of feasting my tummy on meat and drink I feasted my eyes on pictures, statues and other noble works. I returned to my office much refreshed.

The necessity for those jaunts became even greater amidst the stresses of war, and in an occasional lunch-break during the Battle of Britain I spurned food and indulged that other craving instead. So after I crossed the Atlantic Ocean I at first felt a deep nostalgia for the lovely objects lodged in the National Gallery on Trafalgar Square, the Victoria and Albert Museum on Brompton Road, and similar haunts of beauty. After a while, however, substitutes for them began to catch my eye in Canada.

When I felt a longing to gaze upon gracious artistic creations I did my best to appease the hunger by visits to the National Gallery in Ottawa and to the art museums in Montreal, Quebec and Toronto, with not unsatisfactory results. Occasionally I enjoyed an even more sumptuous feast of such fare when I flew to Washington to discuss with our Ambassador and the American authorities current wartime problems of mutual interest and made time to drop into the Mellon Art Gallery for a while. Yet, although those excursions did much to appease my desire to contemplate beauty, they also provoked, without satisfying, my acquisitive instinct to own some such treasures.

This posed a problem. In all the shopping areas of the Canadian cities there was scarcely a store where the English furniture, ceramics, paintings and other objects which I liked were sold. Before long, however, that circumstance gave my aesthetic appreciation an educative jolt in new directions. It caused me to stray beyond the bounds of insular British arts towards the diverse fields of artistic accomplishments by other races of mankind. If there was no English craftsmanship available for me to buy in Ottawa, I needs must cast my eyes around to see what comparable Canadian works might be attractive.

First I toyed with the idea of picking up pleasant specimens of rustic French-Canadian furniture. However, these did not sufficiently lure me, for I felt they would not look congenially at home in my English house after my return to Britain.

I missed one fine opportunity. Eskimo craftsmen along Canada's Arctic coasts were then carving small soapstone figurines representing polar bears, seals, snowy owls and other near-North Pole creatures as well as their own human kind clad in wintry native dress. Their art had not yet been discovered by dealers seeking curios to sell to tourists, and so it still retained a spontaneous indigenous character. If I had seen specimens of it, they would undoubtedly have captivated me, and I would have bought some lovely pieces. But for the reason I have mentioned such items were not on show in shops in the southern cities which I frequented. I did pay three visits to the Arctic, twice in mid-summer when it is the 'Land of the Midnight Sun' and once in late winter when it was just ceasing to be a region of eternal night. On the latter occasion I travelled across the ice-bound ocean on a sledge drawn by a team of vivacious Husky dogs, and I spent hours with families of Eskimos in their igloos. Unfortunately on those excursions I was engaged in official work, with little leisure for relaxed, casual chatter with the people; and I did not become aware of any local crafts beyond their skill in building ice-huts, making clothing from caribou skins (plate 4), and angling for fish through holes bored in the frozen sea. Only several years later did I get acquainted with their robust, exquisite carvings – and by then the figurines' native originality had deteriorated somewhat at the bidding of merchants whose interest in them was not primarily artistic but commercial, and who induced many of the sculptors to produce uninspired 'pot-boiler' imitations of their traditional types for sale to undiscriminating tourists.

That development was a sad example of the decadence which afflicts fine native schools of art when the prime motive for their production ceases to be a creation of beauty and becomes instead the securing of financial profit. Since those Canadian days I have watched the process occur in various other lands where an ancient yet fresh, sometimes naïve but always beautiful indigenous art was suddenly 'discovered' by alien patrons, who promptly – either from misguided friendliness to the local people, silly sentimentality about 'primitive' craftsmanship, or sheer greed for commercial exploitation – sought to organise and 'develop' this charming expression of human genius. Often they only succeeded in damaging and debasing it. That has happened to a significant extent in the cases of such brilliant traditional products as Japanese lacquer, Siamese silverware, Javanese batik and Balinese wood-carving to mention only a few of the casualties.

*

In the National Gallery in Ottawa I found a key which unlocked for me the door to another, very different, extremely distinguished achievement of Canadian artists. The walls of one room there displayed numerous small oil sketches by a painter called Tom Thomson, who was then almost unheard-of outside Canada. I had already noticed some of his larger canvasses hanging elsewhere in the gallery; but although I thought them quite impressive, I did not judge them to be works of outstanding merit. They portrayed wild North American landscapes – some of the rocky islands and wooded shores in Ontario's lake district, splashed in some cases with the glowing hues of a Canadian autumn and in others with the frigid patterns of a Canadian winter. Although pleasantly interesting, they appeared to me a bit stilted.

Yet the group of Thomson's small sketches at once made a very different appeal. They brought his talent brilliantly to life. Painted on small wooden panels measuring only about eight by ten inches, they were spontaneous in composition and vivid in colouring: slightly reminiscent of John Constable's sketches, yet far more imaginative. At first I wondered whether their creator could really be the same man as had painted the larger, more formal canvasses, for these pictures were so vivacious and so consummate. For a while I hesitated in forming a firm opinion, scrutinising them cautiously, rejecting one or two as inadequate, and then catching my breath with excited admiration at others. They really were lovely. Perhaps to a Briton's eye certain of their colours at first appeared too exaggerated, too glamorous, even too artificial – yet were these not exactly the scintillating tints which glow on maple, dogwood and other trees and bushes in the Canadian autumn, when death adorns their foliage with gorgeous pageantry? Yes, the paintings were truthful – and inspired. If their larger versions composed painstakingly later in an indoor studio lacked a touch of spontaneity, these original sketches done out-of-doors amidst the actual scenery showed the 'first fine, careless rapture' of an artist of genius.

Returning to view his bigger canvasses with more enlightened eyes, I still thought the most imposing of them too studied and not satisfying. Now, however, I recognised that some of his medium-sized pictures achieved similar very skilful and beautiful images of nature.

I learned that the pictures had been painted about twenty-five years ago; and I felt eager to meet Tom Thomson. On enquiry, however, I discovered that he was dead. When still a comparatively young man in the year 1917 he drowned in one of the lakes that he loved to paint. Nobody knew the exact cause of the accident, for he was probably alone in his canoe at the time. Yet a suspicion of murder also persisted. The mystery had never been solved. Whatever the correct explanation of it might be, Thomson was inclined to be a solitary character. He spent months every year fishing, boating and painting by himself in the vast untamed lakeland which so captivated him in life, and which claimed him in death.

Yet he was not as isolated in the domain of art as he often was in the kingdom of nature. He had been a leading spirit in a small company of young fellow painters who later, in 1920, formed themselves into an association which became famous in Canada, and is now appreciated through the wider world, as the Group of Seven.

Some of their large canvasses hung alongside those of Tom Thomson in the National Gallery, and for a while I had stood beside them also, partially attracted yet then resisting them as inadequately fine. However, as soon as I saw their small sketches which, like his, appeared here and there, I paid greater heed to them. These, too, possessed a vital, essentially Canadian character, being faithful (though far from photographic) representations of scenery in the Canadian spring, summer, fall and winter. Evidently influenced to some extent by the French Impressionists, they nevertheless had not only in subject-matter but also technique a simple ruggedness evocative of the North American wilds, where pioneering men had engaged in all sorts of novel adventures. These pictures, too, were works by pioneers – artists of fine quality who founded a distinctive Canadian school of painting.

Among them I soon came to like immensely the paintings of A. Y. Jackson, who was still actively alive. Greatly daring, I wrote to him at his home in Toronto, expressing admiration for his works and asking whether I might come and pay my respects to him in his studio. No doubt with misgivings at such an approach from a professional diplomat, he nonetheless kindly answered that I would be welcome. A few days later I knocked on his door, and entered a spacious apartment crowded with artistic bric-a-brac, including large and small sketches scattered all round. On an easel in its centre stood his latest, unfinished canvas.

He greeted me with a courteous grin and a gruff 'How d'ye do?' I thought he looked rather like a polar bear. About sixty years of age, his head was covered with short-cropped white hair, his brow sloped sharply to a similarly slanting nose, and his wide-lipped mouth protruded above a receding chin. His stocky figure clothed in a long white artist's overall above short shuffling legs completed the similarity. Yet there was nothing bear-like about his warm, friendly welcome. With shy smiles and clipped but cordial speech he made me feel immediately at home.

I enjoyed an enthralling afternoon. Jackson's conversation about Tom Thomson and the Group of Seven was fascinating, and he answered many questions that I asked him about his own work. Every now and then I rose to gaze at his paintings lying around on shelves or heaped against walls and when I left the place three hours later I carried away two of his small sketches. In return I gave him a cheque for $60 (the equivalent then of less than £15), which was all that he asked for them. The pair were notable pictures of French-Canadian villages along the shores of the St. Lawrence River; and that evening in my drawing-room in Ottawa I took down two official-style pictures provided by the Office of Works in London, and proudly hung the Jacksons in their place.

During the next few years I gradually collected more than 50 modern Canadian paintings until my house was full of them. They included four Tom Thomson sketches, whilst most of the rest were similarly small pictures by members of the Group of Seven. Among them were sixteen Jacksons, every one carefully selected during a succession of happy visits to the great, modest man in his studio. Another artist in the Group whose paintings I admired was J. E. H. MacDonald, and almost a dozen of these joined the hoard of Canadian pictures which I acquired at remarkably inexpensive prices during those wartime years. In addition to him and Jackson my favourite painter was Lawren Harris, whose style developed along rather different but equally, and sometimes even more lovely lines, until later he turned to producing abstract pictures. I bought two of his naturalistic sketches.

I did not confine my pickings to works by these and other members of the Group of Seven. Wishing the collection to become representative of a wider range of Canadian paintings, I included in it choice pictures by earlier artists like Cornelius Kreighof, J. W. Morrice and Maurice Cullen, and by still living contemporaries such as Clarence Gagnon, Emily Carr and several others. Emily Carr was an extraordinary genius. A spinster who managed a boarding-house on Vancouver Island, but whose chief passion was paintings, she felt deeply attached to British Columbia in general and its native Indian folk in particular. In her early years she produced many pictures of Redskin villages with special emphasis on their dramatic totem poles, and later she wandered into forests filled with giant trees, where she produced exhilarating designs of tall tree-trunks massed together like clusters of nature's totem poles. Her style became more and more vivid, with daring, imaginative, rather Turneresque forms and colours. When in her old age she became too feeble to make outdoor excursions, she laid aside her paint brushes, picked up a pen instead and wrote a few books which are now Canadian classics.

When I left Ottawa in 1946 I suffered my first distressing loss of a work of art. All my Canadian paintings were packed in cases for shipment to England; but when they arrived in London a few weeks later one sketch was missing. Whoever committed the theft had a shrewd knowledge of the respective worth of those various pictures, for he chose his booty with perfect judgement. It was the finest of the four Tom Thomson sketches – a glimpse of a pair of merganser ducks swimming on a lake amidst swirls of mist. I particularly cherished it, partly for its own exquisite artistic sake and partly because it reminded me nostalgically of occasions when, as I paddled my canoe along the Ottawa River, I suddenly caught sight of just such a pair of wild-fowl floating like ghosts among veils of early morning haze.

Chapter 10. The Far East

In April 1946 I moved from North America to the opposite side of the Earth. For the next two years I was Governor General of Malaya, Singapore and the British dependent territories in Borneo, and then my responsibilities were extended to cover also in diplomatic affairs the other lands in South East Asia. There I spent a fascinating decade, constantly travelling from country to country throughout that varied region, and occasionally making journeys into wider fields such as China, Japan and the Antipodes.

In the sphere of art as well as of politics vast new worlds were opened to me. It was an enlightening, thrilling, educative experience. When my preliminary introductions to unaccustomed official duties, a novel tropical climate and many (to me) exotic peoples were over, I began to turn my attention in leisure hours to Asian cultural interests and before long I was running amok among the ceramics, paintings, carpets, furniture, bronzes and other art treasures of the Far East.

My circumstances happened to be propitious for considerable acquisition of these things. One reason was that no such creature as a Governor General had been heard of previously in the area, and when I first arrived no house had yet been found for my lengthy occupation. The local Governors and High Commissioners were comfortably settled in their handsomely furnished mansions; but I had none. I dwelt temporarily in the attractive Residency in Penang, which by chance was almost bereft of furniture. When the Japanese military occupation of Malaya ended, Japanese soldiers helped themselves to many desirable household objects, carrying them away; and in the brief period of chaos which followed, before the returning British authorities restored order, countless additional artistic furnishings were stolen by light-fingered characters who promptly sold them to curio dealers. The Residency was one of the places looted; and it was therefore very inadequately equipped for the accommodation of a Governor General when I first entered its door. Its sparse resources needed quick, considerable reinforcement.

I did not wish to ship my own furniture from England to the tropics, for the hot, humid climate (in those days before air-conditioning got introduced) would damage it. At the same time I thought the British taxpayers should not have to finance the entire furnishing of a house for me. They were already paying me a handsome salary. Moreover, I felt attracted by the notion of collecting for myself pleasing examples of acclimatised Oriental cabinet-making and other crafts; so I proposed to the Ministry of Works that they should provide only beds, chairs, crockery and other necessities whilst I undertook the purchase of the decorative articles required. They agreed.

I could not have assumed this heavy liability were it not for the recent pillaging. The fact was that antique shops in Singapore, Kuala Lumpur, Penang and other centres were generously stocked with stolen properties which the robbers had disposed of quickly and cheaply before their crimes became known to the authorities. In their turn the shopkeepers felt nervous lest the pre-war owners of those goods – many of whom were now returning to Malaya after years of incarceration in Japanese prison camps or absence overseas – would enter a store, recognise a piece of Chinese porcelain, Malay silver, Balinese sculpture or some other enviable *objet d'art* as their property, and reclaim it without payment. Indeed, this was already beginning to happen in the bazaars; and so the traders were eager to sell their recent purchases swiftly at a small profit. As a consequence the prices were low; and over the next several months I bought quite a number of excellent pieces.

Naturally the risk of articles being reclaimed by their rightful owners was then merely transferred from the curio dealers to their clients. I let it be known that anyone who came into the Residency and saw a bit of their stolen property need feel no embarrassment at claiming it, and carrying it freely away. This was all part of the proper rehabilitation of Malaya after the terrible destructions of war; and it was right that newcomers like me should take the risk of loss as well as gain from our acquisitions.

Several times one or another of my lunch or dinner guests – a returned rubber planter, businessman or government official – would suddenly exclaim as he glanced round a room where we sat, 'By Jove, Your Excellency, would you forgive me if I mention that this Chinese scroll painting' – or it might be a Javanese wood-carving, a Brunei gong, a Siamese cabinet or some other item – 'is mine?' as he pointed to one of my recent purchases. I naturally forgave him, and he happily carried the booty away.

The most awkward such occasion occurred several months after I settled in Penang. Shortly before leaving Canada I had become engaged to an enchanting young lady, and I was on the point of flying to Ottawa to marry her and bring her back to preside as hostess in the Residency. In spite of my guests' periodic discoveries the house was now charmingly furnished to receive her, for I had managed to retain many attractive furnishings. On the day when I was due to take wing to Ottawa a party of friends came to lunch with me. As usual after the meal I conducted them through the house on the off chance that they might find some of their lost properties. The principal bedroom was equipped with a set of furniture which the Ministry of Works had provided for me – handsome pieces worthy of a bridal chamber. When we entered that room one of my male guests beamed a glad smile, called to his wife in the corridor outside, 'Oh, what a bit of luck, May! Come and see, darling; here's all our missing bedroom furniture'. When I flew away that afternoon the double-bed, dressing table, chairs and other amenities had been borne away in a furniture van, and the bridal suite-to-be was empty!

*

Early in 1947 my wife Audrey and I left the Residency in Penang to occupy the Sultan of Johore's dwelling in Singapore, and about a year later we moved to one of His Highness's palatial properties in Johore itself. Both were charmingly homely if somewhat regal places, with spacious, sunlit rooms where artistic works could be displayed to advantage. The second in particular, called the Istana Bukit Serene, was a potential private art gallery, and it provoked the connoisseur side of my nature to an exuberantly inflated point. I retained only a slight Caledonian control over its wild indulgences.

I bought decorative examples of Oriental furniture, paintings, carpets and other objects worthy of adorning a Sultanic palace. And I fell in a big way for one of my old loves, although it assumed a new guise. Reverting to collecting ceramics, I switched my affection from English to Chinese pottery and porcelain. This was not my initial acquaintance with those most beautiful of all human potters' achievements. Nearly twenty years earlier they had enticed, and indeed seduced me when I paid a brief visit to the Far East.

One afternoon in 1929 in Japan's ancient capital at Kyoto a friend took me to the famous Yamanaka Brothers' shop. It was not a store alongside many others in a street, but a group of pavilions distributed through a traditional Japanese garden of lawns, rockeries and goldfish ponds. Hundreds of wares arranged in coherent historical order were displayed in them, as if the place were a museum rather than a shop. One pavilion exhibited prehistoric pots, Kansu jars and Warring States objects; the next was filled with products of the Han, Tang and in-between dynasties; and another displayed Song, Yuan, Ming and Qing masterpieces. As I strolled with enchanted gaze through the rooms, I could not resist selecting a dozen of the least expensive bits for further careful consideration with a view to the ultimate purchase of just one perfect specimen. Afterwards I sat sipping tea with the Yamanakas whilst their assistants arranged these where I could contemplate them and make a final choice. An hour later I departed with five pieces! They cost me £20. I could not afford that sum, but neither could I resist the gracious china (plate 5).

However, after my return from that first Far Eastern jaunt, I reverted to a preference for English ceramics. Much as I liked my initial glimpse of the superior Oriental wares, I realised that a truly discriminating appreciation of them – which would prevent my making serious mistakes in buying some – required a scholarly knowledge of Old Cathay which I did not possess. Moreover, my income in those days could not afford the prices which I saw quoted for Chinese pieces when

I gazed into windows of dealers selling them along Bond Street and other fashionable quarters. So I returned to the establishments of friends like Perry and Roberts, and bought their less expensive native British pots. As far as Oriental porcelains were concerned, I contented myself with inquisitive, nostalgic visits to exhibitions of superb *famille rose*, *famille verte*, *sang de boeuf* and other species in public galleries like those in the British Museum.

In 1946, however, I found myself back in the Far East, older, wiser and somewhat richer. Having remained a bachelor for a score of years longer than most young men do, I had been able from time to time to make considerable savings. I never felt inclined to invest these in stocks and shares, for, apart from being an ignoramus where financial matters were concerned, I thought it foolish to buy dull bits of paper which would be hidden away in drawers when I could purchase instead beautiful objects to delight the eye in my rooms. I was not interested in gaining 5%, 10% or any other percent in dividends; to me the pleasure of contemplating works of art was an infinitely more valuable return on financial expenditure. And now circumstances which had previously restrained my half-aroused hankering to gain that enjoyment from Chinese porcelain were suddenly removed. I expected to stay for some years in the East; many of my friends there would be Chinese whose conversations could teach me about their civilisation; and in shops around me were a wide assortment of its gracious artistic creations for sale. I became an easy prey for the courteous, smiling antique dealers who did business along the High Street, Orchard Road, Coleman Street and other such places in Singapore.

At first I bought porcelain sparingly. It took me a while to learn the elementary facts about it that prudence required. Moreover, a certain trait in Singapore's character set limits on my opportunities. That comparatively young trading port had been established little more than a century earlier, and although it boasted a considerable population of vigorous, gifted 'overseas' Chinese I found that few of them had yet developed erudite aesthetic interests. They were preoccupied with such things as commerce and banking, and scarcely any university educated elite existed among them. Millionaires were plentiful; but most of these were the sons or grandsons of coolies who had migrated from the land of their birth to Malaya with no resources except their native wit and eager ambition. Within a generation or two those immigrants or their offspring had soared from poverty to wealth. They were capable and dynamic as well as genial men, but few of them possessed either the time or the inclination for even a skimpy patronage of the arts. Active businessmen in a remorselessly competitive world, they knew a great deal about rubber, tin, real-estate and trading, but little or nothing about paintings, sculptures, porcelains or jades. In their hectic lives they had no leisure for recreational luxuries of that kind.

Therefore almost no market existed in Singapore for fine works of art. Indeed, in those days the place was often described as 'a cultural desert'. Consequently its curio dealers kept no large stocks of genuine antique Chinese bronzes, lacquers, Imperial porcelains, scrolls of calligraphy or other 'museum pieces' for sale. Naturally they stored numerous more or less cunning fakes of these which they were not averse to selling at exaggerated prices to gullible customers; but for the most part they dealt in a different class of goods. They sold pleasant pieces of recently made Chinese furniture, jade ornaments, wood-carvings of Guanyin and other mythological characters, and similar *objets d'art* that would tempt tourists.

Nevertheless, they did stock goodly supplies of one type of ancient Chinese ceramic which happened for historical reasons to be plentiful throughout South East Asia. This was what is called 'export ware', much of it made in the Swatow district (plate 6). At least as early as the seventh century A.D., venturesome Chinese traders voyaged across the oceans, and gradually a regular commerce sprang up between them and the peoples of lands scattered across the southern archipelagos. Among the commonest Chinese articles for trade were jars and dishes which were superior to anything of the kind made locally in those regions. The merchants from Old Cathay did not bring Imperial or other aristocratic porcelains to the 'barbarians' living outside their homeland, but they disposed of coarser, more provincial wares in large quantities. Particularly during the Ming and Qing dynasties this somewhat peasant style of pottery became popular throughout the Philippines, Malaya, Java, Sumatra and Borneo, as well as further afield in the Middle East and along India and Africa's coasts.

Its tough texture gave it a strong survival capacity, and its aesthetic qualities made it coveted in Sultanic courts, peasant villages and even remoter jungle dwellings. Much of it has outlasted all the wear and tear of subsequent centuries. When I first became acquainted with it in the late 1940s a high value was still placed on it in some unexpected quarters. For instance, among the head-hunters of Sarawak – the famous 'wild men of Borneo' – certain large decorative earthenware jars made for storing *padi* (rice) were regarded as marks of wealth, used for special purposes on ceremonial occasions, and sometimes included in bridal price payments. One discriminating collector was Temenggong Koh, the Paramount Chief of the Iban tribe living in Sarawak's jungle interior. From the ceiling of the public gallery in his long-house dangled many skulls of past enemies, for he was the greatest head-hunter of his time; and against the walls of his private room stood a score of ancient Chinese pots which he treasured for their beauty.

On one of my visits to him I took him a three-foot high Ming jar as a gift. After I arrived, and had performed my first ritual duty of preparing a feast to appease the good and evil spirits who (according to local animist belief) haunted the surrounding forest, I told him of it. He expressed pleasure at my friendly thought, but was non-committal about accepting the piece until he could see it. I realised that he thought it might be unworthy of inclusion in his collection. Two of his henchmen fetched the pot from a boat in which I had travelled up river, and he summoned his lesser chiefs to watch its unpacking. We all sat on the floor whilst the sacking wrapped round it got unwound, and as the jar became gradually exposed a lively discussion about its merits began among my naked, supposedly savage companions. When at last it stood wholly revealed, Koh rose, scrutinised it critically, examined carefully the details of a dragon design carved upon it, and then nodded his head in approval. I felt relieved that this knowledgeable connoisseur agreed with my taste in such matters.

I did not myself collect those huge jars; they were too large for shelves in the cabinets where I displayed my pieces. But I started to acquire many smaller samples of Chinese export wares. Certain small, dark-glazed Tang bottles, fine Ming (and occasionally even Song) celadon dishes, boldly painted blue-and-white Ming plates, and both three-colour and five-colour enamelled Qing vases were all attractive. Flasks, ginger-jars, drinking cups, brush-holders and other useful articles also existed in one or more of those variegated styles. None of them had the delicate, highly artistic finish of their Imperial prototypes, but some were brave simulacrums of those more sophisticated masterpieces, and all possessed their own charming character. They bore an unmistakable stamp of the best potters who ever worked on this Earth.

During my ten years in South East Asia I gathered about 120 excellent examples of export wares, nearly always at a cost of less than two or three pounds each. I bought them partly from Chinese dealers in Singapore, and partly from itinerant Malay vendors who picked them up here or there throughout the four quarters of the South China Sea. They looked very much at home in the spacious rooms of my Sultanic palace on a hill-top overlooking the Straits of Johore, with a wide view of Singapore Island, a stretch of Malaya's coast and some distant Sumatran isles all basking in tropical sunshine on the glimmering ocean.

My official duties took me once or twice a year to Hong Kong. Its population's appreciation of antique works of art was much greater than that of the Singaporeans, and as a consequence its shops displayed many enticing samples of Chinese porcelains, as well as of other aesthetic treasures. They soon seduced me.

That seduction had been stimulated by one of the few connoisseurs of such things who lived in Singapore. My Singaporean Chinese friend Dato S. Q. Wong was a man of delightful, gay character whose success in business affairs gave him substantial wealth, and whose appreciation of Man's artistic achievements made him a collector of old china. With a partiality for what Walter Pater called the 'subtle and delicate sweetness which belongs to a refined and comely decadence', he particularly liked products made during the reigns of the Qing Emperors Yongzheng and Qianlong; and show-cases in his house displayed many exquisite samples of these. But he also owned some fine Song, Ming and early Qing pieces.

He was aware of my latent interest, and with his mischievous flair for encouraging other people besides himself to fall for attractive temptations, he gave me a gentle push in the direction of collecting superb porcelains. He threw out a scrap of bait, making me a small gift. With impeccable tact he did not present me with a faultless, priceless specimen of a superlative classical Chinese ware: that would have been too obvious an act of inducement. He merely remarked at lunch in Bukit Serene one day that he had brought me a bit of pottery which he possessed, but which unfortunately had recently got broken, and which he therefore did not himself care to keep any longer. Would I accept the trifle as a token of comradeship between one art patron and another? And he produced the supposedly modest pot. It was true that the piece was damaged – and so rendered of less commercial value – by a chip on its lip. Moreover, a defect in its original firing had in any case caused a splodge in one part of its glaze. Nevertheless, it was an aesthetically pleasing pale blue bowl of Junware made in the Song period nearly a thousand years ago (plate 7). I did not attempt to resist Wong's comradely proposition.

It did not at once persuade me of the supreme quality of Song wares; but gradually over the next few weeks its simple yet rich grace captivated me. The rest of the story flows naturally from that fragmentary beginning. Like a small stream gushing from a bubbling hillside spring, a few bits and pieces of Imperial-style ceramics that I at first haltingly purchased started to flow into my home, and later the stream broadened into a river which in due course became a wide-spreading lake. Some pieces I bought in Nanking and Canton on a visit to China in 1948, others I purchased during trips to Tokyo in Japan, and whenever I went to London or Paris I added one or two choice bits to the steadily growing assemblage. Just occasionally I picked up a good sample that somehow found its way into a dealer's hands in Singapore, and it was not impossible to find worthy specimens in other South East Asian capitals like Bangkok and Djakarta. But mostly I saved my money for a few hours of hectic searching on my periodic jaunts to Hong Kong and every time that I went there I invested all my current savings in antique china. Until some years later when the Communist government in Peking, quite rightly, stopped the export of such national treasures from their homeland, it was easy to find splendid examples of various Chinese works of art in the colony. In numerous shops on Victoria Island and in Kowloon, lying cheek-by-jowl alongside China itself, one could acquire fine jades, bronzes, ivories, porcelains, sculptures, paintings, scrolls of calligraphy and other precious gems. Moreover, their prices were much lower than anywhere else round the world, and the place was therefore a happy hunting ground for connoisseurs. Indeed it was a collector's paradise.

Gradually my taste concerning different styles of Chinese ceramics developed. Dato Wong's instinct about my likely preference proved correct. I am keenly partial to various types of Han, Tang, Ming, Qing or other period pieces, but my unchallenged favourites quickly became – and have remained ever since – the masterpieces of the Song and Yuan dynasties. For me no more satisfying earthenware, stoneware or porcelain has ever been made in all the long history of man's endeavours as a potter, from the beginnings of civilisation in fertile valleys of the Nile, the Tigris, the Euphrates, the Indus and the Yellow River up to this year of grace 1972.

I admire all types of Song wares, but most of all I like Northern and Longquan celadon (plates 8-9), Junware splashed with various splendid glazes (plate 10), Qingbai pieces (plate 11), and ivory white Dingware. I admit that certain Tang figurines (plate 12), blue-and-white Ming porcelain (plate 13), and underglaze red Ming pieces (plate 14) are close runners-up; but in my judgement those Song types generally have no peers. If I were forced to choose between one or another of them, I would give the prize for sheer beauty to Dingware;

and if I had to be even more specific, I would say that the choicest bits of all are its bowls and dishes bearing incised 'secret patterns' of Mandarin ducks swimming among lotus flowers in a reedy stream. But perhaps that is sheer egotistical prejudice – not to mention conceit – because on one fortunate afternoon in a dealer's house in the Happy Valley of Hong Kong I bought a particularly enviable example of it (plate 15). Several distinguished authorities have pronounced it to be as fine as any piece in any private or public collection elsewhere.

For more than twenty years my accumulation of Chinese ceramics – excluding export wares, which I ceased to buy when I left Singapore – continued to grow. It eventually consisted of more than 400 pieces representing most of the well-known types which successively emerged during nearly 4,000 years of the craft's evolution from primitive prehistoric pots (plate 16) and Kansu jars, through various classic styles, to the moment of regrettable decadence in the early nineteenth century. Of all my groups of artistic works it is without question the most distinguished and important. But alas, by the mid-1960s the prices for good pieces were soaring so high that I could no longer afford them, and my collecting of Chinese ceramics came to an end.

Over the years I inevitably made numerous mistakes, buying fakes which at first I thought genuine articles but later suspected, or objects which initially pleased me but afterwards appeared less satisfying. Gradually I weeded several of these out. Nevertheless my erudition was never profound, and when a jury of half-a-dozen true experts sat in judgement on the collection some years ago they returned a verdict of 'guilty' against 14 pieces still among them (plate 17).

Chapter 11. Roaming

Collecting is a hobby indulged in by myriads of people. The precise forms that this common, occasionally fanatical recreation can take are as varied as the multitude of individuals who engage in it. Not only does the taste of each person differ in some degree from that of every other, but the inclinations of each are apt to shift from time to time. No cliché is truer than the statement 'there's no accounting for taste'. Many people collect thousands of postage stamps, some have a passionate urge to accumulate Japanese samurai swords, others cannot resist assorted brass ornaments made for horses' bridles, and yet others unleash their acquisitive instinct with innumerable species of blown birds' eggs, dead butterflies or living Siamese cats. Various artistic connoisseurs concentrate on old Waterford glass, others spend their spare cash buying wooden African masks, others breed every conceivable kind of orchid, and others crave for Meissen porcelains, Hindu sculptures, Russian icons, Oriental lacquers, Oceanic carvings, Mayan pots, and so on and so forth *ad infinitum*. Fortunately both nature and mankind have been for so long such prolific creators of various beautiful or in other ways attractive objects that every taste can be satisfied; and if any particular desirable item is in short supply, it is not beyond the wit of cunning men to make presentable fakes which will appease the voracious hungers of undiscerning customers. Indeed, fakes have themselves now become such skilled products that some odd people collect them as fine works in their own right.

The field open to any collector is therefore as boundless as the stars scattered through the heavens. So much is this the case that a person should set prudent limits to his or her activities if these are to have manageable coherence. One purpose of collecting – in addition to enjoying the pleasure of contemplating (not to mention the pride of owning) attractive objects – is to become ever more knowledgeable about this or that particular type of thing; and if that knowledge is to grow truly deep instead of staying superficial it is desirable to concentrate the effort within a limited field. A prudent collector therefore selects one or at the most two or three kinds of articles to acquire, and confines his activities to them. In the process of making a final, firm choice he may at first flit experimentally from one tempting type to another, like a bee testing various flowers; but in the end he should decide on a definite favourite. This does not mean that he need stay loyal to it for ever afterwards; in the course of years he may accumulate a surfeit of this or that sort of object, and switch his preference to some other. I knew a man, for example, who gathered lovingly over a score of years a magnificent collection of sixteenth, seventeenth and eighteenth century Flemish paintings. It was worth a small fortune, but suddenly he tired of them, suffered an extraordinary revolution in taste, and sold the lot in order to buy in their places modern abstract pictures. I recall another collector who ricocheted from impeccably respectable French Louis Quinze furniture to erotic Hindu sculptures and later to holy manuscripts.

If a man's work sends him at various periods to live in different regions of the world, he is perhaps inevitably inclined to cast his net wider than if he remained stationary in one country. That restless experience occurred to me. Nevertheless, in each land where I stayed for several years I confined my collecting enthusiasm more or less to one or two particular types of local *objets d'art*. My chief successive favourites were old Staffordshire pottery, Worcester porcelain, English furniture and British pictures, modern Canadian paintings, Chinese ceramics of all periods, and – as I shall write later – medieval Indian sculptures, Mughal and related miniatures, and contemporary African wood carvings.

Yet of course one cannot be too rigidly exclusive, too narrowly confined in such matters. Every house needs a variety of utilitarian and decorative articles. If my house, for example, had contained solely the above listed objects, it would have been uncomfortable to live in. Good furniture, paintings, sculptures and ceramics are all very well, but by themselves they provide inadequate amenities in a residence. If the place is properly habitable, other pleasing objects should put in an appearance here and there, many of them being household necessities. Fortunately in the richly endowed Far East many charming specimens of such things were produced by skilled craftsmen in attractive materials like ivory, jade, silver and textiles which added contrasting expressions of beauty to my favourites fashioned in wood, china, stone and paint.

So although the short list that I have mentioned above continued to provide the major themes for my collecting, I indulged also in a number of minor ones. Some were mere variations on a major theme, such as examples of Korean (plate 18), Vietnamese and Thai ceramics which I added as supplements to my Chinese accumulation. Again, I dispersed among the English furniture several Oriental pieces like Chinese red-and-gold lacquer cabinets, multi-coloured Coromandel screens and carved and gilded Thai stools. Similarly I introduced variety into the array of pictures, unrolling here or there on the wall a Chinese silk-scroll painting, a Tibetan thangka painting or a Vietnamese black-and-gilt lacquer panel. One whole room I adorned with Japanese kakemono woodcuts. They numbered less than a dozen, but each was an exquisite example of the art – a chaste Haranobu, two Utumarus of different periods in that master's vivacious evolution, a gracious Eishi, the loveliest Aisho I have ever seen, a flowery piece by Hiroshige, Hokusai's famous view of Fujiyama glimpsed beyond a gigantic wave, and a few more.

As long as I lived in South East Asia I also bought pictures done by living artists in Singapore and Malaya. I wished to play my part in supporting contemporary painters in the same way as I did earlier in the case of the Spencer brothers and others in England. A further reason spurred me in Malaya and Singapore. In the post-war years an unprecedented burgeoning of interest in painting started there. Several art schools opened, many people put brush to canvas for the first time, and what had been called a cultural desert began to blossom like a rose. Several local artists showed distinct talent. Their styles were diversified, for they included Malay sketchers of native kampong scenes, Chinese scroll-painters in the traditional manner of their ancestors, European draughtsmen adapting their techniques to sunlit equatorial landscapes, conventional portraitists of brown, yellow or white skinned models, and aspiring revolutionaries breaking into the realms of abstract art. One at least of them was at that time a performer of outstanding ability, a young man named Cheong Soo Pieng. He was part traditional Chinese and part modern cosmopolitan in his manners of painting – often experimenting, sometimes failing, but frequently succeeding in creating true beauty on his silk scrolls, canvasses or sheets of paper. So parts of my home became an exhibition gallery of contemporary local pictures.

Other purchases in those years had a utilitarian as well as aesthetic purpose. Largely owing to the recent lootings which I mentioned earlier no carpets graced the Residency in Penang where I first stayed, and few existed in the Istana which I occupied later. At the time of my arrival their rooms displayed vast spaces of empty floor. The Ministry of Works was good enough to provide some plain carpets, but gradually over the years I supplemented this by buying a considerable number of Persian and Chinese rugs. The former were splendid and rather costly in Singapore, and the latter were equally superb but much less expensive in Hong Kong.

Domestic silverware was another requirement, and it provided a further admirable field in which I could give encouragement to local craftsmen who were still alive and kicking. In almost all South East Asia's lands the profession of silversmith was ancient and honourable, and guilds of its practitioners flourished in various capitals. Their skills had been handed down from father to son through countless generations. Usually their work was still conducted as a domestic industry, the artisans squatting on the floor in their homes fashioning traditional-style pieces with hand tools. Each country had its own more or less indigenous types of wares. Some finished products were engraved, others embossed, and yet others inlaid. Many were lightly patterned whilst others displayed extravagant all-over designs; and whereas several were thinly, delicately wrought, others were thick and tough. One famous school of silversmiths existed in Kelantan in Malaya (plate 19), another at Bangkok in Thailand (plate 20), a third in Phnom Penh in Cambodia, a fourth at Luang Prabang in Laos, a fifth in Djogjakarta in Java, a sixth in villages of the delectable isle of Bali, and so on. Each displayed its own rather rich beauty.

They all adapted their hallowed techniques to the making of modern tea and coffee services, rose bowls, cigarette boxes, ash-trays, ink-stands, finger-bowls, candlesticks and similar useful objects. Many examples of these were scattered through my house. I also found them very acceptable presents for visiting V.I.P.s, local brides and bridegrooms, and other recipients, so I was an avid customer of silver-workers throughout the region.

My favourite group of those master-craftsmen lived in the small Malay state called Brunei in Borneo. They were an industrious, artistic, charming fraternity of about twenty men led by an accomplished octogenarian named Haji Mohamed. The Sultans of Brunei had sat on their throne and ruled the neighbouring coasts, rivers and jungles for more than a thousand years; and through many generations the royal family had required silver regalia as well as more everyday decorative objects for use in their court. The guild of silversmiths was therefore about as ancient as the Sultanate itself. Certain ritual customs also encouraged their art. For instance, at the time of my early visits to Brunei any especially honoured guest arriving in a local aristocrat's house was presented with a cheroot of native tobacco gripped in a silver cigar-holder. When the visitor finished smoking it he could put the piece of silver in his pocket as a souvenir of his host's hospitality. I puffed numerous such cigars, and still prize their accompanying elegant holders (plate 21).

Often I sat on the floor alongside Brunei's silversmiths in their houses as they squatted beside me hammering designs on pieces of metal laid across hand-anvils. A few feet below us flowed deep water infested with crocodiles, for the old township was built for defensive purposes in the middle of a river. Its grass-thatched, timber-walled, plank-floored huts were raised on tall stilts in mid-stream, and the place's main street and side lanes were channels rippling around them. At the end of my visit I climbed down a ladder to my waiting canoe, and was paddled back to the new town on the river bank where I lodged. Encircling it was the jungle, but there was nothing 'jungley' about the lovely silver wares made in those somewhat wild surroundings.

Other renowned craftsmen in the same Bornean capital were brass-workers. Their trade was also as ancient as history in those parts. In earlier times a wide, almost landlocked inlet nearby called

Brunei Bay was a hideout for pirates who then roamed the South China Sea, and local shipping bent on peaceful purposes had to be well armed. No cannons anywhere around were more efficient than those made by Brunei's brass-workers, and incidentally they were artistically charming. Geometric and floral patterns moulded along their barrels were sometimes enlivened by figures of wriggling crocodiles, squatting birds or drowning human beings. I bought half-a-dozen of them, and got them mounted for the ceremonial defence of my verandas at Bukit Serene (plate 22). Brunei's brass-workers also produced various kinds of more pacific but equally decorative household pots and pans which are now valued museum pieces.

As attractive as any artistic objects still being made during the 1950s by peoples in South East Asia were those produced on the island of Bali in the Indonesian archipelago. That enchanted isle enjoyed a widespread renown in the Western hemisphere, but for a wrong reason. Its fame sang the praises of Balinese women, not because some of those females did indeed have faces of beguiling beauty but because they all walked around naked above their waists. This was typical of the crude, insensitive and sometimes insulting attitude which many Westerners adopted towards native peoples in those times. Bali was illustrious because of its bare-breasted women, whereas its true claim to fame was a much more notable circumstance – the fact that it was the home of a very distinguished culture. Every man, woman and child throughout its small length and breadth seemed to be a born artist. They were nearly all simple peasants who spent their days growing padi, herding cattle, breeding chickens and ducks or tending fruit-trees, as well as doing household chores, for they needs must earn their keep even in that bounteous tropical paradise soaked alternatively with sunshine and rain. But in their leisure hours they devoted themselves to creating beauty. Comparatively few were professional artists who worked all the time at painting pictures, carving stone or wooden sculptures, making musical instruments or designing fabulous theatrical costumes. Yet they were all artistically talented in one way or another, and spent their evenings as members of village orchestras, performers in dance troupes, sketchers of rustic wash-drawings, weavers and dyers of textiles, or just contrivers of bouquets of flowers and baskets of fruit to be taken as offerings to the local gods and goddesses in their temples. Those posies of flowers and pyramids of fruits were constructed with a dazzling aesthetic grace which would have made Constance Spry's students of flower-arrangement catch their breath in envious admiration.

The connection between their art and religion was part of the explanation of their genius. The Balinese were not only blessed with a capacity to create beauty, but also moved by the most inspiring motive in exercising it. Nearly all their efforts were acts of spiritual worship. In their padi-fields they constructed small shrines to lodge hand-made images of Shri, the Goddess of Fertility; their paintings were mostly portrayals of events in the lives of mythological deities (and occasional devils) who presided over mortal men's destinies; their sculptures were figures of divine creatures who guarded sacred sanctuaries; and their music and dancing were usually performed in a roadway outside a temple to pay homage to its holy residents.

I visited Bali on three occasions, staying each time for a few days with the Belgian artist Adrien le Mayeur and his exquisite Balinese wife Polok in their sea-shore home at Sanur, and afterwards for further days with the gay, cultured Tjokorda Agung in his palace at Ubud. Ubud lay at the centre of a district where numerous capable painters, sculptors and skilled craftsmen lived in about a score of villages scattered through the countryside, and I never enjoyed an experience more than walking across padi-fields with the Tjokorda to pay calls on those artists. The sun shone from a speckless blue sky, groves of coconut-palms graced the landscape all around, a myriad padi-shoots protruded above their reflections in the countless miniature lakes where the rice grew, and the thatched roofs of whichever hamlet we were approaching looked inviting. A few minutes later, as we sat sipping drinks and talking with a painter or sculptor in his open-air studio, we heard the music of gongs, xylophones and other instruments thudding and tinkling in a near-by courtyard where the local 'gamelan' or orchestra was rehearsing for an evening's performance. We went from artist to artist in village after village for miles around. Always at the end of those jaunts I had become the owner of a selection of their latest works which I bought.

Alas, those adventures ceased for me in the mid-1950s. But in any case Bali has altered in some important ways through subsequent years. The crowds of tourists visiting it have enormously multiplied, and as a result the chief inspiration for local craftsmen's work has become commercial profit instead of religious worship. The artists produce innumerable pieces for trippers, and since the taste of those human beings is much less discriminating than that of the temple gods, the quality of most of their products has sadly declined.

I could continue almost indefinitely to describe the arts and crafts of the then Far East. Their variety and charms were legion, and many of them lent additional graces to my house. In one room stood a cabinet filled with eighteenth century Chinese jade ornaments, on a mantelpiece in another paraded several old Japanese ivory statuettes, in niches in walls were antique Khmer and Thai stone or bronze sculptures of deities, on a side-table lay an assortment of snakey-bladed Malay *kris* (or daggers), on others were even more formidable, sharp-edged head-hunters' *parangs* (or swords) from Sarawak, on bedroom dressing tables were trinket-boxes of gilded Burmese lacquer (plate 23) and so on and so forth.

I had picked them all up one by one, here and there, often for a mere song and at other times for perhaps exorbitant prices. My reputation as a connoisseur was well-known in the antique shops of a dozen cities, in the workrooms of countless living craftsmen, among itinerant vendors who kept track of my travels from newspaper reports, by rogues travelling in the 'thieves' markets' in Bangkok, and... oh, all over the region. It was not always flattering to my shrewdness in business deals. I remember a tourist friend returning to Singapore one day from a visit in Java and telling me of a conversation he held with a curio seller in Djakarta. He wanted to buy an ancient bronze Chinese bell from the fellow's shop, but his efforts were in vain. The dealer originally asked 3,000 rupiahs for the piece, and in their subsequent bargaining refused to reduce the figure below 2,500. My friend did his utmost to beat him down to a reasonable price of 2,000, but finally gave up when the man remarked, 'I could sell that bell to Mr. Malcolm MacDonald for 4,000 rupiahs'.

Every attractive *objet d'art*, whether antique or modern, that I acquired during my decade in the Far East was made by men's hands with the aid of only simple tools. Their creators never sought help from sophisticated machinery. Many of the finest of them were produced by very poor people who learned their skills from similarly humble, usually illiterate teachers. Those assorted works – strong enough, incidentally, to retain their beauty through many centuries – were a wealth of evidence of mankind's natural artistic capacities. Among mankind's other attributes, good and bad, they are in fact a multitude of creative artists. The assortment of glorious schools of art which have sprung up, one after the other, throughout the last 5,000 years in 'civilised' societies in Egypt, the Near East, China, India, Europe and elsewhere are not the only testimony to this. It appears that almost all – if not all – peoples are capable of making lovely things with their hands. Children's paintings reveal that the talent is inborn in nearly everyone, and the handicrafts of numerous 'primitive' tribes show how it buds, and sometimes blossoms, in even the wildest environments. One need not delve back into the dim, distant past and quote the murals sketched by prehistoric peoples about 30,000 years ago in caves like those at Lascaux. In our own lifetime many tribesmen produce impressive works of art. I have already mentioned the soapstone figurines of seals, loons, snowy owls and other inhabitants of the Arctic which are carved by Eskimos. Additional near contemporary examples are the rock paintings made in not only ancient but also modern times by the nomadic Bushmen of southern Africa.

So far as South East Asian natives are concerned, when I first knew the Ibans, Kenyahs and Kayans in Sarawak a quarter of a century ago, they qualified for similar praise (plate 24). Those notorious 'wild men of Borneo' were still enthusiastic head-hunters. On my first visit to them in their jungles they raised a huge arch of welcome for me, in size and shape a smaller edition of London's Marble Arch. It was made of bamboo poles covered by luscious tropical foliage and decorated partly with beautiful wild orchids and partly with grim heads of Japanese soldiers whom they had decapitated in the recent war. Close-cropped black hair and yellow-skinned flesh remained fresh on those topknots, and beneath their eye-lashes the Japanese looked at me, I thought, rather disapprovingly from their now dull eyes. Yet the Bornean tribesmen's skills in creation were just as impressive as their cunning in destruction. Their swords were not only cleverly forged but also beautifully decorated with engraved patterns (plate 25). With equal capacity they produced more peaceful implements. Some of their wooden oars for paddling canoes were elegantly carved; they cut pleasingly adorned bowls and other household utensils from rough jungle timbers (plate 26); and their graven images for worship had a certain vivid if savage beauty. The rattan baskets that they plaited (plate 27), cotton skirts, jackets and mats which they wove, beaded sunhats that they threaded and hornbill ear-rings which they designed all possessed aesthetic merit. And some of the young warriors stepped dramatic head-hunter dances with a grace of movement and facial expressions reminiscent of the finest performers in a classical Russian ballet.

The artistic skills of all sorts of peoples scattered round the globe were born and bred by the innate cunning of human eyes and hands assisted by small, simple tools, without aid from large inhuman machines. However competent sophisticated modern mechanical instruments may be at manufacturing other types of things, they cannot produce works of art with the same spontaneous, individual quality. Yet our factories nowadays are employed to make countless articles as substitutes for those earlier man-made objects, and in one country after another the local peoples' artistic talent is dying. It will be a million pities – a supreme human disaster – if that process is allowed to continue.

Perhaps I might mention in passing a related matter touching age-old arts and crafts. During my earlier travels in various continents the local populations belonging to different races and tribes still wore traditional native costumes. This was one of the charmingly distinguishing features about them. Their differing exotic styles of dress were designed and hand-made by indigenous techniques, and many of them were lovely adornments particularly suited to their wearers' physical figures and personal characters. One of the sad results of the widespread introduction of modern factories and machines is an increasing standardisation, a dull uniformity in the types of attire which peoples all round the Earth now tend to wear. Many of their earlier customary garbs have virtually disappeared, some of them being worn only occasionally on special ceremonial occasions. Perhaps I shall seem prejudicial if I express regret at the almost entire abandonment of the kilt from Scotsmen's bodies, so let me start with a very different type of dress.

When I first went to the Far East in 1929 and arrived in Tokyo I at once knew that I had landed in Japan because not only all the women but almost all the men strolling in the streets wore Japanese kimonos. It was true that a few gentlemen had begun to adopt an alien style, for although their bodies were clad from their necks to their ankles in those Oriental robes, on their heads they wore bowler hats as if they were bankers in the City of London! Now, alas, that general appearance has completely changed. Not only every man but almost every woman in Tokyo and other Japanese cities wears a Western-type suit, shirt and tie or blouse, skirt or frock. It is very sad that they have cast off the native garments which were eloquent expressions of Japanese character and culture.

A similar disappearance of national costumes is occurring in many other regions. Eskimos in the Arctic no longer wear caribou skins, Malay men appear less and less in sarong attire, Chinese ladies have discarded their gracious cheongsams, inhabitants of the Fiji islands have thrown aside their grass skirts, and all sorts of other diverse characters in numerous lands are rejecting their earlier attractive raiments in favour of plain European-style garbs. Only in a comparatively few cases are traditional racial or national apparels still frequently worn, such as the saris that grace Indian women and the ornate head-dresses and fabulously flowing robes which many men as well as most women display in West African countries.

I know that a lot can be said from the point of view of convenience for this change. Nevertheless, for other reasons the virtual disappearance of traditional costumes, like the decline of many diverse native arts and crafts, is a tragedy. If the process continues many beautiful expressions of hallowed human civilisation will eventually become as dead as the dodo.

Chapter 12. Pains

Whilst I was living in South East Asia some unfortunate events affected the collections of works of art which I had left behind in Britain. I have already mentioned the theft of the best of my Tom Thomson sketches. Worse was to follow.

The old men and women who resided in Hyde Hall during the war treated its contents with respect, and all my possessions survived their occupation without a breakage or even a scratch. When those aged folk returned to their homes in London after peace was declared I expected to reoccupy the house myself. But I got sent to Malaya instead.

I rented Hyde Hall to a well-to-do family. Its head was an officer in a smart Guards regiment; but unfortunately for me his children seemed to be less disciplined than, presumably, the troops under his command. First the youngsters scratched drawings in some of the veneers of my hitherto unblemished pieces of antique furniture. Then they went even further. As I have mentioned, a splendid tythe barn stood in the property's grounds. Considerably older than the Elizabethan manor house itself, it had been built in the fifteenth century. A vast place with lofty timber walls and a vaulted ceiling where original oak beams supported one of the largest thatched roofs in Essex, it was a handsome building which received honourable mention in the official volume describing the country's historical monuments.

Temporarily I allowed the company who farmed the surrounding land to use it for storing machinery and other agricultural objects; but I intended later to have it judiciously adapted as a library and picture gallery for my thousands of books and a selection of paintings and other works of art.

My tenants' children, however, had a different notion. One autumn day they decided to play a game round a bonfire in it. Borrowing a box of matches, they stole into the barn, gathered a heap of the hay which at that season was stacked there, and set it alight.

Soon the timber walls, wooden beams and thatched roof were all ablaze, and before the nearest fire brigade could arrive on the scene the glorious Tudor tythe barn was burnt to the ground.

When the Guards captain's tenancy of Hyde Hall came in due course to an end my agent arranged for its letting, fully furnished, to a group of American Air Force officers working at a base leased to the United States government in nearby East Anglia. I agreed to this proposal on condition that the men were hand-picked individuals who would treat the house and its contents with respect. The first team of airmen were decent, pleasant men who answered to that description. When I visited them one afternoon eighteen months later every picture, piece of furniture and other object in the rooms looked its charming best, obviously being appreciated by the sons of Uncle Sam.

The next batch of officers who replaced them could not have been carefully selected, for they were very different types. Apparently they felt no regard whatever either for an English home kindly made available to them, or for the fair name of their own country which depended partly on their behaviour overseas. My house agent began to suspect that their conduct left something to be desired when a friendly married couple who looked after Hyde Hall during my absence quit the place because they could no longer tolerate the latest tenants' way of life. On enquiries he discovered a very sorry state of affairs.

I do not know entirely what the officers had been up to, and can only guess at their more extreme misconduct. Certainly they and various temporary girl friends who apparently stayed with them must have held a lot of wild parties. When I returned to England many months after they had left Essex some of the consequences were stored in Hyde Hall's attic. Its small rooms and passage-way appeared like wards in a hospital for ailing antique furniture, with a cemetery for dead pieces alongside. Thus, several Heppelwhite dining-room chairs lay there badly broken. Crippled remains of Jacobean, Queen Anne and Georgian stools, side-tables and other furnishings were also dumped upstairs, as if they were tins thrown on a rubbish heap. Some of the tables, cabinets and other fine pieces still in use downstairs had survived fairly well, but others were chipped, scratched or stained by spilt whisky, gin and wines. My Flemish tapestry was ripped, and numerous signs of wanton damage were evident almost everywhere. Charming little objects of utility or decoration like an old Chelsea china inkstand, pieces of a pink-lustre tea set, some Josiah Wedgwood pottery medallions, two Meissen porcelain figures, and a Carolingian needlework picture were conspicuous by their absence – presumably stolen, or perhaps merely cast away in waste-paper baskets after they too got smashed.

Some pleasant new tenants who had moved into the house in the meantime told me that when they first arrived there the grass on the lawn in front of the Hall and in the orchard at its back stood everywhere waist-high, like undergrowth in a tropical forest. They hired a man to cut it with a scythe, but he had to proceed cautiously because hidden in the tall grass were hundreds upon hundreds of empty beer, whisky and champagne bottles. These had presumably been disposed of day after day, week after week and month after month by being drunkenly hurled from the house's windows.

During the war German airmen returning to their Fatherland from raids on London had sometimes dropped undisposed bombs as they passed over Essex, and several times these fell in fields around Hyde Hall. However, none of them hit the house. What the enemy had failed to achieve in the way of destruction among my art treasures throughout five years of warfare was accomplished with gusto by some of our allies during two years of debauchery after peace was restored.

Chapter 13. British Paintings

I wrote earlier about the tardy development of my appreciation of oil paintings. Gradually, however, it budded and then blossomed; and by the time of the outbreak of war in 1939 I had started to be in a small way an admiring collector of them. For reasons which I have mentioned I decided to acquire mostly works by British artists; and always on my occasional brief visits to London during my five years in Canada I made leisure to visit certain picture dealers to see what small masterpieces they might have for sale. Indeed, I sometimes told them of my particular desire for a fine canvas by this or that famous painter; and so they kept their eyes open for these. I continued to do the same throughout my ten years in South East Asia. Slowly my group of charming oils grew.

I have already described the admirable paintings which I inherited from my father. To cut the rest of a longish story short, I progressively added to them nearly a score of creations by various English and Scottish masters. They included carefully chosen pictures by George Moreland, Stubbs, Richard Wilson, Ibbetson, Samuel Scott, Raeburn, Constable, Gainsborough, Turner, Bonington, the elder Crome, James Stark, Etty and an anonymous Tudor portrait. I have kicked myself ever since for not adding to them examples of works by several other men whose renowned names are conspicuous by their absence from that list, such as Zoffany, Davis and Allan Ramsay. This was foolish of me; but I did not realise until too late that their prices were going to soar far above my means. I did for a while possess portraits by Peter Lely and Godfrey Kneller, but they were almost full-length figures of their models instead of the smaller head-and-shoulder likenesses which I would have preferred; and when several years later they turned out to be inconveniently large for any wall in my eventual English home, I sold them.

Among my contemporary oil paintings are a portrait by Augustus John, and Stanley Spencer's picture of magnolias which I have already mentioned. A silly error that I shall always regret was my obstinate, if reluctant, resistance to an offer of a sketch of St. Marks in Venice by

Walter Sickert, for which the price was only £500. However, at that time I had already overspent my current resources.

Sometimes the circumstances in which I bought a picture had a touch of luck. For instance, one afternoon in the Fine Art Society I was attracted by several paintings, but could afford to buy only a single specimen; and so I had to make a choice. After long examination of them I decided in favour of a landscape by Richard Wilson depicting a stretch of the River Thames on the outskirts of London. When I sought to acquire it, however, the dealer who was guiding me round the shop said that unfortunately it was already reserved for an aristocrat who lived in the North of England. The fellow had looked into the gallery on the previous day, eagerly seeking just one painting. He knew little or nothing about works of art, and did not particularly care what piece he seized so long as its size fitted into a certain empty space on a wall in his castle. He thought the length and breadth of the Wilson landscape were just about right; and so he bagged it tentatively, saying that he would either confirm or surrender his ownership after he returned home and could check the exact measurements in feet and inches of the gap on a wall which he wished to fill. He had promised to write within a few days to say whether his final decision was 'yes' or 'no'.

I was due to fly back to Singapore on the following morning, and so would not be handy to learn the reply when it came. When I mentioned this to the friendly dealer he promptly said, 'The picture is yours. You appreciate it, and your rival patron does not care a straw about its merits'. He said he would make some plausible excuse for why he had been compelled to sell it.

At the time I did not realise that occasionally when one of Wilson's paintings was a success he made a copy or two of it. Still less did I know that other versions of this particular landscape already hung in a couple of distinguished collections. When I went to live in India a few years later I took the picture with me, and it graced a wall in my house in Delhi. One day Sir Kenneth (now Lord) Clark came to stay with me. As soon as he caught sight of the painting he approached it, gazed at it closely for a while, and then turned and said to me, 'You rascal! There's a copy of this painting in the National Gallery in London. I bought it when I was the Director. Another version hangs in the Norwich Castle museum. Yours is the best of the three'.

The circumstances in which I bought a J. M. W. Turner were also a bit strange as well as fortunate. On one of my visits from Asia to London I dropped in to see my friend Dudley Tooth in his art gallery on Bruton Street. For two or three years he had known that I would like to secure a Turner, so he had been on the lookout for a possible good example within my means. I felt excited therefore when he told me that morning that he had recently discovered a couple of the great artist's works, one or the other of which might tempt me.

He produced them both, and we contemplated them enthusiastically for quite a while. One was a modest-sized scene of sunrise over Lake Garda in Italy, done in the year 1819 in Turner's early style, whilst the other was a similarly executed period piece, though smaller, showing sailing boats cruising on the sea with a glimpse of Venice in the background. Each was enchanting, and needless to say I would have bought both of them if my purse had been bursting with countless bank-notes. But my resources were much more limited than that. Indeed, I could not afford either painting – yet I could not resist one or the other.

I would have preferred the Lake Garda landscape, but Dudley asked £7,000 for it. The other piece was procurable at £2,000; and after long hesitation I decided that if I economised in my every other financial expenditure during the next several months, I could take the risk of buying it.

'Please give me a signed assurance', I said to Dudley, 'that it's a genuine Turner. Of course, I don't doubt your word; but such a document will be a helpful guarantee if I have to sell this little treasure later'.

He answered that he would readily sign a note, but that this would be useless for the purpose I had in mind. If the document bore only the signature of the interested dealer from whom I had bought the picture, it would carry little weight with authorities. He suggested that

I should get the signature of an impartial, unquestionable expert like Mr. Philip Hendy, the then Director of the National Gallery.

I jumped at the idea, bought the painting, and took it to Hendy. He looked at it and remarked, 'Sorry, but in my opinion this isn't a Turner. I'm not prepared to sign a guarantee of its authenticity'.

Knowing that I had purchased the picture from Tooth, he added, 'What a pity you can't purchase the real Turner that Dudley's got. His painting of Lake Garda is certainly a Turner, and it's a beauty. Indeed, I've tried to persuade two provincial art galleries to buy it for their collections, but they want examples of Turner's later period, not the early one. So they've resisted my urgings'.

I felt greatly embarrassed by his refusal to approve the Venetian scene. However, my long-standing, cordial acquaintance with Dudley was such that he and I could always speak completely frankly with each other. I returned to him and told him of Hendy's judgement.

He disagreed with the Director's verdict, but said that of course in the circumstances I must not keep the picture. He would take it back and return my £2,000. Then he enquired, 'What about buying the Lake Garda painting?'

I answered that this was impossible because I simply could not afford £7,000.

'You can have it for the £2,000 you paid for the other,' he replied, commenting that our friendship was so great, and had been so mutually advantageous on several previous occasions, that in the situation which had arisen he would like to satisfy my ambition to own a Turner.

I felt staggered by this generous offer, but did not refuse it!

I naturally like the works of various English and Scottish artists for different reasons, but if I had to choose who I think is the greatest among them, I would plump for Joseph Mallord William Turner. Close runners-up would be Gainsborough, Constable and Bonington – not necessarily in that order. As regards Gainsborough, I am often, though not always, inclined to prefer his rustic landscapes to his aristocratic portraits; but best of all I enjoy his combinations of the two subjects in such portrayals as his early picture of Mr. and Mrs. Robert Andrews that hangs in the National Gallery in London, and his later painting of ladies and gentlemen strolling in St. James' Park which is in the Frick collection in New York. My own Gainsborough is a delightful, smallish sketch for another of his paintings that hangs in the collection in Trafalgar Square, the much larger scene called *The Watering Place*.

I managed to buy four Constable landscapes, and have gained ceaseless pleasure from three of them ever since. Alas the fourth disappeared in circumstances that I shall describe in due course. Of my remaining trio, one at least is a superb little masterpiece depicting the Newmarket countryside.

Yet perhaps my best gem of a painting is one of two Bonington oils that I bought in the good old days when their prices were still tolerably low. It is a seashore scene of cliffs, boats and sands along the coast of Normandy, very similar to one which is in the Louvre in Paris.

One reason why I was able to buy so many distinguished portraits was that sometime in the 1950s I sold my father's house in Hampstead. Throughout my previous lengthy absence overseas I let it to a succession of tenants, with not consistently happy consequences. As there seemed no chance of returning to settle in England for many more years to come, I decided to be rid of the responsibility of landlording the place, and all the money that I received from its sale I invested in various beautiful paintings.

Chapter 14. More Pains

Throughout my years in Canada two friends stayed in my Hampstead house. They looked after my belongings there with scrupulous and indeed loving care. When they left at the war's end another couple rented the place fully furnished, and they too guarded its contents well. Then they bought a property for themselves elsewhere, and a somewhat different regime was ushered into my London home. I was far away in Singapore at the time, and so could not supervise its letting. The people who looked after my interest during my absence exercised insufficient care, and hired the dwelling to a plausible tenant without adequate inspection of his credentials. He stayed there for about twenty months and then disappeared. Behind him he left wads of unpaid telephone bills, electricity accounts and other of his household debts, all to be settled by me! To this insult he added the injury of having failed to pay any rent for many weeks. When my agents went to the house in due course to remonstrate with him, and to seek the money, they found its front door locked and the place uninhabited. On breaking in they discovered that its rooms were almost bereft of pictures, nearly half the bookcases in its library were empty, and many other gaps existed in the residence's furnishings. In fact it turned out that the fellow had disposed of twenty of my old-master paintings, some precious pieces of porcelain, my only bits of antique silver, several other art treasures, and about 2,000 of my books! All the cash from their sales he had put into his own pocket.

On reporting the matter to the police my agents learned that he was a man with an appalling criminal record for whom they had long been searching, but under an assumed name. Evidently he enjoyed a highly profitable occupation of my home until my representatives began to pester him with what he regarded as excess of zeal for the payment of rent. Then he packed his (and no doubt more of my) belongings, locked the place up, and left it in the hope of disappearing without trace. Fortunately that happened before he had completed his self-appointed task of disposing of all of my properties, for quite a lot of furniture, including the cabinets filled with English pottery and porcelain, continued to put up as brave a show as they could in the pilfered rooms.

Some months later the rascal was traced, arrested, tried in court, and condemned to two years imprisonment.

But what about my stolen property?

Of the twenty missing pictures I eventually recovered sixteen. Their recapture was comparatively easy because each one was a recognisable work of a well-known painter, and by advertising the losses in art magazines they got traced. Some of the dealers through whose hands they had passed helped me to retrieve them, a generous gesture considering that they were then compelled to surrender the money they had received from purchasers, since in the eyes of the law they were – however innocently – 'receivers of stolen goods'. One of the paintings had been bought by the National Gallery in Canada, another was hanging in the Kelvin Art Gallery in Glasgow, a third was on its way to a public collection in Australia, and the others were in the possession of various private owners.

One morning as I sat in my office in Singapore a message came from my Naval Attaché saying that he wished to see me urgently. I suggested a meeting half-an-hour later, and – in order to prepare my mind for the talk – asked my secretary to find out what news concerning our British fleet in the Far East had arrived which the sailor could suddenly desire to discuss with me. No unusual news had come; so I was kept guessing what problem he proposed to raise.

When the Attaché – a genial Commander – entered my room he looked solemn and embarrassed. He said he had received a rather urgent telegram from London which I should see.

'Oh, from the Admiralty?' I enquired.

'No; from my wife', he replied.

'Really, what's that got to do with me?'

'Quite a lot...' he said, looking worried and amused as he handed me the cable.

It read, 'Darling, I have just learned that the beautiful drawing by Augustus John which we bought last year was stolen from Malcolm MacDonald and so belongs to him. Regrets and love'.

My companion grinned and we drank a couple of brandies to drown his sorrows and celebrate my joy. He of course received back from the dealer the cash which he had paid for an excellent pencil sketch of the now illustrious Admiral of the Fleet Sir Caspar John (the great artist's son) as he appeared a few decades ago in his childhood.

Four of the stolen pictures were never recovered. Most valuable among them were an excellent Constable oil painting of a Brighton beach scene, and a brilliant J. M. W. Turner water-colour of the grand canal in Venice. Yet to me the most sentimentally precious was Gilbert Spencer's portrait of Old Kemp, which I described earlier. Alas to this day I have never set eyes on it again. If by good chance a reader of this book possesses it, I shall gladly buy it from him for a fair price.

Nor did I recover any of the missing porcelain, silver or other *objets d'art*. No clue to their whereabouts was ever found, the thief presumably having disposed of them one by one over several months before their losses became known. I kept no photographs and only a skimpy inventory of my possessions. Moreover, I myself was on the opposite side of the Earth when the crime got exposed, and was kept so constantly busy there that many more months passed before I could visit England and check up on precisely what had been stolen.

For this reason I also never retrieved any of my missing books. A dozen handsome volumes which had stood in my library shelves were recovered, but they were a set of beautifully bound Doves Press classics that belonged to one of my sisters. Immediately on learning of their disappearance she went to search for them, and found them in a well-known second-hand bookshop in London. But she was not familiar with the other contents of my library, and so did not know what particular volumes to hunt for. Only when I returned to England half a year later could I check which works were missing, and start to search for them.

I was not an erudite connoisseur of literary *chef d'oeuvres*, and my collection of about 4,000 books had no claim to distinction. Nevertheless, among the 2,000-odd now missing were numerous desirable tomes. They included, for example, several first editions of eighteenth and early nineteenth century classics about travels in Canada and in various lands of South East Asia, such as Stamford Raffles' splendid account of Java; various deluxe copies of authoritative works on English, European and Chinese furniture, ceramics, paintings or other arts; and more than a hundred first editions of the best ancient and modern books about British ornithology and natural history, including many illustrated by Thomas Bewick's engaging woodcuts of birds and beasts. I also possessed complete attractively bound sets of the works of all the celebrated British, French and Russian novelists and short story writers of the last two or three centuries. In addition I prized a number of 'association' copies of famous books inscribed by their authors, such as *An Intelligent Woman's Guide to Socialism and Capitalism* presented by George Bernard Shaw to my father, and *The Life and Times of John Churchill, Duke of Marlborough*, which Winston Churchill had given to me.

When I arrived in England I discovered that all of these, and many other books, had disappeared from my library, like victims of a vast, appalling massacre. I went in search of them in the relevant departments of the bookshop where my sister had found her Doves Press set, but caught sight of none of them. Happening upon the manager in one department, I approached him, mentioned my name, told him of the circumstances in which my books had vanished, and added the titles of several especially important volumes. He replied that the shop had not seen any copies of those famous works in recent times, regretted that he therefore could not help me, and promptly strolled away.

As soon as he departed, a young woman behind a near-by counter, who was an assistant in the place, hurried to me. She said she had listened to our conversation, and could scarcely believe her ears when she heard the manager answer my questions. She told me that all the missing books that I mentioned, and many others, had come to the shop, and been bought and re-sold there. She then described how one morning each week, week after week about a year ago, a man came with a suitcase full of books for disposal, stating that he had fallen into financial straits which compelled him to sell a library which he had gradually collected. She was sometimes on duty when he arrived, and received them under the supervision of the manager. On the fellow's first visit they became suspicious of him because a valuable volume contained my name scribbled on its fly-leaf; but on enquiry he explained that he was a friend of mine, and that I had given the book to him.

I should mention that I never pasted an 'Ex Libris' bookplate in any of my books, and only occasionally bothered to write my name in one, usually in pencil, which the criminal's india-rubber no doubt always expunged after that initial slip-up.

The young lady said earnestly that she spoke to me in strict confidence, and asked me not to reveal to her boss that she had told me all this, otherwise she would probably lose her job. But she said she could not with a clear conscience keep silent after hearing my tale of woe, which at once recalled to her mind their suspicion of the rascal who produced an important volume with my name inscribed in it.

I of course told her not to worry; she could count on me holding my tongue. The thief had already done enough harm to me, and should not be allowed to extend the hurt to her. I thanked her warmly for her candid confidence, which would save me from wasting time during my brief stay in England by searching in other bookstores for my lost properties. Possibly the thief had distributed his loot in several such places, but in light of her information it would clearly be foolish to try to disentangle their scattered whereabouts. In any case most of them had probably been sold already.

I remembered the lesson I had learned during the war, that friendships with people are more precious than possession of valuable objects. Nevertheless I must confess that I harboured a certain resentment against the lofty, we-can-do-no-wrong attitude of at least one official in that immensely profitable business in second-hand books, who had certainly (though, of course unwittingly at the time) received progressively over many months several hundreds of my stolen books.

I have never felt my entirely complete self since being parted from half my collection of books. Some of the lost volumes were irreplaceable; others had ceased to be procurable at reasonably inexpensive prices; and in the case of yet others I was no longer inclined to spend money on them since they represented earlier tastes in my reading which I had now outgrown. Gradually over thirty years I chose those numerous books, ever since I was a freshman at Oxford. A library so assembled becomes in a way an integral part of its owner. It expresses different sides of his personality at successive stages of his growth, and becomes almost as intimate a part of his mental make-up as his arms or legs are bits of his physical character. Without them in my home I still feel irretrievably separated from familiar pieces of myself. For me their disappearance was like a massacre of a multitude of personal friends. Throughout years they had been intimate companions staying in my home and giving me fascinating information on all sorts of subjects whenever we sat together. Every now and then I look on a shelf for this or that book which I know I possessed, and which I wish to consult, and when I cannot find it I realise that it was one of the items stolen.

To add to my sense of grievance, when I sent my insurance company a claim for compensation for that robbery of numerous valuable treasures I received a stuffy reply. My contract with them was an 'all-in' policy covering loss by theft as well as by fire, earthquake or any other natural cause. However, when I explained (in answer to a questionnaire) the circumstances of the calamity, those insurance pundits smiled blandly and declared that my plea was unjustified. They stated that technically I had not been robbed at all! Under the law, as interpreted by them, a thief must break into a house from outside its walls, not commit his crime from within. So this criminal's deliberate, massive acts of stealing did not amount to theft. I permitted him to stay as a tenant in my house; I was therefore responsible for everything he did in it; and so I was to blame for his deed. Or to put it in other words, I was myself the thief guilty of the crime! Thus my 'all-in' insurance policy would remain happily – for them – unconcerned.

The company's directors must have felt a slight pricking of their lordly consciences, for their secretary wrote me a considerately worded letter stating that although they were under no legal obligation to remit me a penny, they would consider sympathetically the possibility of making a payment to me as a gratuitous gesture, since for ten years I had paid my premiums regularly without seeking any previous claim from them. I sent a reply expressing warm thanks, and for several weeks waited hopefully for the arrival of their cheque. However, after another month I received a further note from the secretary regretting that after discussion they had decided they could make no payment whatever to me.

Needless to say, I immediately cancelled my policy with them. Perhaps they were on sound legal ground in adopting their attitude. My lawyer felt dubious about the result of a case in court. However, all I knew was that not only the thief, but also one or more second-hand bookshops and now the insurance company had all done quite well – or avoided doing badly – from his plundering. Eventually the rascal himself suffered at least part of his due by serving two years in prison; but those others (except for the generously friendly picture dealers whom I have mentioned) got off scot free. Incidentally, that is not the only occasion when an insurance company has behaved in a scurvy manner to me.

Chapter 15. India

Towards the end of 1955 I left South East Asia and went to India as Britain's High Commissioner. Before flying away from Singapore I parted with considerable additional sections of my art collection, but this time by my own free will.

In 1949 the University of Malaya had been established, and it quickly became a fine centre of higher education for the rising generation of Malay, Chinese, Indian, Eurasian and other youngsters in Malaya, Singapore and the British Borneo territories. From its start I was its Chancellor, and did everything I could to help stimulate its growth, widen its teachings, and make it a valuable institution in the building of the Malaysian and Singaporean nations-to-be. Among other proposals I suggested establishing in it a Museum of Oriental Art where the undergraduates could study and enjoy noble creations by the ancient civilisations of Asia in general and South East Asia in particular to which they were heirs. I secured support from the University's finance committee, and then recruited some private and public benefactors. Eventually I launched the gallery by presenting to it my collection of Chinese export ware ceramics, numerous artistic objects made of old in Burma, Thailand, Indo-China and neighbouring lands, and also my modern local paintings and drawings. The porcelains totalled about 120 pieces, the pictures counted more than 50, and the other varied articles numbered over a score. Several friends, including genial Dato S. Q. Wong, added gifts from their collections; the most generous of all Singapore's millionaires, Dato Lee Kong Chian, provided a sumptuous Trust Fund from which the museum could continue to purchase more treasures; and in response to diplomatic suggestions by me the governments of India and Cambodia presented many handsome examples of their classical sculptures, paintings and bronzes. From the day of its birth the art museum became a lusty, steadily growing, beautiful child.

I gave numerous other *objets d'art* to the museums at Kuala Lumpur in Malaya, Kuching in Sarawak and the then embryonic one in Brunei. Throughout ten years I had received so much wonderful friendship from the peoples of all those lands that this was a small return for their infinite kindnesses.

The rest of my collection of Chinese pottery and porcelain – then already amounting to about 350 pieces – was packed and sent to Durham in England. Many excellent displays of Old Cathay's superb wares were on permanent public exhibition in art galleries in southern centres like London, Oxford and Cambridge; but I was told that nothing comparable existed anywhere in Britain's North. On enquiry as to where my assortment might be most helpful to young and older students of Far Eastern cultures I learned from my friend Peter Vaughan (of John Sparks) that the recently established School of Oriental Studies in Durham University was an admirable institution, and that the collection could perform a fine service there. So I offered its director the lot on loan, and he accepted. Soon afterwards the Gulbenkian Foundation built an exhibition hall to display it and other groups of various Eastern works of art acquired by the School, and my pieces have filled some of its show-cases ever since. I sadly missed them afterwards in my houses as I flitted from continent to continent round the world; but it was better that they should be enjoyed by a much larger audience than my family and our house-guests.

*

My transfer to India caused yet another extraordinary change in not only my political and diplomatic duties, but also my exotic surroundings and human neighbours. Although Hindu influences had occasionally affected South East Asia's cultures here or there, the Buddhist and Muslim religions were much more powerful and widespread inspirers of art forms throughout that region. Now my eyes slowly began to accustom themselves in many Indian localities to the very different, often predominant and in many places overwhelming architectural and other artistic creations conceived by Hinduism.

I did not fall in love with India at first sight. The distressing human poverty to be seen in some of its cities like Calcutta appalled me; what seemed to me a lack of appreciation by many highly cultured Indians for graceful furnishings in their homes disappointed me; and the visible artistic expressions of Hinduism baffled me. I was an utterly untutored ignoramus regarding their significance. To add to my bewilderment, there was an almost total lack of most of the types of *objets d'art* which had hitherto attracted me. Admittedly some of the 'pukah sahibs' of the now departed British Raj had left behind them a few souvenirs of their rule, for in second-hand curio shops in places like Delhi, Lucknow and Madras I occasionally found bits and pieces of antique English furniture, Sheffield plate or Staffordshire china. For instance, in a store along a back lane off Chandni Chowk market in Old Delhi I came across two Victorian pottery figures of Shakespeare and Garibaldi standing incongruously amidst hordes of bronze Shivas, Parvatis, Ganeshes and other Hindu deities. I greeted them as old friends, bought them for a surprisingly few rupees, and installed them on a mantelpiece in my new Indian home.

Otherwise most of the types of arts and crafts everywhere in sight were strange to my unaccustomed eyes. However, I soon began to adjust myself to them, and to acquire a tentative, groping admiration of their qualities. Within a few weeks I was wandering with rather excited, if still somewhat reserved, curiosity through exhibition galleries in various cities, and poking my nose into shops selling diverse kinds of Indian works of art. I visited with awe numerous venerable palaces, mosques and temples. Of course, it was easy to admire the Mughal architecture. Its superlative gem wrought in marble and named the Taj Mahal was a peerless masterpiece, and scores of other Muslim tombs, pavilions and mansions set in gardens had a dreamlike grace. Just occasionally a room's walls were, in my judgement, decorated with an excess of pretty-pretty coloured-stone inlay patterns, but usually the buildings as a whole had a serene proportion combined with majesty which made it a glimpse of perfection.

The vast, sometimes grotesque and often seemingly over-ornate piles of the great Hindu temples were at first more difficult for a stranger to appreciate. My comprehension of them did not burst from bud into flower until one afternoon as I meandered among the fabulous shrines at Khajuraho. Suddenly I jumped to the idea that they should not be regarded primarily as essays in architecture, but as exhibitions of sculpture. I accordingly paid more heed to the individual statues or groups of statues climbing, tier upon tier one above the other, all over the huge, tall lingam-shaped towers, like a multitudinous stampede of not always very primly behaved mountaineers. Some of them I liked quite a lot. My initiation had begun. Later I readjusted my vision, restoring the statuary to its proper perspective as mere exuberant adornments on a comprehensive sacred edifice. My aesthetic conversion got gradually confirmed during visits to the grand temples in Madurai, Tanjore, Mahabalipuram, Bhubaneswar, Mysore and similar sanctuaries; and it was completed when I viewed the glorious Temple of the Sun at Konark. As I wandered through all those history-soaked places of worship, and became more familiar with not only Hindu but also Jain, Sikh and other artistic expressions of their human and spiritual faith, the power, tenacity and integrity of this Oriental culture laid hold on me. My respect for it, mixed with occasional criticism, was further strengthened when many friendships which I formed with simple peasants in villages around Delhi taught me that the Hindu faith still remained as inspiring in the lives of hundreds of millions of people as it had been through two thousand years.

My fondness for this part-mystical and part-sensuous art burst into bloom. It was a weird and wonderful experience.

*

So far as objects for possible purchase were concerned, I became especially attracted by three different forms of Indian art. First among them were the often exquisitely drawn, vividly coloured, gemlike miniature paintings made during the last few centuries in various princely courts – Hindu and Muslim alike – scattered across wide regions of the sub-continent. Sometimes their subject matter was a mythological or religious scene, and at other times it concerned mundane regal affairs. From many hundreds of samples – including numerous clever fakes – stored in portfolios in antique shops I chose about three dozen. Among them were charming sketches of a Maharajah riding an elephant, an absconding couple flirting on camel-back, courtly maidens performing their toilets, the god Krishna playing his flute to dancing *gopika* (cowherds), an amorous prince dallying in his harem, a hunting party chasing deer in wild country, and scintillating glimpses of crowded pageantry in palaces. They came from various states in the Himalayan foothills and further south.

After a while I decided that I had a surfeit of those miniatures, at any rate so far as accumulating them for private possession was concerned. They were minor book illustrations, not major paintings. I never tired of viewing refined arrays of them in art museums, but felt that I was frittering away my energies thumbing through hundreds upon hundreds of them in dubious curio shops in search of one or two lovely samples of those trivialities.

The second expression of Indian artistry that attracted me were antique bronze sculptures. Pieces varied in size from two or three inches to a few feet tall. The best were those moulded in southern India at various times between the eighth and the fourteenth centuries A.D., the earlier ones usually being the finer. Some were representations of kings and queens, but most were images of gods or goddesses posturing in many different tranquil or lively attitudes hallowed by legend. As impressive as any were the Nataraja figures of Shiva in his capacity as Lord of Dance performing the celebrated jig which brought our Earth into existence.

Numbers of them still abided in the Hindu temples for which they were originally cast. There they lurked almost all the time in shadowy, dimly lamp-lit sacred niches; but every now and then they were carried in daylight processions through the temple precincts clothed on those ceremonial occasions in jewelled costumes as rich as the robes of kings. Others of their contemporaries had been stolen from holy shrines, smuggled into circulation as commercial works of art, and purchased by discriminating, wealthy connoisseurs. I would rather have gathered half-a-dozen of them than dozens of other types of treasure. But the genuine ones were too well-known, too rare, too coveted and therefore too expensive for me. Innumerable fakes stood around in dealers' shops, some of them contrived with cunning skill. Customers had to be very cautious examining them. In my five years in India I acquired only one of true vintage – a small, six-inches high late fourteenth century figure of the infant son of Shiva and Parvati, who usually stands between his parents in family groups of that trinity. Mine had somehow, sometime got separated from his papa and mama, and I secured him at a small price.

My third leaning was towards stone sculptures, and I was more fortunate in gratifying that taste. When I first arrived in Delhi in 1955 they were not so highly appreciated by private collectors as they became within the next few years and could still be bought at low costs. During my first three years I acquired sixteen of them. Had I started a year of two later I could not have afforded nearly so many, for their prices began to soar.

In most countries one would not know what to do with sixteen sizeable sculptures in a comparatively small house. They would crowd the rooms like a group of frigid guests attending a permanent cocktail party. But in Delhi they presented no problem; indeed, they were a form of adornment admirably suited to the style of home life there. Through much of the year the weather was so sunny and warm that one spent leisure hours out-of-doors. Consequently for about six months in every twelve my family, our guests and I ate breakfast, lunch, tea and often dinner in the open air, either on a spacious lawn or wide verandas. And what could be lovelier furniture standing against the walls of those terraces than classical statues? A dozen of my pieces were distributed on pedestals through several verandas leading from the house into the garden.

Unfortunately I found no example of the work of the finest period when the Gupta Empire and contemporary dynasties were ruling their respective parts of the sub-continent between the fifth and seventh centuries. With two exceptions which I shall mention later my acquisitions were all later pieces ranging in origin from the eleventh to the fourteenth centuries (plate 28). Perhaps the best was a headless and almost limbless female torso cut in sandstone in Rajputana about nine hundred years ago. Standing over two feet high, it displayed a voluptuously curving, probably dancing body with splendid breasts, a slim waist, broad hips and strong thighs, all naked except for several strings of jewellery.

The shopkeeper from whom I bought it thought me foolish to desire that faceless, armless and almost legless fragment of an unknown female; and he endeavoured to persuade me to invest my cash instead in a wholly intact and also impressive figure of the Lord Shiva. The dealer was a fairly knowledgeable man, and for a while under his influence I dithered. Yet the vivacious beauty of the broken statue compared with the rather formal rigidity of its undamaged rival made me feel no doubt which was the finer work of art; so I rejected his advice and wrote him a cheque for the fragment. He changed his mind a few hours later when an official of India's National Museum entered the shop, spied the fractured lady and went into ecstasies about her. An expert on ancient sculpture, the visitor immediately tried to buy the piece, judging that it should become a national treasure. He was extremely disappointed when he learned that it had already been sold. Next day I received a message from the Director of the Museum asking whether he could purchase it from me; but, rather reluctantly, I refused his request. I already had another idea about the crippled yet immortal figure's ultimate destination.

Another superb bit of broken sculpture which I bought represented the head and shoulders of a Buddha-like sage. It was an expression of the Buddhist faith which prevailed in parts of India before Brahmanism overtook it as a popular force, and which later continued to assert an influence in some sects. A divine halo encircled the austere, ascetic face. Its nose had been slashed off by some fanatical Muslim – as often happened to statues of 'infidels' in the days when Islamic conquerors over-ran northern India – but formalised curls of hair covered its head, and its slimly curving eyebrows, serenely contemplative eyes and firm mouth were well preserved. Depicting a Bodhisattva, it was probably made in the twelfth century, when that school of art attained its prime.

Another piece that especially pleased me was a carving of Shiva and Parvati dallying together in lover-like poses, with attendant wild animals around them. One of the god's arms embraced his consort's shoulders whilst he touched her under the chin with a finger of his other hand. She showed no unwillingness to be treated so; on the contrary, her ripe body was turned consentingly towards his, and she gazed at his smiling face with responsive affection. Both figures were remarkably undamaged; indeed, suspiciously so. Yet expert tests established that the sculpture was its own original, unrepaired self. Shiva had the sharp features and especially the long, sensitive nose of his images on walls in the temples at Khajuraho, and probably the piece came from that famous region. Qualified authorities assured me that it had almost certainly been created somewhere in Madhya Pradesh during the thirteenth century, which would be consistent with that speculation.

Other of my sculptures represented the elephant-headed god Ganesha and related Hindu deities. They were a distinguished company. Yet perhaps the choicest piece of all was a stucco head belonging to a much earlier period. A fine example of Gandharan work made in the Indus Valley in the fourth century A.D., it represented a Bodhisattva. Although some of its features were undoubtedly Oriental, it also revealed classical Mediterranean traits, almost as if it were a Greek god. Many scholars regard Gandharan carvings as 'Indo-Greek' – a heritage of the time when Alexander the Great conquered northern India – although others believe the Western influence was introduced later, being more Roman than Greek. Whichever view may be nearer the truth, my piece was undoubtedly a lovely example of works done sometimes in stucco, at other times in stone all around Taxila in modern-day Pakistan during the first few centuries A.D. Later I bought another Gandharan Bodhisattva head cut in stone (plate 29); but, although very pleasing, it did not display quite the same quality of perfect beauty.

Minor themes in my collecting in India were various antique *objets d'art* which I bought for utility as well as additional adornments in my house. Among them were several brass Hindu temple lamps.

Usually standing more than two feet high, but sometimes shorter, they were handsomely wrought and appeared like majestic super candlesticks. The summits of their stems were graced with charming images of sacred birds or human figures, and just below these stretched saucer-shaped trays in which several thick wicks floating in oil burned naked flames like those of candles, but more numerous, larger and fiercer. Distributed on the tables at dinner parties, their gleaming, flickering lights gave flamboyant illumination to the gathering.

Other samples of ancient and modern native craftsmanship added attractive touches of local colour to the rooms. Cigarette boxes, ashtrays, inkstands, vases and various knick-knacks made in diverse traditional wares like Bidriware metal-inlay work from Hyderabad, carved ivory from Bengal (plate 30), and papier-mâché from Kashmir stood around here and there. My favourite maker of papier-mâché in Srinagar indulged in the name of Suffering Moses, but both his geniality and his bank balance indicated that his sufferings were a figment of the imagination. Among purely decorative objects in the house were small brass votive offerings carried by pilgrims in olden days, idols which once upon a time presided in family shrines, and miniature children's toys made in the shapes of processional elephants, sacred cows, saintly characters and other such creatures. In addition I acquired a few very distinguished figurines – gilt deities made for worship in villages amidst Nepal's Himalaya Mountains, or beyond them on 'the roof of the world' in Tibet.

During my hunts in curio shops I acquired some attractive fragments of old cotton-print hangings adorned with colourful legendary scenes. But once again a major theme of my collecting was pictures by living artists. I enjoyed friendships with several talented painters whom I used to visit in their studios in Delhi, Calcutta, Madras and elsewhere. Conspicuous among them were the gentle, dark-bearded M. F. Husain, the white haired near-octogenarian Jamini Roy, and the dynamic young artist Krishen Khanna. In the usually clear, dry climate of Delhi pictures can exist out-of-doors with as much impunity as indoors, except during the three humid monsoon months.

So through most of each year many contemporary paintings hung on the ceiling-shaded walls of my otherwise sunlit verandas in company with the medieval sculptures. They were worthy companions of those expressions of an older age of Indian art, and the mixture of ancient and modern works made a happy, congenial harmony.

Alas, sooner or later all good things come to an end. In 1960 I left India. When the time arrived for me to pack my belongings I carried out a plan which for some time had lodged in my mind. With the kind permission of the Indian authorities I sent my medieval sculptures to Singapore as additional gifts for the University of Malaya's art museum. With them also went the collection of modern Indian paintings. My family and I with our guests had been privileged to enjoy their inspiring company for several years, and it was time for them to give enlightenment and joy to a wider audience. What better audience could there be than successive generations of young Malay, Chinese, Indian and other citizens of the newest, most racially mixed, and so in some ways most representative Asian nation? I hoped that the sculptures would help to expand their knowledge of Asia's proud past, and that the paintings would stimulate their pride in Asia's present.

The only carved treasure which I kept was the superlative Gandharan head and two later sculptures given to me as personal gifts by friends. The second Gandharan head I presented to the Museum of Oriental Art in Durham University.

Chapter 16. European Interlude

After leaving India I was compelled to engage in some other disposals of enviable pieces in my collections. For the next several months I took a holiday without pay. The costs of maintaining my family were naturally considerable, and I had no private income of my own. My wife, daughter, step-children and I could not eat the pottery, silver-ware, carpets, pictures, lacquers and other bric-a-brac which I had accumulated during almost forty years of collecting; so I was forced to secure somewhat adequate cash to purchase more digestible substances, as well as to pay household expenses, school fees and other demands. I decided to sell quite a number of my Persian rugs, nearly all my Chinese jades, some of my less desirable English paintings, my Japanese Kakemono woodcuts, and (in a foolish moment) three Zhou dynasty bronze ritual vessels. With them disappeared several other heart-throbs. I hesitated long over their selection, and parted from each and every one of them with deep sorrow.

I confess that a little of the money that I received from their sales failed to get spent on the mundane purposes originally intended. Instead I blew it on certain other *objets d'art*! Returning to London and passing by – or rather, failing to pass by – tempting china dealers' shop-windows along Brompton Road, Beauchamp Place and other such streets, I fell in love again with English eighteenth century pottery and Dr. Wall Worcester porcelain. So I resumed collecting all over again where I had initially begun. However – quite apart from the other consideration which I have mentioned – I had not the means to indulge in more than an occasional spending spree of that kind. I found that the prices of such things had soared appallingly since my similar activities two decades earlier. In many cases the sums asked were ridiculously, and indeed outrageously, inflated, but this was now becoming the practice for even quite modest works of art. Collecting was steadily ceasing to be a comparatively poor man's hobby.

Luckily for my purse my attention soon got distracted elsewhere. At the end of my holiday I went to Geneva, to lead the British delegation at an international conference concerning Laos (plate 31), and for the next fourteen months from April 1961 until July 1962 I lived on the shore of Lac Leman. The civil war between local communist and anti-communist factions there, which had been partly provoked and continued to be stimulated by the rival external great powers, threatened to erupt into a conflict which could drag those powers themselves out of their 'cold' war into a 'hot' one. It was therefore highly desirable that some peaceful settlement of the Laotian problem could be negotiated. I also did duty as one of the conference's two co-chairmen. My colleague was the leader of the Russian delegation, Georgi Pushkin. An indirect descendent of the distinguished writer of the previous century, he was an able diplomat, dedicated communist and a rather delightful man.

Such spare time as I could snatch during occasional week-ends from our difficult negotiations I spent mostly in a motor-car exploring the lovely mountain, valley and lake scenery scattered through Switzerland. Sometimes when I could escape for a whole day or two I dashed across the Alps into southern France or northern Italy, viewing historic sites like the Roman remains at Arles and Nimes or the show-pieces of later European civilisations in such places as Venice or Florence. Those jaunts were enthralling renewals of acquaintances with some of the most splendid achievements of Western culture. Alas, I could find no Renaissance paintings, sculptures or bronzes for purchase within my means, so I temporarily abandoned the fun of collecting and concentrated instead on the joys of contemplation. Hour after hour I tarried in churches, castles, palaces and art galleries in Ravenna, Urbino, Arezzo, Assisi, Venice, Florence, Sienna and similar haunts, gazing with serene happiness on countless works of sublime beauty. It was glorious to glimpse again the creations of Duccio, Giotto, Piero Della Francesca, Donatello, Botticelli, Leonardo da Vinci, Michelangelo, Raphael and many other geniuses. But since I did not acquire any of their works my ruminations on them are outside the subject of this book.

Chapter 17. Africa

At the beginning of 1963 I experienced yet another translation from one corner of the Earth to another. I flew to Nairobi to assume office as Governor of Kenya, and for the next seven years lived and worked in various parts of Africa. After a year as Governor, another as Governor General and a third as High Commissioner in Kenya I became for two years Britain's Special Representative – or roving Ambassador – in the five Commonwealth countries in East and Central Africa. Then my functions were extended for a further two years to cover all the dozen Commonwealth nations distributed across the so called 'Dark Continent', and occasionally my diplomatic duties were stretched into Somalia, the Sudan and other lands as well. I therefore enjoyed a permanent excuse to travel throughout most of Africa. This gave me opportunities to become acquainted with not only its friendly, characterful peoples but also their traditional and continuing cultures. Enthusiastically I resumed activity as an amateur art connoisseur, and among other pursuits added a number of African works to my accumulation of Occidental and Oriental masterpieces.

An absorbing fact about Africa is the recent revelation – largely due to Louis Leakey and his family's excavations of millions-of-years-old skulls, bones, teeth and other relics in Tanzania, Kenya and Ethiopia – that the creature called 'Homo Sapiens' probably first evolved from his ape-like forebears in Eastern Africa; and I never tired of talking with Leakey and his equally erudite wife Mary about the sort of life which existed on Earth during that vital period of Man's emergence. However, I did not get diverted to collecting flint arrow-heads and axes produced by our earliest anthropoid ancestors. So far as craftsmanship was concerned I still limited my acquisitions to more modern products of the last few thousand years.

By-passing for the moment ancient Egypt and the Mediterranean coastlands, it is true that Africa does not possess so rich a heritage of art treasures as do various other areas of long established human habitation. Nevertheless it has a proud, though so far very inadequately rediscovered past. One reason for its comparative paucity of antique relics is that many of its earliest works of art were carved in wood, and through the millennia hordes of voracious white ants kept destroying them. Few of the timber pieces that have been preserved are more than a hundred years old, and most are much younger.

However, the wealth of other surviving African antiquities is considerably greater than many people suppose, and some of them can stand aesthetic comparison with the best of the kind in other regions round the world. For example, many ancient rock paintings still visible in various regions scattered across north, central and southern Africa are as fine as those in the caves at Lascaux or elsewhere in Europe. Again, the Nok terracotta figures created in what is now central Nigeria between 500 B.C. and 200 A.D., the brass and terracotta sculptures made at Ife (also in Nigeria) during the thirteenth and fourteenth centuries, the best of the bronze busts and panels produced in Benin from about a hundred years later, and the ivory masks, bracelets and similar ornaments carved there at the same periods have superb qualities.

It is extremely difficult for present-day addicts to acquire specimens of these for private ownership. Many were whisked out of Africa in colonial times around the beginning of the twentieth century, and are now mostly lodged in museums in Britain and Europe. Quite rightly, the independent African governments prohibit any further export of such treasures from their native lands, so that they can be cherished for display in their own public art galleries. I for one therefore possess no worthy pieces. My sole attempt to gain a tolerable sample ended in failure. Once in a curio shop in Lagos I saw an attractive, antique looking Benin bronze figure of an Oba's courtier. I assumed that it could not belong to a classic period, but hoped it might have been made by a skilled craftsman towards the end of the last century. I bought it on the off chance, and took it for examination by the authorities in Nigeria's National Museum. They enlightened me. It was a competent but slightly inaccurate and entirely recent fake.

For the rest, I bought many examples of modern African craftsmanship which made no pretensions to an older vintage. They included two ebony carvings by a talented living sculptor named

Idabur in Lagos. One of these was a characterful figure of a rogue elephant, and the other a charming head of a tribal girl with an extravagant traditional hair-do. Several of my pieces were products by Makonde wood-workers in Tanzania, who are in my judgement the most gifted artists still devising carvings in customary native techniques and forms. Some of their products are more or less naturalistic human figures, whilst others are fabulous, rather nightmarish mythological creatures who nonetheless possess an abstract-style beauty. In addition I picked up numerous soapstone and wood carvings made by Kisii and Wakamba tribesmen respectively in Kenya, ivory figurines cut by skilled workmen in Malawi, and decorative pieces of leather-work and silverware produced in Gambia. Some of these are specimens of what is sometimes called, rather contemptuously, 'airport art' made for tourists; and a lot of such stuff is indeed cheap in every sense of the world. Yet if you keep a discriminating eye open when examining supplies of it on traders' stalls you can find every now and then a piece of high merit. One of my carvings representing a warthog – of all ugly yet endearing creatures – has a touch of artistic genius about it.

I also purchased splendid Kikuyu, Luo and other tribal shields, spears and drums to help me adorn my home in Government House in Nairobi. When I first arrived there that stately mansion was furnished entirely with characteristically British tables, chairs, sofas, pictures, ornaments and other attributes. Except for two Zanzibar chests hidden away in an upstairs corridor no glimpse of Africa appeared anywhere. The place might have been the dwelling of some plutocrat in London's Mayfair, with no connection whatever with Kenya. Yet it was the official residence of Kenya's head of government, which should therefore be at least partially expressive of the Kenyans' character and culture.

I at once began to 'Africanise' much of it. Naturally a lot of the functional furniture could not be banished; but I took down English landscape paintings adorning its entrance hall and replaced them with decorative tribal shields and spears; removed bits of English porcelain, silver and other objects from cabinets and mantelpieces in numerous rooms and substituted attractive examples of Wakamba, Kisii and other local craftsmanship; put the handsome Zanzibar chests in prominent positions in the drawing-room; spread zebra-skin and other East African carpets on the floors; and introduced traditional African creations like Congolese masks, Ghanaian stools and Nigerian sculptures. To help give the place an appearance of a house that was truly playing an important part in the making of a new African nation in which black and white citizens co-operated as friends together, I also bought paintings by contemporary Kenyan artists, African and European alike, and hung them on the walls of the state rooms. Among them were several of the admirable batik pictures of Masai and similar scenes done by the outstandingly gifted Miss Robin Anderson.

Among local craftsmen whom I sought to encourage were prisoners in Nairobi's gaol who were being taught carpentry and similar skills in workshops there in the hope that after being released they would pursue creative occupations instead of resuming criminal careers. I bought useful small tables and stools made by them, and also sent pieces of damaged furniture from Government House for them to repair. One morning whilst touring the prison I thanked a genial rascal for the ability with which he had renovated half-a-dozen of my dining-room chairs. Evidently pleased by my appreciation, he asked whether I would arrange for his discharge from prison so that he could re-join his family and engage in productive employment outside. I replied that I had no power myself to make a decision on this plea, but that I would mention his case to the responsible authorities. When I did so I learned that he was a murderer who had killed multiple people on an occasion when he ran amok.

When I left Government House at the end of two years residence in it I presented many of my pleasing examples of Kenyan arts and crafts to the newly independent nation. They still help to adorn the stately home of its great President Jomo Kenyatta.

Sometimes during my African years my diplomatic duties took me to Addis Ababa, with opportunities to travel widely in Ethiopia. Certain of that country's characteristics are very impressive. Some of its northern Rift Valley scenery is as dramatically grand as any landscape anywhere, and the Ethiopians' historic culture is eminently distinguished. This is natural, since His Imperial Majesty the Emperor Haile Selassie, who is also the Lion of Judah and King of Kings, claims descent through a line of 255 previous rulers from King Solomon and the Queen of Sheba, and his kingdom was already an imperial power in the early years of the Christian era. Splendid relics of its subsequent continuous civilisation survive in the ancient stone steles at Axum, rock-hewn churches in Lalibela, castles in Gondar, and other antique monuments on various sites. Incidentally, the handsomeness of many of its men and beauty of its women – whether they be immaculately dressed aristocrats or poverty-stricken peasants clad in rags – is as noble as that of any people round the Earth.

On jaunts in Addis Ababa's shops I bought some attractive traditional-style religious paintings. Other pleasing curios were elaborately decorative Christian crosses cast in silver in the eighteenth century, which used to dangle from the necklaces of pious worshippers. One afternoon I picked up from different stalls in an open-air market nearly a dozen variously designed examples of these. On my return to the British Embassy where I was staying I showed them proudly to my host and hostess. The Ambassador was an experienced diplomat, his wife was a native of Athens who once upon a time in a national beauty competition had been chosen Miss Greece, and both were generous as well as charming friends. On the following morning I was surprised to see beside my plate on our breakfast table a parcel with an affectionate message scribbled by them. Opening it, I found several similar Christian crosses made in gold which made my silver ones look like poor, if still graceful, relations.

*

Periodically when I flew from Nairobi to London or back I stopped in Cairo for two or three days. In the museum there, at the pyramids and in tombs at Saqqara, as well as during a visit to Luxor and the Valley of the Kings, I viewed many glorious artistic and architectural remains of one of mankind's earliest great civilisations. My unappeasable appetite for beautiful things inevitably made me eager to acquire some *objets d'art* which would represent it alongside those from various other cultures in the Occident and Orient that graced my home; and slowly over a few years I found, one by one, four small bronze images of the goddess Isis nursing her infant Horus, the divine cat Bast, the demi-god Imhotep, and a funerary vase. I failed to find a good example of a similar Sacred Ibis; which I would have especially liked. The quartet that I collected were all allegedly produced in some classic period of the Pharaonic age, but I daresay each one is in fact a counterfeit effort. However, they put up a good pretence.

I did manage to buy one truly genuine treasure made in the Nile Valley sometime during the historic Middle Kingdom. A two feet high slab of stone broken from the wall of a tomb or temple, it displayed a finely carved figure of a hallowed mythological character surrounded by a few hieroglyphics. I paid quite a lot for it, being assured that I would receive permission from the Egyptian authorities to transport it from the country. I left it temporarily in the dealer's shop to be packed and sent to me in Nairobi when the document granting that permission arrived. For a considerable time I heard no more about it, and then learned that the dealer had been suddenly arrested and expelled from Egypt, and that all the goods on his premises were confiscated. Nevertheless, some months afterwards I got written permission from the appropriate government department in Cairo to receive my lovely purchase, and a while later a heavy package arrived for me in England, where I had then retired. Eagerly I opened it. The slab of stone inside was similar in size and shape to mine, but the carving on it was different. Artistically inferior, it represented a commonplace human courtier, and was a modern fake. I could not tell who was responsible for the substitution, nor why it had been made. Realising that a protest would be undiplomatic and probably fruitless, I concealed my shocked disappointment and accepted the bogus dummy.

One day in an antique shop in Cairo I saw an object that switched me into a new field of collecting. Throughout my years in India and Switzerland I had continued to buy on occasional visits to London pieces of Chinese porcelain to add to my assembly of them in Durham, seeking especially bits that would fill some of the gaps in the historic types of ware represented there. I continued to do this for a while after I went to Africa, but soon the prices for desirable specimens soared so high that I could no longer afford even the least expensive of them. With deep sorrow I gave up the pastime of collecting these lovely things. Yet I could not complain; through nearly two score years I had managed to acquire far more than I or any other individual deserved to own. My collection now contained more than 400 pieces representing almost all the significant types of pottery and porcelain produced in Old Cathay from prehistoric times until towards the end of the Qing dynasty.

However, pots continued to exert an irresistible attraction over me, and that morning in a shop in Cairo I glimpsed something indicating that practicable opportunities to indulge the taste still lurked around. On a shelf I spied a ceramic object which had originated not in the Far East but the Near East. It was a medieval Persian bowl decorated with a black-painted pattern beneath a turquoise glaze. Many years earlier I had formed the opinion that the best potters after the Chinese through several dynasties were the Persians of the Middle Ages. I fell for the bowl, discovered that it cost very little, and carried it away.

That pushed me into a fresh acquisitive track. I knew that Roger Bluett, the charming, scholarly dealer in old Oriental porcelain in London who (like his father before him) had sold me some of my most distinguishing Chinese pieces, kept securing fine ceramics from Persia as well as China – and that the prices for the former were a small fraction of those for the latter (plate 32). After my new initiation, therefore, whenever I flew from Africa to England for a few days of official consultations with my political masters in Whitehall I dropped in for at least a few minutes chat with him in his show-rooms in Davies Street. I viewed his current stock of Persian pottery, and usually left the place with one, two or more additions to my novel group of possessions. I need not weary the reader with details about them beyond remarking that during the next several years I accumulated about fifty attractive examples representing various important types made between 1500 B.C. and the fourteenth century A.D.

*

Perhaps I should mention that my admiration for beauty was not confined to works of art made by Man, but extended also to many of God's creations. When I was still a schoolboy I became very fond of wild flowers, and picked large assortments of them, from common daisies to rare orchids, which I pressed and arranged decoratively on the pages of albums. Other objects that I collected at different periods of my life included numerous species of cowrie shells, exotic corals, goldfish and marine animals. One of my favourite recreations in every country where I lived was bird-watching, not merely because of these winged creatures' interesting life histories but also because of their sometimes simple and at other times flamboyant beauty in shapes and plumages. Such species as the Robin Redbreast in England, the Snowy Owl in Canada, the Paradise Flycatcher in Malaysia, the Golden Oriole in India, the Greater Flamingo in Kenya and hundreds of other types here, there and everywhere present an astonishing diversity of magical beauty. Indeed, many phenomena in nature are blessed with a fantastic grace that is almost incredible. The exquisite, gorgeous, sublime (and various other adjectives) patterns of countless butterflies, wild plants, tropical fish, sea-shells, snowflakes and other small objects; and of larger creatures like gazelles, leopards, giraffes; flowering trees, stalactite caves, mountain ranges and other sights in landscapes, reveal touches of fabulous beauty which have to be seen to be believed. I assembled many assortments of the tinier ones for viewing in show-cases, drawers and other receptacles in my rooms.

One type of God's creations was not so confined, but roamed freely through the place. They aroused comments which were always appreciative but sometimes also a trifle critical. Gracious female human beings of any age from one to a hundred years, and of any skin colour from white or ivory through various shades of brown to black, were always welcome visitors. Many of my guests who belonged to the so-called fair sex were in fact plain and even ugly, but I liked them because of their vivacious personalities, intelligent minds or gentle spirits. I confess that others were invited because they possessed enchanting faces. If I discovered later that they were endowed with unpleasant personalities, empty minds or nasty spirits, they usually did not receive further invitations. But many of them were blessed with genial intellects or pleasing characters which made them all the more agreeable. They added extra aesthetic distinction, fresh dimensions of beauty to a room, as if they were lovely portraits who had stepped from their frames on walls and joined in active life in the house. Incidentally, their husbands were also good friends of mine, and accompanied them. Yet occasionally their presence caused insinuating whispers, and in some scandal-mongering quarters their frequent appearances at my parties gained me a flattering but undeserved reputation as a Don Juan. Probably I was too inclined to gather many of those vivid human works of art in my home, for only one thought jumps into some people's heads when they observe fond, however innocent, friendships between such goddesses and a male mortal. Nor do I deny that my partiality for them was to some extent a case of sex rearing its ugly (or beautiful, or whatever description is correct) head; but it was due mostly to my devotion to aesthetic grace in all its manifestations. Why should a man be praised for liking to see exquisite works of art arranged static in his rooms, yet criticised for enjoying the sight of others moving vivaciously through them?

Yes, I like Beauty, I love Beauty, I worship Beauty in all its earthly forms.

Chapter 18. Envoi

My purchases of Persian pottery were my last fling in the field of art collecting. Towards the end of 1969 I retired from the public service, and thereafter lived mostly on a pension which, if adequate to keep the wolf from the door, pay for my daughter's university education and finance various other requirements, did not permit indulgence in further artistic acquisitions. The only additions that I have since made to my previous accumulations are a few inexpensive examples of modern Chinese craftsmanship which I bought during visits to China in 1962 and 1971. I was delighted to find how those everlasting artists still maintain their traditional skills in producing certain beautiful things like silk needlework embroidery in Suzhou and shell decorations in Qingdao.

Through nearly a whole lifetime I had been able to indulge my artistic tastes quite generously, not merely because prices were low during much of that time but also because over many years I enjoyed a handsome income. Through almost four decades I held a succession of official posts which were very well paid – sometimes too well. When I became Governor and afterwards Governor General in Kenya, for instance, I decided that my salary and allowances were too high, and that it was unfair on the local tax-payers that I should be remunerated so excessively. Without publicising the fact – so that my colleagues in the colonial service would not be embarrassed by my action – I reduced my pay by £2,000 each year.

This still left me a sumptuous income. My official expenses in Kenya – as in every other country where I served – were of course very heavy. Audrey's and my social entertaining was enormously costly. Almost always VIPs or other visitors were staying with us in our mansion. Every day about a dozen guests came to lunch, for this was the best way for us to meet informally large numbers of Kenyans whom we would otherwise never get to know, or only have opportunities to greet on formal occasions. Often a crowd of youngsters came to tea with us beside our tennis court or swimming-pool, where University students, school children and others like to bash tennis balls, float in the water, or laze in the sunshine. Each week we gave several dinner parties; frequently groups of people came for drinks in the evenings; and now and then we held the ridiculously large cocktail parties which had become an apparently unavoidable part of diplomatic existence. And on special occasions two or three times each year thousands of guests came to garden parties where tribal dancing was performed and tea and drinks were served. Such was the high gubernatorial life in those days. Similar obligations when I lived in Malaya and Singapore often made me remark that my correct title should be not Britain's Commissioner General in South East Asia but Britain's Hotel Keeper there. However, I greatly enjoyed much of that exuberant social activity.

I myself lived in some ways simply, and even frugally. Indeed, certain of my personal habits tended to be rather Spartan. Thus, I ate moderate meals and drank little, never being a connoisseur of foods or wines, still less a gourmet or a tippler. In some fields of expenditure I was economical, and may even have been positively stingy. But I was not a miser. On the contrary, I believed in spending every shilling that I owned, but not in frittering it away on small, unimportant things. I blew it on big things that in my opinion really mattered, such as adding desirable books to my library. And two sorts of spending sprees in particular I favoured. One was providing bounteous hospitality to acquaintances of every class, colour and creed, for I felt this was not only very enjoyable in itself, but also helpful in the supreme cause of promoting mutual understanding and friendship between peoples of every race and culture around the world. The other field in which I liked spending my money was that of art collecting.

But now those days were over. I had stepped down from the seats of the well paid mighty, and must live in a much more modest way. Indeed, far from being able to buy more artistic treasures, I was forced to sell many of those that I already possessed. Having lived away from Britain for almost thirty years, I no longer kept a house there. Sometime earlier I had sold Hyde Hall, for I could not be bothered to cope any longer with the problems which tenants – whether good or bad – produce for their landlord. So now I had to purchase a new family home. Never having saved a penny as such, I commanded no ready cash for this purpose. Nor had I invested money in stocks and shares which I could sell to secure the necessary resources. Throughout decades all my spare earnings had been squandered on antique teapots, old master paintings, aged bits of furniture, medieval Indian sculptures, modern pagan carvings and all sorts of other fantastic things. Nor had I chosen any of them because of its commercial value, but only for its aesthetic grace. Yet by a stroke of good luck this turned out to be conduct worthy of a supreme financial genius – one of the very last characters whom I could claim to be. Purchases of works of art through the 1920s, 1930s and 1940s, and even in some parts of the world where I chanced to dwell through the 1950s and early 1960s, were more profitable investments than almost any dealings, however shrewd, in bonds on stock exchanges.

I had hitherto hoped that I could eventually give my whole collection of Chinese ceramics as a gift to the School of Oriental Studies in Durham, but now I realised that this was impracticable. I needed quite a lot of money to buy a house. I could have secured a sumptuous sum by selling the collection in an auction; but I wished it to remain intact and if possible to stay for ever at the service of the students in Durham. So I suggested to the University authorities that if they would care to buy it, they could do so for one-third of its valuation. I added that I would ask an expert to calculate its worth according to what one willing buyer – not several fervently competing buyers in a sale – would be prepared to give to a willing seller, and to err in his reckonings on the low rather than the high value. They promptly agreed. On the basis laid down the valuer calculated the collection to be worth £90,000; and so I received £30,000. That was in 1967. I am happy (and indeed mightily conceited!) to say that its value has since rocketed to a vastly higher figure.

I still required more money for the charming house that I had my eye on; so I sold then and later considerable quantities – though by no means all – of my Worcester porcelain, Indian miniatures, Canadian paintings, antique English furniture, Persian pottery and various other treasures. It was sad, but unavoidable. With the proceeds I bought the tempting house, which stood in a spacious garden surrounded by peaceful woodland on a hilltop overlooking the Weald of Kent. It was a residence larger than was needed for sensibly simple living, and in some ways I would have preferred to settle in a charming cottage. But I chose it partly because its rooms would be plentiful and sizeable enough to accommodate all the fine antique furniture and works of art that I had gathered on various continents. They had never previously been assembled all together, since many of them were lent to friends or kept in storage during my absence overseas. Now at last I wished to live with them all around me, and to enjoy their distinguished company.

Carefully arranged through the house, therefore, are the remnants of my art collections which I have (so far!) been able to keep. As I indicated earlier, they are not limited to purely decorative objects like paintings hanging on walls, bronze statuettes standing on mantelpieces, and pots marshalled in show-cabinets. Almost every utilitarian article was also bought by me sometime, somewhere during the last fifty years, such as an old Spode dinner service, an early Wedgwood dessert set, Kashmiri papier-mâché trays, Cambodian silver pepper-grinders, Javanese silver sweet dishes, and various other such items. Those comparatively unimportant, often small pieces give me and my family almost as much pleasure as the more significant art gems, because in their own ways they also achieve engaging beauty. And with sentimental nostalgia I recall exactly when and where I acquired each object in the house, whether I had to bargain hard for it, what controversies may have ensued among experts about its merits, and all the other circumstances of its and my association.

Certain of them possess little artistic merit and no commercial worth; but they have such sentimental value for me that I shall never part with them. One, for example, is a cheap theatrical china figure of a Peking Opera singer which one of my Chinese houseboys in Singapore insisted on giving me after I helped his family through a crisis during the jungle war in Malaya. He said he knew how much I loved Chinese porcelain, and that he would like to add it to my collection. Another piece is an image of Christ hanging on the Cross made by Anton Lang, the potter in Oberammergau who had acted the part of Jesus in the Passion Play when I first viewed it as an 8 year old boy with my parents in 1910, and who was Leader of the Chorus on the stage when I returned to see the drama during its tercentenary performance twenty-four years later.

My galaxy of works of art comes from many different corners of the Earth and many contrasting periods in human history, having been made in ancient or modern times by an immense variety of artists and craftsmen. Distributed through my drawing-room, for instance, are objects from twenty-two different countries scattered across four continents. Their coming-together in the same room is accidental; when I arranged the interior furnishings of the house each one happened to look just right in the place it now occupies. One of the lessons I have learned during my collecting career is that – with rare exceptions – any work of art which is truly beautiful can live harmoniously alongside any other lovely piece, regardless of the countries or centuries where or when they were made.

I wrote a few paragraphs above that in my home are all the remaining works of art which I have so far been able to retain. Not all the missing ones are absent because I had to sell them. Some of the pleasures of collecting abide with me, but so do some of the pains. Thus I gain constant pleasure from contemplating the objects which still remain, but I frequently have to dispose of more. And twice in the last three years gangs of thieves have broken into my house at night and helped themselves to some of its contents. On both occasions they were disturbed before completing their raid, but managed to escape promptly with a quantity of precious things, leaving more pieces lying around on floors where the thugs were presumably packing them when they heard people moving upstairs. On the first occasion the police quickly discovered the receiver of the stolen goods, and most of the properties were recovered. On the second none reappeared, but the robbers themselves were caught a while later. Each time the missing pieces were mostly my charming South East Asian and other exotic silverwares.

For a while after becoming unable to buy more *objets d'art* I bought as an alternative numerous of the beautifully illustrated books about various artistic Occidental, Oriental and other cultures which are being published in these times. Until a few years ago they were not unduly expensive, and gazing at their exquisitely coloured pictures was a not unsatisfactory substitute for contemplating the original works of art themselves. But now those volumes' prices have also risen above my means, and so this method of appeasing my acquisitive instinct has also passed away. However, with the steady advance of old age, that eagerness in me, like all my other capacities, is slipping into decay. My longing to acquire new possessions grows ever feebler, and I am content to confine my activities to viewing the masses of glorious art treasures which are housed in public collections.

So I linger in my hilltop home. When the sun shines from a cloudless blue sky and the atmosphere is clear the view from it is as pleasant, widespread an English landscape as one could desire to see. At other times the hill's summit is encircled by mists which hide that scene and make me imagine that I live on a small, solitary island in a boundless sea such as could exist anywhere round the world. And after night falls a myriad lights from a town and farms strewn across the weald sparkle in the darkness beneath my windows, as if the Earth had vanished and I were suspended somewhere in the Milky Way in outer space. At all seasons the place has a serenity in which it is pleasant to spend one's last few years, months or days on this planet, waiting curiously for whatever new experience – if any – follows after death.

Malcolm J. MacDonald, 1972

Editor's Afterword

Malcolm wrote these final words of this, his most personal book, in 1972. He passed away on 11 January 1981, but his lifetime's achievements as a diplomat and collector live on. Despite the feeling of closure embodied by his last few paragraphs, Malcolm still had a great deal left to give the world. In 1975 and 1979, he returned to China as President of the Great Britain-China Centre: a Foreign Office-sponsored think-tank dedicated to building cultural relations with China. Malcolm led teams of archaeological, museums and art experts for productive discussions with their Chinese counterparts. On the first of those trips, he became one of the very first Westerners to be told of the discovery of the now famous Terracotta Army. The other members of the delegation were a little jealous at the reception given to Malcolm by the Chinese authorities who were generously funding their visit. It was no accident that the best hotel rooms, and most expensive personal gifts, were always reserved for Malcolm. Whilst the other British delegates were in China to forge new relationships, Malcolm was enjoying the opportunity to reconnect with old friends. The Curator of the Palace Museum (within the Forbidden City) warmly greeted Malcolm, with whom he had become friends during Malcolm's important diplomatic visit of 1971. He gave Malcolm a fine Ming dynasty blue-and-white bowl, repaying the generosity with which Malcolm had donated the funds to buy an exquisite celadon piece for the Palace Museum in 1962. Unfortunately the bowl was damaged in transit to Xi'an, but was expertly restored by the regional museum in that city, and Malcolm received another piece of porcelain to compensate him for any worry he had suffered. Malcolm loved China and the Chinese people. His visits during the 1970s also gave him the opportunity to bid farewell to old friends such as Prince Norodom Sihanouk (then living in exile in Beijing), his 'twin' Chen Yi, and the venerable statesman Zhou Enlai.

Malcolm MacDonald was as human as the rest of us and sometimes made mistakes. This happened in his pursuit of beauty, where he at times fell prey to forgeries, and also in his work as a politician and diplomat. Some of the conflicts which Malcolm tried to resolve proved too intractable, and some of the initiatives he sponsored less than successful. Despite these mishaps, Malcolm's legacy today is testament to his many successes. As a diplomat, he played an important role in promoting peaceful and mutually beneficial Anglo-Chinese relations; as a colonial administrator, he worked to end the anachronisms of empire; and as a lover of art, his collections remain on public display across the world. In Durham, students and visitors continue to be inspired by his love of beauty, captured for posterity in the collections now held at the Oriental Museum. After selling his collection of Chinese ceramics to the museum at the end of the 1960s, Malcolm continued to make donations of his South East Asian artefacts throughout the final decade of his life. Temenggong Koh's head-hunting sword, Sihanouk's xylophone and Malcolm's favourite Dingware bowl remain some of the highlights of this wonderful museum. Further afield, Malcolm left behind a positive cultural and political legacy in all the corners of the world in which he worked. In Canada as well as Durham, Singapore, Malaysia and Brunei, visitors to many museums continue to enjoy the antiquities as well as contemporary art-works which he bequeathed. The very existence of Malaysia owes something to Malcolm's vision as one of the first people to dream of a practical, united Malay state born out of the former British colonies of South East Asia. Likewise, many students of the University of Malaya and its successor institutions benefitted (and still benefit) from his passionate belief that decolonisation must be cultural as well as political, and that Asian peoples should celebrate their artistic heritage of the past whilst seeking inspiration for their future. In chapter 15, Malcolm relates the story of how he helped to set up an art museum for the University of Malaya, then based in Singapore. Today these collections are split between the University of Malaya Asian Art Museum and its affiliated Art Gallery in Kuala Lumpur and the National University of Singapore Museum in Singapore. The magnificent sandstone sculpture of Shiva and Parvati described in chapter 15 can be found amongst the exquisite collections of the Asian Art Museum. The almost limbless female torso recounted in the same chapter today resides in the National University of Singapore Museum.

In Kenya also, Malcolm stood apart from previous conservative, aloof Governors and forged a unique relationship both with Kenya's first independent president, Jomo Kenyatta, and its people. He had already achieved something similar in India, where his conversations with statesmen helped to shape the form of the modern Commonwealth relationship between Britain and its former colonies, whilst his talks with villagers helped to consolidate the independent state. On one memorable occasion Malcolm found himself trying to convince an old villager that an independent India was much better than a British colonial India. For perhaps any other British representative, this would have been an ironic situation; but Malcolm was a lifelong believer in decolonisation.

Lastly, two of Malcolm's greatest abiding legacies relate to his service in the cause of international peace during the Cold War. In 1961 -62, he defused a dangerous crisis in Laos which had the potential to escalate into another Vietnam War. His reward from one of the Laotian princes is the beautiful army baton which can be seen in the colour plates of this book. Then, in 1971, Malcolm's unofficial intervention broke through two decades of diplomatic deadlock and enabled the appointment of an old acquaintance and fellow ceramics collector – Sir John Mansfield Addis – as the first British Ambassador to communist China. Malcolm's negotiations took place at the same time as Henry Kissinger's, but China and America did not exchange ambassadors until 1979. As a true believer in diplomacy and peace, Ramsay MacDonald would have been proud of his son's achievements: a pride which should be shared by Durham University, where Malcolm served as Chancellor from 1971-80.

In between admiring his remaining collections, visiting China and officiating at various functions in Durham, Malcolm also devoted some of his retirement to writing. After this manuscript was rejected by his publishers, he embarked on three more book projects, only one of which – *Inside China* – was successful. His attempt at a romantic novel set in 1940s Thailand and Cambodia – *A Khmer Smile* – tells us more about Malcolm's personal passions (most of the romance taking place against a backdrop of Malcolm's favourite South East Asian museums or the temple complex at Angkor Wat which he visited with his friend Sihanouk) than his talents as a writer. Also currently unpublished,

Malcolm attempted to write a detailed memoir of his adventurous career. Unlike *The Pleasures and Pains of Collecting*, that book – *Constant Surprise* – proved elusive to Malcolm. He worked on it intermittently from 1973 until 1981, more because of the naggings of his publisher than through genuine desire. The memoir which Malcolm most wanted to write was the one which you have just read.

To end Malcolm's narrative, perhaps there are few words more fitting than those composed for his memorial service, held at Westminster Abbey on 3 March 1981. Representatives of the Queen, the government and many foreign nations attended to bid farewell to a man whose love of beauty, and even greater love of people, has left a positive impression upon many corners of our world.

> *We meet to remember before God with affection, admiration and respect, Malcolm MacDonald, a unique person who performed a unique work. Modest, highly talented, his burning passion was the welfare of his fellows without discrimination of colour, class or creed. We give thanks for his caring concern on behalf of the Commonwealth; his faith in its future which he helped to mould; the absence of pomp and circumstance in his daily life and the satisfaction which he found in simple pleasures. We recall his openness to the culture and spirituality of China and the Far East and his deep love and understanding of Canada, India and Africa. A man for all seasons, we pay tribute to his delight in beauty, whether of nature or of art, and his enjoyment in the friendship of young people of many races. Patriot and citizen of the world, sensitive to the unity of the spirit in the diversity of its manifestations, we shall ever remain grateful for a life so well lived, distinguished throughout by a high integrity. May Malcolm MacDonald inspire us to labour unceasingly for the ideals which he cherished.*

Alexander Nicholas Shaw, 2018